Greece
at the Polls
The National Elections
of 1974 and 1977

Edited by Howard R. Penniman

D1456952

American Enterprise Institute for Public Policy Research
Washington and London

Library of Congress Cataloging in Publication Data

Main entry under title:

Greece at the polls.

    (AEI studies ; 317)
    Includes index.
    1. Greece. Boule—Elections. 2. Legislative
bodies—Greece. 3. Greece—Politics and government—1974. I. Penniman, Howard Rae,
1916–   . II. Series.
JN5123.G67   324.9495'076   81-8026
ISBN 0-8447-3434-9   AACR2
ISBN 0-8447-3435-7 (pbk.)

AEI Studies 317

Printed in the United States of America

Contents

PREFACE *Howard R. Penniman*   ix

ABBREVIATIONS   xiv

1 ELECTIONS AND POLITICAL MODERNIZATION IN GREECE   1
    Roy C. Macridis

   The "Common Mediterranean Profile" and Greece   2
   The Political Forces Present in the Late 1970s   9
   Conclusion   19

2 GREEK ELECTORAL LAW *Phaedo Vegleris*   21

   The Right to Vote and to Run for Office   22
   The Electoral System   29
   Validation of Parliamentary Elections   40

3 NEW DEMOCRACY: THE NEW FACE OF CONSERVATISM   49
    J. C. Loulis

   From the People's Party to New Democracy   49
   The New Democracy Party in Government: Ideology
      and Performance   59
   The Organization and Structure of the New
      Democracy Party   68
   New Democracy and the 1977 Elections: Campaign
      and Results   73
   Postscript and Conclusions   79

4 THE UNION OF THE DEMOCRATIC CENTER *Thanos Veremis*   84

   History of the Party   85
   The Elections of 1974   89

Between the Two Elections   92
The 1977 Campaign and Elections   97

5   PASOK AND THE ELECTIONS OF 1977: THE RISE OF THE
    POPULIST MOVEMENT   *Angelos Elephantis*   105

    The Charismatic Leader   106
    Political Orientation   110
    The Ideology of Populism and its Social Roots   116
    The Organizational Structure of PASOK   122
    PASOK as the Main Opposition Party   126

6   THE CRISIS IN THE GREEK LEFT   *Michalis Papayannakis*   130

    Aspects of KKE and Left History   134
    Toward the 1974 Elections   149
    The 1977 Elections and Future Perspectives   152

7   DEFINING GREEK   FOREIGN POLICY OBJECTIVES   160
    Theodore A. Couloumbis

    Greek Foreign Policy since 1974   165
    Political Parties and Their Foreign Policy Programs   170
    Prospects   183

8   CONCLUSION   *Theodore A. Couloumbis*   185

    APPENDIX A   Greek Ballots, 1977   193

    APPENDIX B   Greek Election Returns, 1974 and 1977
    Compiled by Richard M. Scammon   198

    CONTRIBUTORS   211

    INDEX   213

Preface

Greece at the Polls: The National Elections of 1974 and 1977 is another in the continuing series of studies of national elections in selected democratic countries published by the American Enterprise Institute. Underlying the series is the belief that public policy makers and students of elections in each democracy can profit from a knowledge of electoral practices in a wide variety of other democracies. The greater their understanding of the political consequences of the conduct of elections in other countries, the deeper their insights into the impact of electoral rules and practices at home.

As of mid-1981 the *At the Polls* series includes books on at least one election in Australia, Canada, France, West Germany, Greece, India, Ireland, Israel, Italy, Japan, New Zealand, three of the four continental Scandinavian democracies, the United Kingdom, and Venezuela. Volumes on more recent elections in Canada, France, West Germany, India, Italy, and Japan are nearing completion. Books on elections in Belgium, Colombia, Jamaica, Luxembourg, the Netherlands, Portugal, and Spain are in progress or planned. AEI has also published two studies of referendums and *Democracy at the Polls: A Comparative Study of Competitive National Elections* on the conduct of elections in twenty-eight democracies. A volume on the election of representatives from nine countries to the European Parliament will appear in the winter of 1981–1982. Finally, a new group of books will approach aspects of electoral politics cross-nationally. Volumes underway on left-wing parties in Western Europe, women in national politics, public financing of election campaigns and political parties, and candidate selection and its impact on party systems will combine essays already published in the series with a new analysis of the similarities and differences among them. A complete list of the titles in the series can be found at the back of this book.

Greece is one of three Western European nations that returned to democratic institutions in the mid-1970s after a period of authoritarian rule. The military junta in Greece was shorter lived than the authoritarian governments in Portugal and Spain, but for the seven years it lasted it was, according to Roy Macridis, "one of the most naked and repressive dictatorships in the post–World War II history of Europe." Shortly after the Turkish invasion of Cyprus in July 1974, the junta abruptly resigned, turning the government over to civilian control, and in November Greek voters elected a new government. Three weeks later by a margin of more than two-to-one in a national referendum they blocked the return of the king, who had "contributed decisively to the crisis of parliamentary democracy" in the period preceding the original coup and then bungled an attempt to oust the colonels.[1]

Before the junta, Macridis tells us, the "fragility of the party system" had been striking: aside from the Communist party (KKE), the parties were decentralized, personal organizations with no mechanism for selecting leaders and little power to control the votes of their representatives in Parliament. The distribution of the popular vote fluctuated wildly from one election to the next, and dozens of groupings vied for public support. In the hope of reducing this fragmentation, the architects of the new constitution designed an electoral system that rewards the two largest parties to the disadvantage of all others: in the 1974 election the two parties that together took 74.8 percent of the vote were awarded 93.3 percent of the seats in Parliament, and in 1977 the front-runners parlayed their combined 67.1 percent of the votes into 88 percent of the seats. While all electoral systems tend to award the two largest parties a share of seats that is greater than their share of the popular vote, the Greek variant of proportional representation clearly does this more than most. It does so even more than some plurality systems with single-member-districts, generally the least prone to ensure proportionality.

Under this system the extreme fragmentation of the prejunta years has not returned, but it is not yet clear how great the changes have been or how long they will last. The evidence so far is mixed. In 1974, partly because of the election rules discussed above, four parties or coalitions won all of the parliamentary seats; in 1977 the same four won all except nine of the seats, but there were major

[1] Juan Linz, "Europe's Southern Frontier: Evolving Trends toward What?" *Daedalus* (Winter 1979), pp. 175-209.

shifts among them and some evidence of fragmentation. New Democracy (ND), led by Constantine Karamanlis, won a comfortable majority of votes and seats in the first election; three years later, though still the majority party in Parliament, ND was reduced to a plurality of the popular vote and lost 49 of its 220 seats. The center's loss of seats was even more striking—from 60 to 16. And the rise of the Panhellenic Socialist Movement (PASOK) was positively spectacular: after winning only 12 seats in 1974, PASOK jumped to 93 in 1977. The KKE gained a handful of new seats in the second election.

Moreover, all of the parties except the KKE were still personalized organizations with no usable mechanism for choosing leaders and often without a means of controlling the votes of their members in Parliament. J. C. Loulis says that New Democracy "was far less significant as a mass organization than as a group of leaders and professional politicians." He adds that "despite ND's serious organizational efforts on the eve of the 1977 elections, all power still rested in the hands of the party leadership and the parliamentary group. The membership, limited in number, stood powerless and inactive on the sidelines."

PASOK too—though Angelos Elephantis describes it as "an entirely new political formation, substantially different from any other party in Greek political history"—has some of the weaknesses that have characterized most earlier parties. For one thing, Elephantis argues, it "is not the organization but the glamour of the leader, who is the sole decision-maker," that binds PASOK's followers to the party. Andreas Papandreou not only selects the candidates and decides which ones will receive the full backing of the party in the decisive battle for preference votes, he also determines the party's program virtually single-handed.

PASOK's motto is "National Independence—Popular Sovereignty—Social Liberation." The party opposes Greek participation in NATO and bitterly criticizes what Papandreou calls American imperialism, the force behind the "privileged Greeks" who make money at the expense of "nonprivileged Greeks." PASOK maintains working relations with left socialist parties in Europe and elsewhere while criticizing the social democratic regimes of Germany and Austria. Papandreou also rejects the Eurocommunist parties, which in his view include the Communist party of France as well as those of Italy and Spain. On the other hand, he speaks highly of "the genuine anti-imperialist forces of the Arab countries," among which he counts Libya, Syria, Algeria, and the Palestine Liberation Organization (PLO). Elephantis points out that "whereas Papandreou is lucid and categorical on the role of American imperialism, his views on the Soviet Union remain considerably more elusive." In general he avoids all criticism of the U.S.S.R. He has sought support from Greek military leaders by advocating ultranationalistic positions; from poor voters by proposing what Elephantis characterizes as an "exceedingly generous social policy." In spite of his strong platform statements, Papandreou is flexible enough to modify his language to meet the practical demands of a campaign. In 1977, for example, he did not use the word "socialism" in his radio and television speeches or his final address in Athens's central square.

PASOK differs not only from earlier Greek parties, but also from its socialist counterparts in Europe. We have already noted its criticism of social democratic and Communist parties. More important, although European socialist parties have had charismatic leaders, each of them, unlike PASOK, is based upon a strong, active organization of long standing that ensures the party's future strength independent of the leader. The future of a party based solely on its leader is often problematic.

Only the highly organized Communist party breaks the pattern of personalistic politics—and it has been a diminishing factor in Greek politics. According to Michalis Papayannakis, government suppression, party splits, and the party's ties to the Soviet Union have all contributed to the KKE's stagnation. Today, the party has "very limited influence on the Greek electorate, including the left one." It is closer to Moscow and less important in national politics than the Communist party of any other southern tier European country including France. Furthermore, PASOK apparently presents increasingly formidable competition on the left and seems more likely than the Communists to benefit from any leftward shift of sentiment among the voters.

The contributors to this volume are Roy C. Macridis, professor of political science at Brandeis University; Phaedo Vegleris, professor emeritus at the University of Athens specializing in constitutional law and jurisprudence; J. C. Loulis, director of studies at the Center for Political Research and Information in Athens; Thanos Veremis, lecturer on modern Greek history at the Pantios School of Political Science; Angelos Elephantis, editor of the monthly review O Politis; Michalis Papayannakis, lecturer on development economics at the Mediterranean Agronomic Institute at Montpellier; and Theodore A. Couloumbis, professor of international relations at the School of International Service of the American University. The statistical appendix was compiled by Richard M. Scammon, director of the Elections Research Center in Washington, D.C.

Most of the chapters in this book were originally written in Greek. To the extent that the final text is both accurate and readable, much credit goes to Theodore Couloumbis, Theodore Kariotis of George Mason University, and Dino Panagides of the Embassy of Greece, who kindly helped our staff with the innumerable questions that arose in the course of editing.

HOWARD R. PENNIMAN

Abbreviations

EA	Enomeni Aristera, United Left
EDIK	Enosi Dimokratikou Kentrou, Union of the Democratic Center
EK-ND	Enosi Kentrou-Nees Dynameis, Center Union–New Forces
KKE	Kommunistiko Komma Elladas, Communist Party of Greece
KKE-Interior	Kommunistiko Komma Elladas–Esoterikou, Communist Party of Greece–Interior
ND	Nea Dimokratia, New Democracy
NF	Neofileptheroi, New Liberals
PASOK	Panellinio Sosialistiko Kinima, Panhellenic Socialist Movement
SPAD	Symmachia Proodeftikon ke Aristeron Dynameon, Alliance of Left and Progressive Forces

1

Elections and Political Modernization in Greece

Roy C. Macridis

Greece returned to democracy in August 1974 after seven years of one of the most naked and repressive military dictatorships in the post–World War II history of Europe. Parliamentary elections were held on November 17, 1974, and on December 9 the same year a referendum resulted in an overwhelming vote against the monarchy and the king's return. The Parliament (Vouli) drafted and voted a new democratic constitution favoring reinforced executive power, somewhat along the lines of the French Fifth Republic. It came into force in June 1975, when a president of the republic was duly elected by Parliament for a period of five years. The courts meted out sentences to some of those responsible for the military coup of April 21, 1967, and some accused of torture, but also to those among the military who in February 1975 had conspired to unseat the government. Freedom of the press and of association have been respected and political parties have been free to organize and prepare for various electoral contests.

Again on November 20, 1977, legislative elections were held in an orderly fashion under circumstances that could be envied even by countries with a long tradition of democracy. The electorate, despite a number of significant shifts, showed stability. While the opposition parties, and especially the new Socialist party (PASOK), could boast a marked increase—due largely to the collapse of the center— the "majority" remained in power with 171 seats in the legislature out of a total of 300. Finally, the new constitution was again tested in the April–May 1980 presidential election: failing at first to receive the required two-thirds of the votes in the legislature, the only candidate, Constantine Karamanlis, had to have recourse to a third ballot, which gave him three votes over the 180 he needed to be elected president. Barring unforeseen developments, the new legislative election that must take place not later than November 1981 will be held in an orderly fashion. And by then Greece will be a full-fledged member of the European Economic Community.

Thus, compared with other countries in the Mediterranean, but also with Portugal and even some of the established democracies of Western Europe, Greece's reborn democracy seems to have functioned well. It is quite conceivable that the last decade may prove to be a watershed in the rather turbulent political history of Greece.[1] What might be termed the "generous" hypothesis about the future would hold that party reorganization and consolidation along national lines, together with the new constitution that strengthens the executive, will pave the way to both political participation and political stability.[2] These developments could provide the proper participatory and integrative mechanisms for consolidating a democratic regime. On the other hand, the "niggardly" hypothesis would be that basic conflicts over the regime and internal divisions among political parties will continue to run just as deep as in the past and will eventually surface again. New demands are pressing upon what are still fragile party and governmental structures, and genuine participatory mechanisms may be unavailable. If so, instability may push Greece in the direction of Sam Huntington's "praetorian politics" model.[3]

The "Common Mediterranean Profile" and Greece

First, a few words about the "Mediterranean profile" of which Greece partakes. As countries go through economic and social modernization, their governments—whether authoritarian or parliamentary—are unable to meet new demands. This makes for a high degree of instability, and serious internal or external shocks are manifested in severe institutional strains (such as occur periodically in Italy) or in the actualy breakdown of government structures, whether authoritarian (as in Portugal, Spain, and Greece in the mid-1970s) or parliamentary (Greece in 1967). Political parties remain (except for the Communist parties) parties of notables, forming and reforming coali-

[1] The two best available contributions on recent Greek politics are Keith R. Legg, *Politics in Modern Greece* (Stanford: Stanford University Press, 1969), and Jean Meynaud, *Les forces politiques en Grèce* [Political forces in Greece] (Lausanne: n.p., 1964), translated into Greek as *Politikes Dynameis stin Ellada* (Athens: n.p., 1965). See also Pavlos Bakoyiannis, *Anatomia tis Ellinikis Politikis* [Anatomy of Greek politics] (Athens: n.p., 1977).

[2] The text of the new constitution and a commentary on it can be found in *Syntagma tis Ellados* [Constitution of Greece] (Athens: Nees Ekdossis, July 1975).

[3] Samuel P. Huntington, *Political Order in Changing Societies* (New Haven: Yale University Press, 1968).

tions clustered around individual leaders. Elections and governmental decisions follow patron-client patterns that, in a period of economic and social modernization, are highly unstable. The bureaucracy develops along the patron-client lines that Joseph LaPalombara has described so well for Italy.[4] New demands, associated with modernization, constantly press upon the parties and the governmental structures, resulting in party splits and cabinet reshufflings, breakdowns in governmental management and administrative performance, and cabinet instability—or in authoritarian regimes, palace revolts, and even the complete collapse of the governing cabals or juntas. Greece has experienced both. In 1967 the parliamentary machinery broke down, making way for the military; in 1974 the military authoritarian structure simply collapsed.

The "profile," then, can be drawn and studied in terms of two basic factors: economic modernization, with all its social implications, on the one hand, and political modernization on the other. The latter can be reduced for the purposes of this discussion to its simplest possible components: (1) participation and participatory mechanisms including the formation of national and integrative political parties, (2) the development of rational governmental and bureaucratic structures, and (3) regime-acceptance—legitimacy.

Economic and social changes have been very much in evidence in Greece. Since 1949, when the Civil War ended, gross domestic product has increased seven-fold, with the manufacturing sector growing five-fold while the agricultural sector only doubled. However, given the particular character of investment—mostly from the United States —this remarkable growth did not always correspond to the needs of the country: it was concentrated in a few manufacturing firms, tourism and construction, and in general in enterprises likely to provide high short-term returns. This became abundantly clear by 1970 when the export of capital from Greece in the form of profit repatriation—but also a heavy trade deficit—began to exceed by far the rate of capital imports. What is more, overall economic growth did not increase employment opportunities; given the exodus of young workers to various Western European countries, employment as a whole remained stationary. Nor did it bring about a corresponding increase in real wages. Agricultural production remained pitifully inadequate, for unlike most other cases of rapid economic growth, that of Greece did not bring a rise in the productivity of the farmers. Finally, income inequalities remained sharp, and little has been done to attenuate them.

---

[4] Joseph LaPalombara, *Interest Groups in Italian Politics* (New Haven: Yale University Press, 1964).

Thus, Greece in 1975 had a dependent economy in which foreign investments had been made and solicited under very attractive conditions for the investor, with little consideration for the long-range interests of the economy. Nevertheless, the country had profited greatly—for the foundations of a modern economy had been laid out. It had developed much faster than other countries whose socio-economic profiles and rates of modernization before World War II had been analogous, notably Turkey and Portugal, and perhaps Southern Italy. But the major problems—how to increase the opportunities for employment, how to modernize agriculture and increase the productivity of the farmer, how to avoid disparities of income at the very time when the growth of the national wealth made the aspirations of many more pressing, and, finally, how to plan the economy and gear it to national needs in order to make the country at least relatively less dependent upon outside financial help—all these problems remain. They all have a direct impact upon the social structure of the country and upon the demands that are generated. They are likely to put a heavy strain upon the political system.

The social considerations, many of which stem from rapid but unplanned economic growth, are easy to outline. First, "traditional" groupings have been undermined, perhaps faster than in any other Mediterranean country. This is particularly true of the village which has progressively declined in population as well as in political, social, and economic influence. Second, there has been marked geographic mobility, which again tends to break down isolated, parochial units and produces a greater degree of national homogeneity. Third, urbanization has been particularly rapid. More than 60 percent of the Greeks live and work today in middle-sized or large urban agglomerations. Five and a half million live in urban centers, another million in small towns (3,000–10,000 pop.) and less than 3 million in villages (2,000 and less) and the countryside.[5] The social implications of urbanization have been stressed by a number of authors. In Kornhauser's words, the "rapid influx of large numbers of people into newly developed areas incites mass movements."[6] According to Black, it is related to the last stages of development when a society reaches political "integration."[7] It is also a clear sign that the "segmented"

---

[5] *Statistical Yearbook of Greece*, 1971 (Athens: 1973).

[6] William Kornhauser, *The Politics of Mass Society* (Glencoe, Ill.: Free Press, 1959), pp. 143-144.

[7] C. E. Black, *The Dynamics of Modernization* (Princeton: Princeton University Press, 1964).

society has given way to social and political integration.[8] Urbanization is generally linked with education and the spread of literacy, with role differentiation, and with intense associational activity—all of which lead to a renewed interest in politics and political organization.[9]

Greece has been on the way to economic and social modernization—at times quite rapid—for the last twenty-five years. Its social structure was more receptive and conducive to this process than that of many other countries. Agrarian reforms had already done away with the large landowner, except in isolated cases, and emphasis upon trade and small-scale manufacturing averted the concentration of wealth in family-owned companies that has occurred elsewhere. The pattern of land ownership has been much more like that of France than of Italy or Spain: few big landlords, many—too many—smaller plots and individual farmers. At the same time, the still relatively low degree of industrialization, combined with the rapid growth of the tertiary sector from tourism, accounted for the lack of an industrial proletariat. Out of an active population of 3.5 million, not more than 900,000 are "technicians and workers," and fewer than 40 percent of these are industrial workers.[10] They live and work in large urban centers, and the majority work in factories that employ fewer than fifteen workers.

The second aspect of modernization is political development. In the absence of survey work, I would venture a thought based on my understanding of the historical forces that have shaped the modern Greek states but also on some recent politcal trends: namely, that the Greek political culture is more homogeneous, and integrated with a higher level of political awareness, than that of any other Mediterranean or Latin American country. The individual is more drawn to participatory political action and has a more positive view of his own role in influencing politics and political decisions. In contrast to Italy[11] and other Mediterranean countries, Greece achieved national independence through a common national and popular effort; and a long irredentist movement—despite, but also because of, many reverses—kept the feeling of national unity intact. *Le pays réel* is a

---

[8] Samuel H. Beer, *Modern Political Development* (New York: Random House, 1974), p. 72. Also Dankwart Rustow, *A World of Nations* (Washington, D.C.: Brookings Institution, 1967).

[9] Daniel Lerner, *The Passing of Traditional Society* (Glencoe, Ill.: Free Press, 1958).

[10] *Statistical Yearbook of Greece*, 1971, pp. 73-74.

[11] Joseph LaPalombara, "Italy: Fragmentation, Isolation, Alienation" in Lucien Pye and Sidney Verba, eds., *Political Culture and Political Development* (Princeton: Princeton University Press, 1965), pp. 282-330.

living force in Greece no matter what the divisions have been about *le pays légal!*

Many other factors reinforced this strong integrative force of national identity. One has been the lack of sharp regional differences. There is nothing comparable to the separation between north and south that continues to be so much in evidence in Italy, for instance. But there is also nothing comparable to the sharp distinction between a "church culture" and a "lay culture." The church, even if a conservative force in many parts of the country, never became a separate political culture. Nor did the villagers separate themselves from the rest to form parochial enclaves *against* or outside the state.

There are a number of forces, however, that have impeded the realization of a stable and efficient political system. One stems from the disagreements within the middle classes about the political regime itself. A second, perhaps even more fundamental, is the Greek elites' tradition of "dependence" on outside powers (England, then the United States from roughly 1947 to 1974) and the overt intervention of these powers in Greek politics. A third is the failure thus far of the political parties to develop effective national organizations.

It is naturally impossible to analyze here in any depth the character and relationship of these forces. The division of the middle classes accounts for the perennial conflict between the monarchy and the republic. A different style of government is associated with each, and different socioeconomic and political forces cluster behind them. The monarchy (even a constitutional monarchy) was fundamentally a semiauthoritarian system in which some basic powers—indeed, what may well amount to the commanding heights of the polity—remained in the hands of the monarch and his advisers, often in close cooperation with a foreign ally. Foreign policy and defense remained invariably in the hands of the king. The monarchy was backed by the upper bourgeoisie, some of the middle classes, and the peasantry, especially in some of the backward areas of the country. A democratic regime, on the other hand, has been traditionally supported by the majority of the middle classes, the urban centers in general, and the workers; for historical reasons, it has also found strong support in some sections of the country—notably the island of Crete. When the conflict reached a high level of intensity as in the years between 1963 and 1967, with neither the proponents of parliamentary democracy nor the supporters of the monarchy able to prevail, the army stepped into the picture to establish military dictatorship.

The "Foreign Factor" and "Dependence". Virtually all modernizing societies—especially since the end of World War II—have aimed to attain full and unqualified independence, be it from a former colonial power or from military occupation or from indirect military and economic control and domination. Greece, however, attained its independence in 1831 largely as a result of direct foreign intervention, and this left a legacy of dependence. For a number of reasons related to Greece's past but also to its more recent efforts to carve its proper territory out of the Ottoman Empire and develop national boundaries that correspond to the territories where the ethnic Greeks live, the extension and the integrity of the nation's territory depended upon benevolent neutrality, intervention, or protection from outside. The Greek elites learned to live with it and even to solicit it. Important decisions could not be made without the direct intervention of a foreign power, which deprived the political leaders, the parties, and ultimately the people of the responsibility for making major political choices. This also affected major economic and social decisions related to the procurement of capital and investment policy. Capital formation and investment became, as we noted, dependent upon foreign loans or aid rather than upon domestic effort and planning. In this sense Greek society remained in a state of dependency, which in the last analysis is incompatible with the logic of full political development.

The Fragility of the Party Structure. Since World War II there have been nine legislative elections in Greece, in which a total of at least thirty-five different parties have participated. On the right, the old "People's Party"—the anchor of all right-wing coalitions—appeared under a variety of labels such as National Radical Union and, in 1974, New Democracy (ND). It formed coalitions with a host of satellite parties. Its platform was attachment to the king, anticommunism, a strong pro-American and pro-NATO stance, and a conservative economic and social outlook. In the center the confusion was greater. There were at least fifteen different party labels, and the various groupings did not always manage to form coalitions. The Liberal party splintered —sometimes into as many as six factions, some of which managed to form the Center Union party in 1974. Its leadership has always been uncertain, its organization invisible, and its membership virtually nonexistent. On the left, the Communist party of Greece (KKE), but also left-wing splinters and occasionally even centrists, managed to form a coalition under the label United Democratic Left (EDA), which gave way in 1974 to the Communist party under the label United Left and to a new party, the Panhellenic Socialist Movement (PASOK).

The results of the nine postwar elections highlight the internal instability of the party system. Except in the election of 1964, no party won a majority of seats, and party alliances were unstable.

Between 1946 and 1951 fifteen cabinets were formed under six different prime ministers. Five times the legislature was dissolved before the expiration of its term—in 1952, 1958, 1961, 1963, and 1964. If we cluster some ten parties on the right and fourteen parties in the center, their shares of the vote at the elections between 1946 and 1964 changed from as little as 62 percent to as much as 95 percent. As for the parties comprising the left, they changed from as little as 5 percent to as much as 23 percent. The average shift of the popular vote from one political "family" to the other amounted to thirty percentage points.

Party fragmentation is, of course, one indication of the fragility of the party system and of its inability to translate demands into policies and become an integrative mechanism for the realization of common aspirations. Lack of membership, lack of internal organization, lack of institutionalized forms for selecting leaders and for establishing leader and rank-and-file relationships, party decentralization with emphasis upon local and regional party barons and bosses, the lack of even a modicum of programmatic coherence, the tendency of members to vote differently in Parliament even if they belong to the same party, and, finally, the frequent desertions of powerful figures and their followers to join other formations, are all part and parcel of the same phenomenon. All have been present to an inordinate degree in Greece. Parties have been "personal" creations, holding together as long as the leader remained present; membership has been virtually nonexistent; meetings of party congresses and executive committees, required on paper, have not taken place; continuous reshufflings among party groups have both demonstrated and aggravated the inherent instability of the parties and made them increasingly susceptible to extraparliamentary pressures— whether from the monarch, the army, or a foreign power.

In recent years, however, there has been a noticeable reduction in the number of parties. The late Jean Meynaud,[12] in his study of Greek politics prior to the military junta, listed a total of ninety-seven "parties" active in one form or another in the period between 1946 and 1964. Keith Legg, using a more parsimonious classification, identified thirty-two party formations.[13] In the election of 1964 the trend toward the consolidation of parties and electoral coalitions and the increasingly national as opposed to regional and local character of the parties were unmistakable. The number of parties dropped

[12] Meynaud, "Politikes Dynameis stin Ellada," pp. 78, 91, 94, 98, 103, 109, 117, 121, and 511-527.
[13] Legg, *Politics*, pp. 328-332.

gradually, as the larger parties seemed to absorb the splinters—and Greece's party system began to resemble those of Western Europe.

The Political Forces Present in the Late 1970s

An analysis of the period of the military junta (1967–1974) hardly belongs here. However, we shall not be able to evaluate the election and the referendum [14] that took place in 1974 and the election of 1977 without a brief reminder of the colonels' efforts to do away with political parties, to imprison, exile, or intimidate all political leaders at the national, regional, or local levels that did not support them, and to infiltrate and control the major instrumentalities of government and the most important centers of administrative, cultural, and educational life—the bureaucracy, the judiciary, the church, and the university. Political activity froze, and the only movements that could be detected were either palace intrigues and conflicts among conspirators or variations in the intensity with which repression and intimidation were meted out. Few could have predicted that within a matter of weeks after the junta's fall in August 1974 the old parties would come back to life; that within a matter of three months the most open and free elections the country had experienced since the end of World War II would have taken place; and that they would give an overwhelming majority to a center-right government.

The Revival of the Parties. With the fall of the junta and the return of some of the old politicians, the parties hastily reorganized. Some reappeared with the same labels, some with new ones. The trend toward simplification held, with four major parties running in every electoral district in the nation and only a very few independents and regional leaders competing for the vote. A right-wing extremist party and *all* the independents running throughout the country received less than 3 percent of the total vote.

All four parties appealed to the voters across local and regional issues; thus, behind their competition there was a unifying and nationalizing element. Further, despite the parties' rhetoric, there were a great number of issues on which they seemed to be in agreement, including the most divisive issue of Greek political history—the nature of the new regime. Thus there was noticeable convergence. In fact, except in the case of the one new party—the Panhellenic

---

[14] In the analysis that follows I rely on the accounts and figures of the Greek daily press. I also use the very competent tabulations and analysis of the vote published in the weekly *Tachidromos*, March 27, 1975, Athens.

Socialist Movement founded by Andreas Papandreou—ideology gave way to concrete options and choices. Even the Communist party put the accent on specifics and developed a program stressing incremental solutions that would lead *ultimately* to the establishment of a socialist society

Yet past practices and patterns were again very much in evidence. To begin with, the hastily reorganized parties remained "personal parties." This was clearly the case with New Democracy, the center-right formation established by Karamanlis upon his return; it was, at least in its inception, a replica of the Union for the New Republic founded by Charles de Gaulle when he returned to French politics in 1958. But the same was true of PASOK, whose organization and inspiration came from its founder. Only the centrist groups met to designate the leader of the Center Union. As for the Communists, they were divided into competing factions, though they managed to establish a coalition, the United Left. In addition, though ten years had passed since the last election, the parties, including even PASOK, continued to rely upon old-time local and regional political leaders. Death had taken many leaders, and some 50 percent of all the candidates were new. But in many instances political influence had simply passed from father to son or to some other family member. To be sure, there were genuine newcomers. Yet, by and large, control remained in the hands of the political class that had been pushed aside by the junta. As a result the parties remained—despite their nationwide appeal—loose federations and alliances of political leaders and local notables rather than centralized and disciplined entities. They were and still are prone to factionalism and fragmentation, especially if "the leader" disappears. They remain prone to internal quarrels and likely to splinter. This was true both for the left and for the right.

By the beginning of October 1974 the parties had designated their candidates and entered the electoral campaign. The election was set for November 17. What were their programs? Areas of convergence first: among all but the minuscule extremist groups, an affirmation of democracy with political freedoms and civil rights; a quasi-unanimous desire to purge the military of all elements that had cooperated with the junta and to place the defense establishment under civilian control; an overwhelming commitment to the republic as opposed to the return of the monarch—all parties except New Democracy opposing the king's return and ND itself avoiding the issue by claiming that it was not a matter for the legislative elections but one to be decided later in a referendum; a virtually unanimous stand in favor of moving the Greek military forces out of NATO, reducing the number of U.S. military bases, and limiting the legal and other prerogatives of American personnel; a strong affirmation of national unity vis-à-vis Turkey and Turkish demands in the Aegean and elsewhere and a concomitant unanimity in favor of strengthening control over monopolies and bringing some key economic activities under state direction; and, finally, general support for larger appropriations for education and the overhauling of the educational system. Curiously enough the Cyprus issue—although 40 percent of the island was occupied by Turkish forces—did not play a significant role in the election. All parties paid lip service to a return to the territorial status quo ante but avoided studiously (and wisely) either demanding a timetable or adumbrating the tactics that could bring it about.

These powerful unifying themes did not, of course, hide differences—ideological, pragmatic, and tactical. As was to be expected, New Democracy emphasized the personality of its leader. Karamanlis stressed gradualism in the purging of the army and the related services and promised to punish only the major offenders. He was reluctant to commit himself to any pronouncements that might jeopardize the Atlantic Alliance and suggested few basic economic reforms. Like Valéry Giscard d'Estaing, then the newly elected president of France, he emphasized the need for change "without risks," while affirming the party's commitment to national independence. And he promised to immediately resume negotiations to make Greece a full member of the Common Market. Otherwise New Democracy appealed to the forces that had traditionally supported the right—but, again as in France, it was to be a renewed, reformist right. Its appeal had widened toward the center and even toward the left.

It was PASOK, of course, that attracted public attention. It proved to be—at least in its policy statements—the only ideological party. But its ideological positions were couched in strong nationalist terms. It was the party of national independence par excellence, arguing for withdrawal from NATO *and* the Alliance, the immediate removal of all American bases, but also withdrawal from any European entanglements such as the Common Market. It favored the settlement of the Cyprus conflict by the United Nations without any interference from, or any benefit of the good offices of, the United States. It was blatantly anti-American in every pronouncement of its leader. PASOK asked for a sweeping purge of the state administration, the military, the judiciary, the universities, and the civil service and demanded that all legislation passed in the seven years of military rule be declared null and void. But it was in the social and economic fields that PASOK struck its true ideological note: it favored a sweeping socialization of industry and even of trade, the nationalization of banks, a national health service, the nationalization of the educational system to include private schools and colleges, comprehensive social security for all, and broad welfare benefits. It demanded the right to work for all, equality of men and women, and drastic measures of decentralization verging upon "community control."

The United Left, quick to point out that Greece was not ready for socialism, outlined a gradualistic program. It asked for state control of all foreign monopolies and multinationals, public control of oil imports and oil production if oil indeed were found in the Aegean, the cancellation and reconsideration of all trade and economic agreements with foreign companies, and sweeping tax reforms. Only the "preconditions" of socialism could be laid down. The Communists, after almost forty years of uninterrupted persecution, were simply trying to reorganize their party, to unite the factions that had grown up and bide their time. They took a cautious, reformist approach, sensing, perhaps correctly, that the fall of the junta had not brought a strong swing to the left as had happened elsewhere.

The Electorate. What were the major changes in the national electorate since 1964, and what inference could one draw from them for 1974? There were two major changes—both favoring a shift to the left. About 1 million young men and women who had been between eleven and twenty in 1964 (the year of the last election) were now entitled to vote. In the same period about 750,000 voters who were sixty-four or over in 1964 may be presumed to have died. Thus, while the overall age distribution of the electorate was about the same, a smaller percentage remembered anticommunism and the cold war. How would these new voters vote? There was a prima facie reason to expect that a good percentage would vote left, and there is no doubt that the strategy of Papandreou and his party was predicated on this assumption. There was a reinforcing factor: the movement of population within Greece showed that as many as 1 million people had moved from the country and the villages into urban centers. The population of greater Athens alone had increased from almost 1.9 million in 1961 to over 2.5 million in 1971—a net increase of almost 700,000. In the same period greater Thessaloniki had grown from 380,000 to 557,000, a gain of 177,000. Again it was expected that these voters would lean to the left. Thus *at least* 1 million and perhaps as many as 1.5 million—15 to 20 percent of the electorate—might shift to the left. With voting participation ranging between 75 and 80 percent of the registered voters, it is my conclusion that potential left supporters, and especially the younger people who are generally the most active and interested in politics, may well have amounted to as much as 20 percent of those *who actually voted*—almost 1 million. This trend to the left would be strengthened, it was expected, by other factors: this was a genuinely free election; there was no pressure or intimidation from the police or the gendarmerie in the countryside where it had played an important role in the past, or from army officers and servicemen—a practice that had accounted for huge majorities for the right-wing parties. The only factor working in the opposite direction was the greater number of women, who normally vote more conservatively than men. About 2,850,000 men and 3,150,000 women were registered.

There were no other factors that made any particular trend to the right or to the left seem likely. The only new and significant ingredient was intangible—the people's reaction to the fall of the junta and the restoration of democracy. It could have led to intense factionalism, but this, as we have seen, was avoided in part thanks to the simplification of the party system. It could have ushered in an irresistible movement of protest against past abuses and led to a left-wing surge, from which PASOK and the Communists would profit. But it could also have found expression in an affirmation of "democracy without risks" and a preference for moderate and cautious leadership that would unify rather than polarize the country, especially in the face of a Turkish threat. It was, I believe, this last consideration that played the preponderant role in the outcome of the election.

The Results. As table 1–1 shows, the result was a landslide victory for Karamanlis and New Democracy. They carried every region except Crete by overwhelming pluralities and frequently by absolute majorities. In 1964 the National Radical Union—the core of what later became New Democracy—had won only 36 percent of the vote; New Democracy received 54.5 percent. The Center party, which had received 52 percent in 1964, was reduced to 20 percent. It managed to win a plurality only in Crete and fell below 20 percent in many parts of the country. PASOK came a poor third with 13.6 percent, and the Communists (the United Left) retained their hard core supporters with just a little under 10 percent. The combined vote of the Communists and PASOK was just over 23 percent. The electoral landslide translated into overwhelming control of the legislature by New Democracy. It secured 220 out of the 300 seats, while the Center Union received 60, PASOK 12, and the United Left 8. Had the election been held under a straight proportional representation system, the corresponding strength of the parties would have been 167, 62, 41, and 27. Had it been held under a majority system, however, it would have given New Democracy 285 seats and the Center

Table 1–1
RESULTS OF THE PARLIAMENTARY ELECTIONS OF
1974 AND 1977

	Popular Vote	Percent of Vote	Seats
1974			
Registered voters	6,241,066		
Votes cast	4,963,558		
Valid votes	4,908,874		
Turnout	79.53%		
ND		2,669,133	54.4	220
EK-ND		1,002,559	20.5	60
PASOK		666,413	13.6	12
Left		464,787	9.5	8
Other		106,082	2.2	0
1977			
Registered voters	6,403,738		
Votes cast	5,193,891		
Valid votes	5,129,771		
Turnout	81.11%		
ND		2,146,365	41.8	171
PASOK		1,300,025	25.3	93
EK-ND		612,786	11.9	16
KKE		480,272	9.4	11
NA		349,988	6.8	5
Left		139,356	2.7	2
New Liberal		55,494	1.1	2
Other		45,485	0.9	0

NOTE: For details of "other" vote and district breakdown see appendix B.

SOURCE: Election Directorate, Ministry of the Interior, *Apotelesmata ton Voulef-tikon Eklogon tis 17is Noemvriou 1974* [Results of the parliamentary elections of November 17, 1974], vol. 1 (Athens: National Printing Office, 1976), and Election Directorate, Ministry of the Interior, *Apotelesmata ton Vouleftikon Eklogon tis 20is Noemvriou 1977* [Results of the parliamentary elections of November 20, 1977], vol. 1 (Athens: National Printing Office, 1979).

Union 15, allowing no representation to the other parties.

The Monarchy and New Democracy. Three weeks after the election the referendum was held, as promised, on the king's return. Technically the people were asked if they wanted a democracy headed by a monarch—along the lines of the British prototype—or a democracy headed by a president, whose powers were to be defined by the new

Table 1–2

RESULTS OF THE REFERENDUM ON THE MONARCHY,
DECEMBER 8, 1974

Registered voters	6,244,539
Votes cast	4,719,787
Valid votes	4,690,986
Abstention rate	24.4%
Yes to king's return	1,445,875
	30.8%
No to king's return	3,245,111
	69.2%

SOURCE: General Secretariat for Press and Information, *Postwar Elections in Greece* (Athens: n.p., n.d.).

legislative assembly, which was given also the power to revise the constitution. The presidency might be patterned after the Italian or the German model, but the model of the French Fifth Republic was also under serious consideration. The response was overwhelmingly against the monarchy: 70 percent of the voters were opposed. The vote, despite some regional variations, showed a nationwide consensus (see table 1–2).

All parties except New Democracy had come out before the legislative election against the king. The leader of New Democracy had decided to downplay the issue. He did the same in the referendum, taking a neutral stance, while all his opponents urged a vote against the king's return. Virtually all the elected representatives of New Democracy—215 strong—remained silent, though a good number favored the king's return. This was a remarkable display of discipline on such a politically emotional issue. The reasons are not difficult to find. By muting the issue, New Democracy averted an intraparty split.

A glance at the regional distribution of the referendum vote shows that wherever New Democracy had been strong in the legislative election there was also a significantly higher (though virtually nowhere a majority) vote for the king; wherever New Democracy's vote had been low, the vote for the king was low as well. Given the fact that practically all voters for PASOK, the Center Union, and the United Left, accounting for about 45 percent of the vote in the legislative election, were opposed to the king, most of those who voted for his return must have come from among the supporters of New Democracy. As many as 50 percent of the latter were royalists. Thus unless the royalist and antiroyalist forces within the ND reconcile their differences, the possibility of a party split on the question of the regime remains.

November 20, 1977. The election of November 20, 1977—almost exactly three years after the first election—virtually reproduced the basic left-right voter alignment. New Democracy, under the same leadership, won only a plurality and suffered a decline of thirteen percentage points. In fact, however, about half of these defectors went to an extreme right-wing party, the National Alignment, and thus remained close to New Democracy, which could count on their support. Its real loss, therefore, amounted to not more than six or seven percentage points. If we add the votes of the New Democracy, of the National Alignment, and of the centrists (the Center Union), the total strength of the center-right in 1977 amounted to about 55 percent. On the left the most noticeable phenomena were the stability of the Communist vote (around 10 percent) and PASOK's gains from 13.6 percent to 25.3 percent. Many of the PASOK votes came, therefore, directly from the center, but some may have also come directly from New Democracy. Without survey research it is impossible to tell what was the percentage of transfers from New Democracy to the Center and from the Center to PASOK. But whatever the case, the combined vote of PASOK, the Communists, and the other leftists did not amount to more than 42 percent. Even a straight proportional representation system would have given a center-right coalition a majority to govern, though not the 180 seats in the legislature that are the minimum needed to elect a president of the republic.

The overall stability of the vote should not hide the elements of potential instability. The first was the split of the extreme right from New Democracy. Under different electoral circumstances the National Alignment—even as a splinter—may have a weight that is disproportionate to its electoral strength, enabling it to hold New Democracy hostage to its policies. The second element of instability lies in the collapse of the Center, which has only been confirmed since 1977, and the ensuing polarization between right and left. This is further aggravated by the rise of PASOK, from 13 to 25 percent— another trend that appears to have continued since the election.

Basically the issues before the electorate in 1977 were the same as those in 1974. PASOK and the Communists refused to cooperate with each other, but they both harped on powerful nationalist slogans with regard to Turkey and Cyprus; they both exploited dissatisfaction with the United States and NATO; they both argued strongly against Greece's entry into the Common Market. On economic and social issues Papandreou continued to sound farther left than the Communists, advocating socialization and social welfare measures that the Communists were not yet ready to endorse. New Democracy stood on "its record"—prosperity, full employment, democracy, and political and social tranquility. The military had been brought under control. The European vocation of Greece, the ND claimed, was consistent both with the nation's traditions and with its future orientation. A cautious foreign policy had averted a confrontation with Turkey, and Greece had continued to maintain its distance from NATO. Karamanlis's personality and his ability to tame the generals and the colonels, to reorganize the armed forces, and to remain within the framework of the constitution and the political liberties it guaranteed continued to play a dominant role.

Karamanlis Becomes President of the Republic. A new presidential election had to be held five years after the first president of the republic, Constantine Tsatsos, was elected in June 1975. The new election was held in late April 1980. Karamanlis was the only candidate, and three ballots were required in his election. In the first and second ballots he received fewer than 180 votes. On the third and final one he received 183 votes—three more than the required minimum. New Democracy, the National Alignment, and some centrists voted for him. The other parties abstained. Thus a legislative election was averted, and at the age of seventy-three the most popular leader assumed the highest office in the land. He pledged to be the president of all Greeks and, in the Gaullist tradition he admires, promised to remain "above party." Like de Gaulle, however, he may play an active leadership role.

Institutions never function exactly as their framers intended. They change to fit changing circumstances. This is especially true when a constitution embodies contradictory provisions and principles—as does the constitution of the Fifth Republic, from which the Greek constitution draws its inspiration. Both embody two potentially contradictory principles—one parliamentary, the other presidential. In France under de Gaulle, fundamental changes occurred well outside the letter of the constitution. The presidency, despite all the disclaimers of Giscard d'Estaing, has been *politicized*—the president is the leader of a majority in Parliament, which often is "his" majority. "If you vote for 'my' deputies," de Gaulle often said, "you vote for me!" Second, the office has become personalized. It is the man—his leadership, integrity, courage, and intelligence—that the people accept or reject. The party often is overshadowed by the appeal of the president and the support he elicits. Third, the presidency of the

17

Fifth Republic has become the *real government*. De Gaulle developed the theory of *la domaine reservée*—the proposition that certain affairs of state, namely foreign policy and overall strategy, were "reserved" for the president. Giscard d'Estaing also makes his own foreign policy; the minister of foreign affairs simply executes it. Last, the ascendancy of the presidency has amounted to the *hierarchization* of the executive branch—the presidency is the superior office; the premiership and cabinet are inferior. The first decides on broad policies; the second implements them. In essence, the real prime minister in France is the president himself. A vote against the prime minister and the cabinet in the National Assembly is likely to be construed as a vote against the president and will lead him to dissolve the legislature and call new elections.

Any reading of the Greek constitution, when we keep in mind the French one, will easily show that it contains many presidential elements. The Greek president can dissolve Parliament; he can call for a referendum; he appoints the prime minister (and may even be able to dismiss him, as French presidents do); he can veto legislation (something that the French president cannot do), in which case it cannot become law unless voted by three-fifths of the legislature; by virtue of article 48 (the same number as the fateful article of the Weimar constitution . . .) he can declare a state of emergency and rule by executive order. A strong and popular president, in other words, even under the letter of the Greek constitution, may assume real powers and play the dominant role in policy making. This is particularly so if he has majority support in the legislature—or if the legislature is fragmented into many groups and parties. Only if and when there is a strong and cohesive majority *against* the president will presidential leadership become difficult, if not quite impossible.

With Karamanlis as prime minister, the Greek constitution developed in the parliamentary direction. The prime minister, supported by a majority, governed, and the president limited himself to the ceremonial affairs of state. But now it is Karamanlis who is president of the republic. Will he play the same role *under* a prime minister that his predecessor played under him? Will he let the constitution continue to develop in the parliamentary direction that he himself imparted to it after 1974? Or will he rather make use of the "presidential powers" that the constitution sets forth and assert his presidential prerogatives and leadership over the prime minister and the cabinet? Will Karamanlis play the role of de Gaulle? The latter when elected for the second time was seventy-four years old. In June 1980 Karamanlis was only seventy-three!

The question is extremely important. If Karamanlis decides to give the constitution a Gaullist interpretation and uses the powers of the office against a prime minister—especially a leftist one—then the old conflict between the prime minister and the crown will reappear as a conflict between prime minister and president. This might have grave repercussions for the stability of the regime and the future of constitutional government.

The Appeal of Populism. Andreas Papandreou's PASOK has managed to provide a powerful appeal to many groups—university students, farmers, people in the small towns, environmentalists, nationalists and xenophobes, the poor and the dispossessed, and the aged living on pensions. It has appealed to anti-Americanism, exploiting the charge that the United States was responsible for the military junta (just as, according to the Iranians, it was responsible for the Shah and his crimes). It has mounted a strong anti-American and anti-European campaign in foreign policy coupled with a strong nationalist campaign for an independent Greece seeking its identity and vocation in its own past and history. A powerful protest movement, PASOK has all the characteristics of a populist crusade and courts all the attendant dangers. It is a movement that has received considerable support from the Greek middle classes as well, and from some of the most important newspapers.

Herein lies another element of instability; just what it means will be revealed in the legislative election that must be held before November 1981. If PASOK continues to gain in votes and in popular support, a confrontation with the president will be unavoidable. The latter will want to preserve Greece's position in the European Economic Community and in the Atlantic Alliance and to shelter the country from the sweeping social and economic reforms to which Papandreou is committed or to which he pays lip service.

Conclusion

There is little in this essay to allow for anything but the most qualified concluding remarks. The party configuration has been simplified. Though New Democracy remains divided between "royalists" and "democrats," the overwhelming vote against the king may have paved the way, barring serious internal or international crises, to the development of a broad national consensus on the form of the regime. In Parliament a classic dichotomy has developed between "majority" and "opposition" analogous to the one that grew up in France and West Germany but that has failed to materialize in Italy, Spain, or

Portugal. The opposition parties have a leader in the Assembly—Papandreou. They managed to combine their forces in the municipal elections held in March 1975 to back a single candidate in each contest (often successfully) against the "candidate of the majority." This may initiate a movement—which did not materialize in the legislative election of 1977—in the direction of further simplification. Elections may well offer a choice between two rival coalitions. If they do, the parties—even broad coalition parties—are likely to develop into participatory mechanisms mobilizing the electorate in favor of or against certain policies and national options rather than fragmenting it into a plethora of groupings from which no national direction and choice can come. It follows that under such circumstances the party coalitions will become less ideological and sectarian and, by trying to attract as many of the voters as possible, will compromise their respective positions in order to present national programs. They will become more pragmatic and in so doing will be forced to blunt the sharp differences that have separated them in the past. In other words, Greek politics may begin to follow the Western model. That is what I have called the "generous" hypothesis.

But the reader should also consider the "niggardly" hypothesis. Despite the simplification of the party system, the parties might remain internally weak and continue to stress personal leadership at the expense of organization and structure. Party divisions are likely to reappear—and foremost among them the division within New Democracy between royalists and republicans. A breakup of the new majority—resembling the breakup of the centrist majority in 1965—is a distinct possibility. It would usher in a period of instability and sharp cleavages over the regime. This would mean in effect that the second prerequisite of political modernization—regime-acceptance and legitimacy—had failed to mature. The socioeconomic demands following in the wake of rapid modernization, but also the social and economic problems that economic growth had failed to solve, would press harder and harder upon governmental structures, themselves weakened by the dislocation of the majority party. The need for the restoration of the king, especially if confrontation developed between the president and a prime minister, would be voiced and echoes would reverberate through the military establishment. Any international crisis, especially a clash between Greece and Turkey, would be likely to heighten the effectiveness of the monarchists, especially if, in the name of NATO unity, powerful foreign forces lent them their weight. Such a development would again undermine the third prerequisite for political modernization—a modicum of national independence.

2

Greek Electoral Law

Phaedo Vegleris

Parliamentary elections in Greece are governed by the constitution, which is a self-sufficient text superior to the acts of all public authorities,[1] by laws,[2] and by decrees supplementing the laws. Customs and convention add little to the provisions of the constitution and the laws in the Greek electoral system.

In terms of their effective stability, the electoral rules can be divided into two categories. First, the rules expressly laid down in the constitution together with the laws supplementing them provide for the existence of a Parliament representative of the whole electorate, the maximum and minimum number of its members, the principles of universal suffrage, freedom of association in political parties, and equal representation, the right to vote and to run for office, and the impediments to eligibility for either.

Second are the rules initiated by the legislature in areas not covered by the constitution. These refer mainly to the electoral system in the technical sense, the way in which the parliamentary seats are distributed between the parties and candidates in each constituency and

[1] Greece belongs to the group of states (the overwhelming majority) where the constitution is not only written but also "codified." See the definition in S. E. Finer, *Comparative Government* (Harmondsworth: Penguin, 1974), p. 146. The superiority of the constitution means in Greece not only that laws cannot be enacted by any body or procedure other than those provided by the constitution, but also that laws must be consistent with the broad principles and specific rules of the constitution; consequently the courts, which must not enforce an unconstitutional law, perform a function very similar to judicial review in the United States.

[2] Under all the Greek constitutions, laws have been made by Parliament and by the head of state (the king, or the president of the republic in the years 1924-1935 and today), who makes them public and has a veto power. During periods of military rule, however, laws have been made by "legislative decree" and governments have essentially ignored the constitution.

21

in the country as a whole. In fact, a peculiarity of the present constitution, which was retained from the constitution of 1952, is that it expressly authorizes the legislature to define the electoral system (though this power had never been denied it). This provision ensures that, for questions regarding the electoral system and the constituencies, Parliament cannot delegate its power to the executive.[3]

These two categories overlap. For example, the constitution acknowledges the right of all Greeks to vote but allows the law to determine the conditions under which this right is acquired and exercised. Again, the constitution specifies that one-twentieth of the total number of members of Parliament may be elected in a different way from the others, to be determined by Parliament. Moreover, the constitution itself has evolved, so that even its provisions cannot be considered absolutely constant. But above all, an internal relationship binds the constitution's essential guarantees of representative government to the electoral system proper. This relationship constitutes one of the most serious and neglected aspects of Greek electoral law.

The discussion is organized around these two categories because they correspond roughly to two lines of development. A third section of the chapter, devoted to the validation of parliamentary elections, will make evident the connection between constitutional and statutory electoral rules and the problems that arise from it.

The Right to Vote and to Run for Office

Democracy in Greece. Some of the features of Greece's present government have their roots in the first constitution of the Kingdom of Greece of March 18, 1844, which put an end to the absolute monarchy.[4] Others were introduced by the second constitution, of October 31–November 17, 1864, when, after the installation of a new royal house, a combination of monarchy and democracy evolved, following a compromise formula which began to spread through continental Europe toward the beginning of the third decade of the nineteenth century.[5]

---

[3] Constitution of January 1, 1972, article 68 b; constitution of June 9, 1975 articles 5 para. 1, 43 para. 5, and 72 para. 1.

[4] The absolute monarchy, under the Regency and later under a Bavarian king, lasted from 1832 to 1843. The first modern Greek state was a semi-sovereign state under the suzerainty of the Ottoman sultan, established in 1828; the Protocols of London of February 3, 1830, gave it full sovereignty.

[5] The models for the first two constitutions of the Kingdom of Greece were the French constitutional charter of August 14, 1930, and, more directly, the Belgian

The constitution of 1844 made the separation of powers a general organizing principle of the state. Legislative power was vested in the king and in Parliament (at that time an elected Chamber of Deputies and an appointed Senate), the executive power was vested in the king, who exercised it "through his ministers," and the judicial power was vested in judges named by the king for life (articles 15, 20, and 21). The same constitution contained a list of individual rights and liberties under the heading "Public Law of the Greeks," which began by declaring: "All Greeks are equal before the law and all without distinction contribute to the public expenses in proportion to their property" (articles 3 to 14).[6] The formulation of these guarantees was inspired by the first European constitutions of the nineteenth century.[7] The political reform of 1862–1864 made Parliament unicameral and established direct, universal suffrage and the secrecy of the ballot for Chamber of Deputies (and municipal) elections (constitution of 1964, articles 22 and 66).[8]

The interpreters of the constitution of 1864 gave particular emphasis to a new provision, one contained in the Belgian constitution of February 7, 1831, but omitted from the Greek constitution of

---

constitution of February 7, 1831. But to these, provisions of indigenous origin were added, some of which echoed provisions of constitutions voted by assemblies of combatants and local chiefs during the Greek revolution (1821-1827) in the liberated territories of the Peloponnesus and of Sterea (mainland Greece). It should be noted that, as in most countries, particularly in continental Europe, revisions of the constitution are not required to leave intact the original text, merely appending new provisions; that requirement is peculiar to the American system of amendments. Constitutional revisions may either add provisions or modify existing ones with the exception of those declared unalterable. The distinction between "fundamental" and "nonfundamental" provisions, highly uncertain in the past, is spelled out in the 1975 constitution, which states which of its articles and paragraphs may be revised (article 110 para. 1).

[6] After the revision of the constitution of 1864 in 1911, the last phrase became "according to their capabilities." This wording has been retained ever since (constitution of 1975, article 4 para. 5).

[7] French charter of 1830, article 2; Belgian constitution of 1831, articles 6 and 112.

[8] One event had smoothed the way for the adoption of universal suffrage in parliamentary elections: by a resolution of November 19, 1862, the provisional government formed after King Othon was expelled had called upon the Greek people to elect by universal suffrage the new King George of the Danish royal family (whom the Protecting Powers, England, France, and Russia, had already chosen).

It is worth noting that each time a dictatorship was imposed in Greece, the provision of the constitution regarding the election of Parliament was suspended and so was the provision on the election of the local authorities; however, while the government confined itself to dissolving or not convoking Parliament, it actually dismissed mayors and local councils and proceeded to appoint persons of its own choice in their stead.

1844. The provision read: "All powers emanate from the nation and are exercised in the manner defined by the constitution." Another new provision of the same origin states: "The king has no other powers than those which the constitution and those particular laws which are in accordance therewith expressly accord him" (article 44). From these provisions scholars have concluded that the constitution of 1864 marked the evolution of the government of Greece from a constitutional monarchy to a democracy where the head of state was hereditary—a "crowned democracy," to use the name that the constitution finally adopted after the revision of 1952. Eventually the referendum of December 8, 1974, would determine the demise of the monarchy, and the first provision of the constitution of June 9–11, 1975, would call the new government a "presidential parliamentary democracy."[9]

The Principles of the Representative System. These general provisions were not essentially altered by the constitutional revision of 1911, the new constitution of June 3, 1927, or the post-World War II revision that produced the constitution of January 1, 1952. The constitution of 1975 in turn emphasizes the fundamental principles of liberal representative government. Thus, directly after the first article, which names the form of government, and before the old declaration "All powers emanate from the nation . . .," the following proposition has been added: "Popular sovereignty is the foundation of the form of government" (article 1 para. 2), a statement of democratic theory never before included verbatim in the text of a Greek constitution.

This provision should be correlated with two others, placed right at the end of the text, as if in a last attempt to safeguard democratic government. The first of these determines that action may be taken against persons accused of "usurping popular sovereignty" after legal institutions are again functioning (article 120 para. 3). The second enjoins the Greeks to resist "by all means" whosoever attempts by force to overthrow the constitution (article 120 para. 40). For the first time, a modern Greek constitution acknowledged a popular right which the French Revolution had considered fundamental: *la résistance à l'oppression.*[10] Whatever the practical value of these

[9] This phrase was probably preferred because the present head of state (1) is elected for a finite period (by Parliament, with a two-thirds majority, for five years) and (2) has powers enjoyed neither by the king nor by the president of the republic during the short-lived Greek Republic of 1927. The phrase seeks to identify a form of government halfway between a British-style parliamentary system and the American presidential system. The influence of the French constitution of 1958 is also conspicuous in many respects.

[10] The Declaration of the Rights of Man and of the Citizen of August 26, 1789,

paragraphs, their presence in the constitution of 1975 is indicative of the framers' purpose.

Freedom to found political parties has always been recognized as essential to representative government and deriving from the principles of freedom of thought and expression, which are explicitly guaranteed by the constitution. That is why, when the Communist party was outlawed in 1947, a "constitutional act" or "decree"—a law formally of equal validity to the constitution although contrary to it—was required. The 1975 constitution confirms the freedom to organize political parties on condition that they not interfere with the free functioning of democratic government.

Since the constitution of 1864, the parliamentary term in Greece has always been quadrennial, and it remains so under the constitution of 1975, according to which the term may only be prolonged in the event of war (article 63). But at the same time Greek constitutions have always acknowledged the right of the head of the state to dissolve Parliament before the expiration of its term. Until the constitution of 1975, the only conditions to which such dissolution was subject were that the decree be countersigned by the Council of Ministers, that the voters be called together for the election of a new Parliament within thirty days, and that the new Parliament be convoked within thirty days of the election (article 41 para. 3).

One of the notable innovations of the new constitution is that it enumerates the situations in which the president of the republic can make use of his right to dissolve Parliament. These are (1) when Parliament "is found to be in evident discord with popular feeling," (2) when "its composition does not secure the stability of the government," and (3) when "a national issue of exceptional importance" has to be faced. It also prohibits the dissolution of Parliament twice for the same reason (article 41 para. 4). All these conditions were inspired by the experience of political crises where the head of state had refused to dissolve Parliament and call new elections (1965) or, inversely, had insisted on two successive dissolutions (1915), with disastrous consequences.[11]

---

gives this as one of the four basic rights, together with freedom, property, and personal safety (article 2). The preamble to the French constitution of June 24, 1793, regards it as flowing from the other Rights of Man (article 33).

[11] The dual dissolution of Parliament in 1915, by which the king twice manifested his belief that Greece should remain neutral in the First World War and his opposition to the prime minister's policy of alignment with the Entente, created a profound and lasting polarization in the nation, with disastrous immediate and long-term consequences. In 1965-1967, the king's persistent refusal to dissolve Parliament and call new elections intensified the crisis, which then culminated in the military coup of April 21, 1967.

There is already some indication, however, that these conditions will not, in practice, hamper the executive. The first dissolution of Parliament after the constitution of 1975 came into force took place one year before the expiration of its term of office, and the government, relying on a solid majority of more than two-thirds of the parliamentary seats, offered no reason for it beyond a general reference to "extremely important national issues" that had long been pending, such as "the question of Cyprus, difficulties with Turkey, and the final decision on the entry of Greece into the European Economic Community" (decree of October 22, 1977). By deciding to dissolve a parliament that ensured governmental stability and that was not suspected of having become estranged from "popular feeling," the president and the Council of Ministers ignored the explicit restrictive provisions of the constitution and acted as if they still had unqualified discretion.[12]

The Right to Vote. Universal suffrage makes the right to vote an attribute of citizenship—indeed, the constituent element of citizenship under representative government. The 1975 constitution, to remove all doubt about the bounds within which the law could restrict the franchise, not only makes voting compulsory (article 51 para. 5) but also provides that the only admissible limitations are a minimum age requirement and incapacity flowing from a court judgment (article 53 para. 3).

Women were first granted the vote in Greece in the municipal elections of 1934 (implementing a decree of February 5, 1930), though with a more restrictive age limit than men (thirty years). They acquired the vote on the same terms as men in 1952 and voted in the parliamentary election of November 16 that year. The new constitution states firmly that "Greek men and women have equal rights and obligations" (article 4 para. 2).

Every Greek is a *demote-citadin*, a registered citizen—registered in one of the "demes" or "communities," the local government units into which Greece is divided.[13] Unless he is registered no Greek

---

[12] The question whether a dissolution of Parliament, either past or planned, is justified under one of the conditions of article 41 is only of theoretical interest. The courts do not have the jurisdiction to review a decree of dissolution for either its form or its substance.

[13] *Deme* is the name given to agglomerations of more than 10,000 inhabitants or those which have been recognized as the administrative capitals of *nomes* or departments, and which are under a territorially based local administration. *Communities* are settlements with fewer inhabitants. There are 51 nomes, 256 demes, and over 5,700 communities. The administration of the communities is simpler than that of the demes; the *mayor* of a deme enjoys a certain local

can prove his citizenship, whether he has it by birth or by naturalization. From the introduction of universal suffrage until quite recently the voting age, like the age of civil majority, was twenty-one. In June 1977 it was lowered by one year (though this step did not affect the composition of the electorate for the elections of November 20, the period between the publication of the law and the day of the poll being insufficient for the registration of the new voters).[14]

Various laws, mostly penal, provide that the right to vote may be rescinded in connection with a criminal conviction or serious mental incapacity; it may also be suspended during an inquiry held on suspicion of the perpetration of a crime or of military desertion or insubordination. In all these cases forfeiture of the right to vote is the result of a court judgment and, except in the case of life imprisonment, is provisional or at least revocable.

Voter Registration. Only a citizen registered on an electoral roll may exercise the right to vote. When he is registered the voter receives a personal election booklet, which he must present to the Supervisory Committee at the polling station. The booklet is initialed and stamped and constitutes proof that the voter has fulfilled his civic obligation. It also guarantees that he has not already voted and that he will not vote again at another polling station. The requirement to produce the booklet may be waived in exceptional cases, but only if the voter's name appears on the electoral roll. Special electoral rolls are drawn up for particular categories of state employees (judges, civil servants, the armed forces, personnel of the urban police and of

---

prestige—even some influence in the eyes of the central authority—while the *president of the community* holds a more modest position. But there is no difference in the degree of initiative with respect to the central state authority which the demes and the communities may exercise. This initative, significant enough in the general definitions of the constitution and of the Municipal and Community Code, is in reality very limited for many reasons. The point which must be made clear is that all of Greece is divided into demes *or* communities, and that each nome—a simple administrative division and not a self-governing territorial unit—includes within its borders a number of demes *or* communities whose authorities are subject to the control or supervision of the *nomarch*, the chief of the nome, who is appointed by the government.

14 The law lowering the voting age was number 626, June 25-29, 1977. Information given hereafter in the text without particular reference to the constitution or to a specific law has as its source the codification of the provisions of the electoral legislation (last assembled in decree 650/1974) which was valid during the elections of November 20, 1977, with only two modifications (mentioned in the text) resulting from law 626/1977. Reference to the articles of this codification—which we will cite hereafter as "Electoral Code" or, for the sake of brevity, "EC" —will only be made as an exception.

the fire brigade) who happen to be serving outside the deme or community where they are registered.

Voting was first made compulsory by law in 1932, but the penalties for "unwarranted" breaches of the obligation were light. After 1946 the penalties for failure to vote started to become more severe. Since 1975 the civic duty to vote has been prescribed by the constitution itself (article 54 para. 4). Under current law the penalty prescribed for "unwarranted" failure to vote in parliamentary elections is imprisonment for one to twelve months. The same penalty is imposed for failure to submit an application for registration. Moreover, this penal liability is accompanied by a series of particularly onerous administrative penalties, such as deprivation of the right to receive a permit for any sort of professional or generally lucrative activity, a driver's license, a passport, or even a police identity card (Electoral Code articles 6 para. 2 and 108 paras. 1–4).[15] The excessive severity of these penalties is evident; indeed, one wonders whether they actually obscure the significance of the citizen's "right" to vote.

However, Greek citizens who are abroad on polling day are still unable to vote. Their exclusion became increasingly significant after World War II with the growth of the Greek labor force working in other countries. The new constitution authorizes Parliament to provide for absentee voting (article 51 para. 4 line b), but so far it has not done so.

Elections are held simultaneously in all constituencies and all polling stations in the country. They are held on just one day, a Sunday, from sunrise to sunset, with the possibility of two more hours' balloting if voters are still waiting (constitution article 51 para 4, EC article 42 para. 1). The principle of the simultaneous ballot can be waived in certain cases, including the invalidation of the ballot in particular polling stations or constituencies, and by-elections. There is one polling station for every few hundred (seldom more than 700) voters on the electoral roll. A supervisory committee observes the balloting in each polling station.

Eligibility for Holding Office. Under Greek law the qualifications for holding electoral office differ on three points from the qualifications

---

[15] The explanation for the exceptional severity of these penalties and for the adoption of compulsory voting in the constitution may be the fear that some parties would call on the public to boycott elections. Boycotts were formerly (1946) considered anarchic, and an election booklet showing that the bearer had not voted was taken as evidence of his political convictions. Since the ballot is secret, of course, the voter is free to cast a blank vote; thus the compulsory vote is in fact compulsory appearance at the polling station.

for voting: (1) the constitution sets a higher age requirement, twenty-five complete years (article 55 para. 1),[16] (2) registration on an electoral roll is not required for candidacy (article 55 para. 1, EC article 29 para. 1), and (3) to run for Parliament certain public officeholders must resign their functions, while others are ineligible in certain constituencies for a specified period of time. The former group include salaried civil servants, officers of the armed forces and security forces, mayors and presidents of communities, presidents of the administrative councils of certain other legal entities, and notaries; the person resigning cannot resume his public office for one year (article 56 para. 1). Public employees and officers of the armed forces as well as administrators and employees of certain legal entities cannot become candidates in constituencies where they have served for more than three months during the past three years. This obstacle does not apply, however, to the new "deputies of the state" (article 56 para. 3), which we will come to later.

In addition, the constitution declares to be incompatible with the office of member of Parliament certain positions with any commercial enterprise under a government concession, subsidized by the state, or enjoying special privileges. Holding one of these positions does not prevent an individual from becoming a candidate or winning election, but he must choose between his commercial position and his seat in Parliament within eight days of his election's being confirmed (article 57 paras. 1 and 2).

The Electoral System

The Electoral Laws. As we noted in the introduction, the definition of the *electoral system* and the division of the nation into *constituencies* are two matters that Greek constitutions have always left to the law. The legislators have taken their mandate to heart—so much so that since 1926 no two consecutive elections for Parliament have been carried out under exactly the same electoral system.

Before its term ends, each parliament takes care to modify the electoral law to a greater or lesser extent in view of the forthcoming elections. In particular, the parliamentary majority tries to devise changes that will help it win, drawing on its experience in the previous contests. Whether its calculations have always produced the desired result is another question.

---

[16] For voting purposes anyone is considered to have reached the required age after January 1 of the year in which his twentieth birthday falls (EC article 4 para. 1).

YUGOSLAVIA

BULGARIA

ALBANIA

43.
Drama
3

46.
45. Xanthi
Kavalla 3

47.
Rodope
4

38.
Pella
5

37.
Kilkis
3

40.
Serres
8

35.
Thessaloniki—
Remainder

41.
36. 2.
Elorina
Castoria
1

33.
Imathia
4

39.
Pieria
3

42.
7. Chalkidiki
3

29.
Kozani

27.
Grevena
1

5

23.
Ioannina

32.
Thikkala
5

30.
Larissa
8

24.
Corfu
3

22.
Thesprotia

31.
Magnesia

50.
Lesbos
4

2
26.
21. Arta
Preveza 3

28.
Karditsa
6

2
25.
Lefkas
1

17.
Evritania
1

8.
Phthiotis

15.
Aetolia-
Acarmania
9

9.
Phokis
2

6.
Beotia
4

7.
Euboia
6

5.
Attica—
Remainder
6

52.
Chios
2

20.
Cephalonia
2

16.
Achaia
8

12.
Corinth
4

19.
Elia
7

10.
Argolis

18.
Zantthe
1

11.
Arcadia
5

3.

49.
Cyclades
4

14.
Messinia
7

13.
Laconia
4

4.
Piraeus-
Suburban
8

2.
Athens-
Suburban
28

1.
Athens-
Central
22

3.
Piraeus—
Central
8

34.
Thessaloniki-
City
12

56.
Canea
4

55.
Rethymnon 53.
3 Heraklion
7

Lassi

SOURCE: National Center of Social Research, Athens.

30

FIGURE 2–1
THE ELECTORAL DISTRICTS OF GREECE, PARLIAMENTARY ELECTIONS OF NOVEMBER 20, 1977

NOTE: The electoral district's name and number are shown in italic type; the number of parliamentary seats for each district is shown in roman type.

For the second distribution of seats, the country is divided into nine "major electoral districts," which group the electoral districts as follows:

Electoral Districts	Major Electoral District
1 to 9	1st
10 to 14	2nd
15 to 20	3rd
21 to 26	4th
27 to 32	5th
33 to 42	6th
43 to 47	7th
48 to 52	8th
53 to 56	9th

At the same time, the number and boundaries of the constituencies have undergone many changes, some prompted by the demographic upsets and displacements of population which have repeatedly shaken Greece, particularly in the years 1922–1923 and during and after World War II; but others have been motivated by party interests and effected without regard to objective criteria.

A full enumeration of Greece's successive electoral laws does not belong in this chapter.[17] It will be sufficient here to trace the general evolution of the electoral system used in the last elections—however short-lived it turns out to be.

Until 1926 Greek parliamentary elections were held under the majority system; sometimes the constituency was the province (an administrative unit that is a subdivision of a nome) or an even smaller division; sometimes it was the nome or a group of nomes. The first was called the "narrow district" system, the second the "broad district" system. The second finally prevailed. According to legislation currently in force, each nome is a constituency. An exception is made for the two nomes whose populations have increased disproportionately in the last forty years: the Nome of Attica (which includes Athens and suburbs and some nearby islands) is divided into five constituencies, while the Nome of Thessaloniki is divided into two. The total number of constituencies is fifty-six (see figure 2–1).

Since 1926, when a proportional electoral system was first used, Parliament has wavered between the majority and the proportional systems—and once even went so far as to prescribe one system for some constituencies, a second system for others, and a third for the remaining constituencies (1958). Nevertheless, most elections since March 31, 1946 (1946, 1950, 1951, 1958, 1961, 1963, 1964, 1974, 1977) have been carried out under a proportional system of some kind. On the whole, politicians seem to be satisfied that it provides the degree of proportionality attainable or expedient in present-day Greece.

The Greek Parliament has 300 members, whom the constitution defines as "representing the nation," implying that they should not be swayed by the particular interests of the constituency in which they have been elected. Three hundred is the maximum number of seats allowed by the constitution (the minimum is 200; article 51 paras. 1 and 2).

[17] For a studied account of these electoral laws from the establishment of the Greek state until the colonels' seizure of power, see Ion Contiades, "Griechenland" [Greece], in *Die Wahl des Parlaments u. anderer Staatsorgane* [Elections for Parliament and other state organs], D. Sternberger and B. Vogel, eds. (Berlin, 1969), vol. 1, pp. 554-603.

The "Reinforced Proportionate System." Proportional representation (PR) systems aim to produce a distribution of parliamentary seats between all parties participating in the elections proportional to the electoral strength of each. They may attempt to respect proportionality within districts and/or within the nation as a whole.

The Greek PR system, adopted in 1926 and again in 1932 (after a return to the majority system in 1928), follows the basic lines of the Hagenback-Bischoff system.[18] This method requires two series of mathematical exercises:

(1) The first division has as dividend the number of valid votes each party has received in the constituency and a divisor either fixed beforehand for all constituencies (in Greece this divisor was 15,000 in 1926 and 1932, 20,000 in 1946, 30,000 in 1950, 25,000 in 1952) or formulated for each constituency by dividing the total number of valid votes by the number of seats allotted to the constituency or (sometimes) by the number of seats plus one (the divisor adopted in Greece in 1977, law 626/1977). The quotient of this division, with one divisor or another, is the "electoral quota." Each party is assigned as many seats as the number of times that this quota goes into its electoral strength in the constituency. This exercise or series of exercises results in the "first distribution" of seats.

(2) If, as usually happens, the first distribution leaves seats not allotted, a second distribution takes place. Sometimes only certain parties may participate; the conditions for eligibility in Greece are discussed in the next section. For the second distribution, the constituencies are clustered into "major constituencies," of which there are nine in Greece under the current law. Within each major constituency, the total number of seats remaining is divided into the total number of votes cast for the eligible parties, to give the electoral quota. This quota is then divided into each eligible party's total vote to determine how many of the remaining seats it will receive. The assignment of particular seats to particular parties is done at the level of the original constituency, where another quota is calculated and remainders are also considered.

(3) The seats still unallocated at this point pass on to the third distribution, which in Greece is closely supervised by the Supreme Supervisory Committee. This time, the total vote for the eligible parties in the whole country is divided by the number of seats remaining, to produce the quota for the third distribution. Each party's total

[18] Hagenback-Bischoff, *Die Frage der Einfuhrung einer Proportionalvertretung staat des absoluten Mehrheit* [The question of the introduction of proportional representation instead of the absolute majority] (Basel: n.p., 1888).

for the whole country is then divided by this quota to determine the number of seats it will receive. Here again, constituency remainders are considered in the assignment of particular seats.

Finally, which candidates will occupy the seats awarded after the successive distributions is determined, in most PR systems, by either (1) the order in which their names are printed on the ballot, which reflects the party's priorities, or (2) the number of "preference votes" they receive, marks the voters may note beside the name of one or sometimes more candidates for whom they wished to express a preference. The second method has always been used in Greece.

Characteristics of the Present Greek PR System. "True" or "simple" proportional representation is sometimes modified by the statutory requirement that a party win a minimum percentage of the vote in the country as a whole in order to participate in the second distribution of seats—or sometimes even in the first. This requirement is inspired by a concern (mixed sometimes with political expediency) to discourage very small political groups and thus promote governmental stability.

In 1946, Greece adopted a threshold for participation in the second distribution. Since then the system has had two peculiarities: (1) the percentage of votes required for participation in the second distribution of seats—high from the beginning—was soon increased, and (2) since 1951 this threshold has been higher for coalitions than for single parties. In 1958, the threshold for coalitions of more than two parties was raised to an almost prohibitive level.[19]

The following data show the development of the electoral system in Greece on this critical point:

Election	Threshold
1946 and 1950	10 percent for parties and coalitions
1951	17 percent for parties, 20 percent for coalitions
1958	No threshold for parties, 35 percent for coalitions of 2 parties, 40 percent for coalitions of more than 2 parties

[19] The electoral law authorizes a competent branch of the Supreme Court of Appeals to determine whether a group purporting to be a party is in fact a "disguised coalition." The court deals with this question *ex officio* and issues a final and irrevocable decision as soon as the candidates are declared. Thus it is the responsibility of a section of the highest civil court to judge, in doubtful cases, under what conditions a party shall participate in the second distribution (EC article 89 para. 6).

1961, 1963, and 1964	15 percent for parties, 25 percent for coalitions of 2 parties, 40 percent for coalitions of more than 2 parties
1974 and 1977	17 percent for parties, 25 percent for coalitions of 2 parties, 30 percent for coalitions of more than 2 parties

The official justification for these thresholds, which prevent small parties from gaining representation in Parliament and actually penalize electoral cooperation between parties, is that they safeguard governmental stability. The true reason—borne out by the history of Greece since World War II—is that they safeguard the stability of one particular government. Their purpose is to cripple the left-wing parties and prevent the formation of a "popular front." The three graduated thresholds reflect the major parties' estimate of the left-wing parties' and coalitions' chances of success, with an added safety margin.[20]

Be that as it may, the exclusion from every distribution except the first of parties that fail to attract 17 percent of the votes ensures a systematic and organic overrepresentation of the larger parties and underrepresentation or nonrepresentation of the smaller ones; this effect is not fortuitous, as in other electoral systems. (The results of the elections of 1974 and 1977 are illustrative. In 1977, for example, the two largest parties saw their showing in the popular vote magnified in the distribution of seats: ND went from 41.8 percent of the vote to 57.4 percent of the seats, PASOK from 25.3 percent to 31.0 percent. The opposite was true for the two parties that came in third and fourth: EDIK dropped from 11.9 percent of the votes to 5.0 percent of the seats, the KKE from 9.4 percent to 3.7 percent.) Since it would be absurd for only one party to enjoy the spoils of the second distribution, however, the law provides that, if only one party or coalition obtains the statutory percentage, then the single party closest to it in strength participates in the second distribution whatever its share of the vote; all coalitions are excluded from this provision—a further indication of the legislators' intent to discourage coalitions.

This system was dubbed the "reinforced proportionate system" by its political supporters. The elegance of this label may account for

[20] The margin is exceptionally large considering the present-day strength of the stronger of the two Communist parties in Greece, the KKE. In the 1974 elections it won 9.47 percent of the votes in coalition with the other Communist party, the KKE-Interior, and the United Democratic Left (EDA), and in 1977, running alone, it took 9.36 percent.

the fact that its fairness has been discussed so little by theoreticians and political commentators. It is worth noting that the "reinforced" proportionate system has been used in Greece for the last twenty years and would thus seem to be widely accepted as an appropriate formula for electing a representative government. It is clear, however, that it is not *proportionality* that the system "reinforces," but the representation in Parliament of the political tendencies prevailing at a given moment.

One more minor peculiarity of the Greek proportional system must be noted. A provision of the electoral law of 1951 (law 1878/1951 article 12 para. 2) states that the leaders of the parties are considered to have received as many preference votes as their party's total valid votes in their constituency. This provision has been retained in all the electoral laws providing for the reinforced proportionate system. Today, candidates who have served as prime minister and have also been elected to Parliament once in the past also enjoy this privilege.

State Deputies. The first election after the junta marked the appearance of a new category of member of Parliament, known as "state deputies." This category was created by a "constituent act" of the transitional government of July 1974 in view of the elections due later that year and was confirmed by the electoral law that preceded them (law 65/1974); the constitution of 1975 allows the legislature to retain this feature (article 54 para. 3), and it did so for the elections of 1977. The system is as follows: Up to one-twentieth of the parliamentary seats (twelve seats, under the law in force for the 1974 and 1977 elections) are reserved for candidates that each party or coalition is entitled to propose as state deputies. These candidates neither belong to a particular constituency nor compete for election: their fortunes are tied to those of the party that has nominated them, and they are elected in proportion to its success throughout the country. A controversy arose over whether the twelve seats of the state deputies should be distributed among all parties or only those that passed the threshold for participation in the second distribution. The latter solution was accepted by the Electoral Court after the elections of 1974, and the seats of the state deputies were divided nine to three between the two parties participating in the second distribution, New Democracy and EK-ND. All the state deputies again went to the two largest parties after the elections of November 1977, this time seven to New Democracy and five to PASOK. This new modification of the proportional system gives the largest parties or coalitions yet another privilege. The twelve state seats are a kind of additional bonus for them—and they reduce to 288 the number of seats available at the first distribution.

Caretaker Governments. One fact noted by all those who have studied them is that the results of many Greek elections have been distorted by large-scale or local violence or electoral fraud. This situation bred mistrust of the government in power at the time of the elections and resulted in a custom (which some writers date from 1867) not prescribed by the constitution: the appointment of caretaker governments, whose task was to ensure the impartial and smooth conduct of the elections and whose term expired on the day the new government took office. This custom presupposed an agreement between opposition and government parties that the head of state would receive the resignation of the government and appoint a caretaker government composed of nonpolitical personalities—high court judges, civil servants, university professors, presidents of institutes, high ranking retired military officers, prominent businessmen, and so on.

Without ever being required by law, recourse to caretaker governments during elections has been frequent in the last thirty years. Of the eleven elections held since the end of the foreign occupation, six were conducted by caretaker governments (1950, 1952, 1958, 1961, 1963, 1964) and five by the government in office (1946, 1951, 1956, 1974, 1977). Whether caretaker governments have always justified their existence cannot be discussed here. The 1975 constitution seems to admit and to disavow a past in which the fairness of parliamentary elections was anything but secure when it proclaims in article 52 the duty of all public officials to ensure the "free and unadulterated expression of the popular will."[21] It can be argued that this makes recourse to caretaker governments superfluous and perhaps inappropriate.

The Referendum. The referendum made its appearance in modern Greek politics shortly after World War I. It was not provided for by the constitution then in force and therefore required extraordinary legislation. In most Greek referendums including the last on December 8, 1974, the question put to the voters has been basically the same: whether or not the state would continue to have a king as its

---

[21] The Universal Declaration of the Rights of Man states in article 21 para. 3 that "the will of the people" must be demonstrated *"par des élections honnêtes"*; the Protocol of the (European) Convention of Human Rights and Fundamental Freedoms (1952), to which Greece is a contracting party, says in article 3 that elections must take place "under conditions which will ensure the free expression of the opinion of the people in the choice of the legislator."

head, and even a specific king (who was usually in exile). This was as much a constitutional question as a judgment about a person and a dynasty, and it has been intensely controversial ever since 1915.[22] The referendum held by the military dictatorship in 1968 for the first time put a more complicated question to the electorate (restored to life for just one day): the acceptance or rejection of a constitution drawn up by the government. In 1973, a similar referendum was held on various modifications to the already ratified text—in particular the move from "crowned democracy" to presidential government. It must be added that the validity of all Greek referendums except the last (December 1974) has been generally doubted by the public.

The constitution of June 9, 1975, makes the referendum a permanent institution, but only for exceptional use. The authority to announce referendums "on critical national issues" thus is a prerogative of the president (articles 35 para. 2, and 44 para. 2), who enjoys the sole right to decide what is "national" and what is "critical," as well as to choose the time, though it is unlikely that he would attempt to exercise this authority against the wishes of the government. While this provision of the constitution has been criticized for giving the president excessive discretion, it can also be argued that direct recourse to the people's will is the ideal way of resolving questions of general interest in a democracy.[23]

Nothing in the letter of the constitution prevents the president from putting more than one question to the electorate in a referendum. It also leaves him free to judge whether the referendum should precede a governmental decision and the introduction in Parliament of the relevant bill or ratify a decision or law which has been provisionally passed. Indeed, law 350 of June 16, 1976, which regulates referendums, places as few restrictions as possible on the president's power to put a "critical national issue" to the electorate. It specifies that the decree announcing the referendum must formulate the question and determine explicitly the method by which the citizen will express his answer—"by the words YES or NO, or in any other way defined in the presidential decree" (article 1 para. 3). The issues must be simple and the questions direct and clear, so that this recourse to the judgment of millions of people of different levels of education

---

[22] In 1915 a disagreement arose between King Constantine and Prime Minister Eleftherios Venizelos over Greece's policy toward the two opposing blocs in World War I. Since both these leaders enjoyed high popular prestige, their disagreement split the nation profoundly. Referendums on the monarchy were held in 1920, 1924, 1935, 1946, 1973, and 1974 (see also note 11).

[23] The usefulness of referendums for resolving problems on which the electorate is uninformed or that are abstruse, technical, or very controversial is less clear.

and perception will retain those elements of sincerity and fairness that are essential to the institution.

Local Elections. Like elections for Parliament, local elections are held every four years by universal suffrage; unlike parliamentary elections, they are held on a fixed date: the first Sunday after October 10.

The purpose of local elections is the selection of a governing body with general competence for local matters in every deme and community. In the smaller communities the local Council has five members (including a president), while in the larger ones (with populations over 5,000) it has eleven. In the demes the Council is composed of eleven to sixty-one members, plus the mayor.

The qualifications for voting in local elections are the same as those for parliamentary elections. For local office, the minimum age of twenty-five completed years applies. The electoral system for local elections has undergone alterations and transformations, but it has retained one important characteristic ever since the major reform of municipal legislation in 1912: it allows different tendencies and outlooks to be represented in the local councils. Since all candidates run on lists, local elections have taken on a strong political coloration and reflect, at least broadly, the wider party divisions. This is the case despite general agreement that local politics ought to be non-partisan—and some politicians' insistence that it actually is.

The electoral system, regulated now by the Municipal and Community Code of 1980 (law 1065, art. 61ff), presents the following characteristics: *In the demes* the names of the candidates for municipal councilor and mayor are put forward in lists. These lists contain at least one and one-half times and up to twice as many names as there are seats on the municipal council and the name of the candidate for mayor. *In the communities* the lists contain the same minimum and maximum number of candidates, one of whom is designated as the candidate for president. The seats on the councils, in both the demes and the larger communities, are allocated two-thirds to the list receiving an absolute majority and one-third to the list immediately following. If no list obtains an absolute majority, a runoff is held the following Sunday between the two strongest lists.

As in parliamentary elections, the number of preference votes determines the order in which candidates are awarded seats. Like the party leaders in parliamentary elections, candidates for president and mayor are considered to have come first in the preference votes. For the rest, the rules governing parliamentary elections also apply to municipal elections except with regard to disputed elections. Disputes are judged in the first instance by Peace Courts for elections in the communities and by District Courts for elections in the demes. As we shall see, the venue for disputes is different in the case of parliamentary elections.

Validation of Parliamentary Elections

The Principle of Judicial Validation. The validation of parliamentary elections is entrusted to a judicial body once the voting is completed, the results announced, and the winners declared by the District Courts.

From 1844 until the first revision of the 1864 constitution in 1911, the authority to validate parliamentary elections was vested in Parliament itself. The revision of 1911 removed this competence from Parliament and entrusted it to a special court assembled ad hoc after each election to determine the final composition of Parliament.[24] Since then, this question has become and remains an object of litigation and of judicial consideration. As was to be expected, the belief has grown—though it is something of an illusion—that the validation of elections can and must be conducted in a cool frame of mind and with legal precision. The validation of parliamentary elections now takes the form of a legal action which may be instituted only following an application by a person concerned; other concerned persons and their attorneys may intervene both for and against the announced result, and an irrevocable decision with validity of the *res judicata erga omnes* is issued.

Under the constitution of 1975, these electoral matters lie within the jurisdiction of a body which articles 58 and 100 call the Supreme Special Court (SSC). Its composition differs slightly from that of the electoral court provided for in the constitution of 1952; in fact, beside the president of the Council of State (C of S), the Supreme Special Court includes four members of the C of S, four members and the president of the Supreme Court of Appeal (SCA), and the president of the Audit Court. But what makes this one of the major innovations of the last constitutional revision is that the SSC is not exclusively an electoral court; it also has four other main spheres of competence,

[24] Under article 73 as revised in 1911 and law 3955/1911 which followed, the special court was composed of members of the Supreme Court of Appeal and of the lower appeals courts. The constitutional revision that took place after World War II changed the composition of the special court. Its members became the president and five members of the Council of State (which, as we have noted, was established in 1928 as the highest court of "administrative justice") and five members of the Supreme Court of Appeal (constitution of 1952 article 73, and LD 2202/1952).

three of which are entirely new to the Greek judicial system, introducing matters which did not formerly constitute objects of judicial consideration.[25] Another competence of the SSC which the electoral court did not enjoy under the constitutions of 1911 and 1952 will be discussed below.

Scope of the Judicial Validation of Parliamentary Elections. As far as the object of validation is concerned, the constitution of 1975 repeated the definition used in the constitution of 1911 when it transferred election disputes from Parliament to a special court. According to article 58, "the review and investigation of parliamentary elections against the validity of which *objections are lodged* with regard either to electoral violations as to the carrying out of these, or to lack of the required qualifications" are within the jurisdiction of the SSC (see article 100 para. 1, a and c). We shall deal here only with the way in which the question of the validity of an election is brought before the SSC.

Every person declared a candidate is legally entitled to lodge an objection, but so is the ordinary voter; that is, any citizen registered on an electoral roll. The application must be submitted within fifteen days of the publication of the decision declaring a candidate elected and must pertain specifically to the election of one or more members of Parliament or runners-up. When the objection is lodged by an ordinary citizen, the only requirement is that he be registered in the constituency where the disputed election took place (EC, article 119)—though this limitation does not apply when the legitimacy of the election of deputies of state is disputed (as it was after the elections of November 17, 1974, when such members were elected for the first time).[26]

---

[25] The three new spheres of competence are: (1) "the validation of the results of a referendum," (2) the resolution of disagreements between court rulings on the constitutionality or interpretation of a provision of the law, and (3) the determination—binding on other courts—of which rules of international law are "generally accepted" when this qualification is in dispute. A new provision of the constitution (article 28 para. 1) gives significant practical force to this point: it grants to the "generally accepted" rules of international law (and to treaties if they have been ratified by law) superior validity to that enjoyed by common laws. The fourth sphere of competence not connected with elections which the constitution of 1975 handed over to the new court is the resolution of conflicts between administrative courts and ordinary courts with regard to the limits of their respective jurisdictions.

[26] The electoral court judged two such objections after the elections of November 17, 1974. We shall deal below with the substance of these cases.

Grounds for Objection. The grounds for recourse to the Supreme Special Court on a question concerning the composition of Parliament fall into four categories.

Procedural violations and errors. The first includes all irregularities taking place during the electoral proceedings until the voting is finished and the results have been delivered to the competent court for the constituency by the Supervisory Committee and the judicial representative (EC article 121 para. 1; law 345/1976 article 32 para. 2). Such regulations include any event disturbing the order, tranquility, secrecy, and freedom from coercion in which the votes are cast, even if it is fortuitous or due to *force majeure,* and errors in the counting of the ballots or preference votes. The objections that fall into this category of electoral violations are upheld only if the irregularities in the proceedings or in the circumstances surrounding them are likely to have altered the outcome. The alleged irregularity must have affected the conduct of the election either to an indeterminate extent or enough to give the decisive advantage to another party or another candidate.

Errors in the distribution of seats. The second category of grounds for challenging "the validity of elections" consists of complaints about the allocation of seats to parties or coalitions or their assignment to candidates within lists which the Supreme Supervisory Committee has effected in the second and third distributions of seats. Most of these complaints turn on the interpretation of the relevant provisions of the electoral law (in particular the interminable and extremely detailed articles 89 and 90 of the EC). In the second and third distributions the system is so difficult to describe with precision that the law really remains open to different interpretations, and legal precedent is no sure guide.[27]

Lack of qualifications. The third category of grounds for objection consists of charges that declared members of Parliament or their runners-up lack "the legally required qualifications."[28] In one celebrated case the declared member of Parliament was charged with

---

[27] One commentator on the decisions of the electoral court after the elections of November 17, 1974, notes that twelve of these interpreted the daunting paragraphs 7 and 8 of article 89 in one way and three in the opposite way—for the same elections! (One explanation is that in some sessions one or two judges had been replaced by substitutes.) C. G. Raikos, *Dikonomikon Eklogimon Dikaion* [Electoral procedural law] (Athens: n.p., 1977), pp. 497 et seq.

[28] We recall here that nonregistration in an electoral roll is not an obstacle to eligibility for election.

being under age,[29] but the great majority of complaints in this category have as their legal basis the obstacles to election, relative or absolute, general or local, defined in article 56 of the constitution.

Loss of qualifications. As we have noted, the reform of 1911 transferred the validation of parliamentary elections to a judicial authority, but Parliament remained competent to ascertain that elected members of Parliament met the conditions set down in the constitution, in particular those concerning offices incompatible with membership in Parliament (article 57 of the present constitution). The authority for declaring the forfeiture of a member of Parliament when he held one of these offices was the exclusive competence of Parliament until the new constitution transferred this competence also to the SSC.[30]

The code of the SSC implementing this provision states that such a matter (even if other grounds for the intervention of the court exist concurrently) can be introduced through an application by the would-be member of Parliament entitled to occupy the seat falling vacant if the forfeiture is announced, and also by any voter registered on the electoral roll of the constituency where the contested member of Parliament was elected (article 39). Thus the question of the influence of events subsequent to the elections and challenges to their validity both take the form of judicial disputes between persons. The decision of the SSC is final. However, on the publication of its decision the authority of the SSC comes to an end. In cases where it accepts the objection as well founded, it is up to Parliament—on whose Speaker the decision is served—to execute it, calling upon the first declared runner-up to take over the seat of the member pronounced forfeited. As a permanent court, and not a periodic body like the old electoral court, the SSC has jurisdiction over the composition of Parliament throughout its term of office.[31]

[29] The declared winner was the son of a former politician. The electoral court, disposed to benevolence, decided to overlook the lack of this one qualification, which time would soon amend!

[30] When the Supreme Court of Appeal gave its interpretation of articles 70 and 72 of the constitution of 1911, according to which "the members of Parliament forfeit their office by law" when they assume certain incompatible duties or jobs, it judged that Parliament had exclusive jurisdiction to decide on forfeitures. The electoral court was competent to rule only on the validity of elections, and ordinary courts could not encroach on the competence of the "legislature" even on a matter preliminary to a case under their jurisdiction (Supreme Court 42/1952, *Themis* 73, 213).

[31] The tendency toward the broadening of the role of the "judicial authority" within the state is manifested in other provisions of the new Greek constitution as well. There are local reasons for this phenomenon, but their study belongs

Disputed Referendums. The constitution states that the SSC "validates the results of a referendum" (article 100 para. 1, b). An objection to the referendum result can be raised by a voter registered on the electoral roll of any constituency, on the grounds of violations of the law during the carrying out of the referendum and errors during the counting of the votes (code on the SSC articles 35 and 36). It can be argued that here too, only irregularities likely to have altered the final result will be examined by the court. The question hinges on the meaning of the word "result": is it whether "yes" or "no" wins, or merely the precise distribution of the votes, which in the final analysis has only historical significance? The logic of things, and the provisions of the code on the SSC defining the authority of the court and the consequences of its decisions on this matter, lead us to accept the first interpretation. The involvement of the court would be fruitless if it ended only in a more accurate calculation of the difference between majority and minority; it would have no more importance than a correction to an opinion poll. Therefore, in order for an objection to fall within the court's jurisdiction, the plaintiff must cite irregularities or errors extensive enough to change the final balance between "yes" and "no," and this presupposes a narrow margin between the two sides. However, since the new provision of the constitution with regard to referendums has yet to be applied, no precedents are available.

Consequences. If an election violation is judged to have been substantial, the SSC invalidates the results and orders a new election to be held in the polling station or constituency affected. The new ballot is carried out within one month of the ruling. The same electoral rolls are used, and the candidates whose election was invalidated and all those who lay claim to their seats compete. If, however, proven violations are such that no further evidence is required to show which candidate should have been the winner, then the SSC itself sets in motion the latter's declaration (law 345/1976 article 32 paras. 2 and 3; EC article 92 paras. 1 and 2). A court ruling on an error in the counting sufficient to alter the result of the ballot also proceeds by invalidation and declaration.

When the SSC accepts as well founded the claim that a declared member of Parliament or runner-up lacks the necessary qualifica-

---

to legal sociology and to political science, if not to straight politics. It is possible that another influence also had its effect: the excessively high regard in which the judicial institutions created by the Basic Law of the Federal Republic of Germany on May 23, 1949, and their evolution and application are held by eminent Greek legal scientists.

tions, the law specifies that the court shall "declare null and void the declaration" (code on the SSC article 32 para. 1), but it does not expressly grant the court the authority also to declare the qualified candidate with the next most votes the winner.

Judicial Review of Electoral Laws. We have already noted that under the Greek judicial system, the constitutionality of a law cannot be directly challenged. On the other hand, the courts are bound to examine the conformity or nonconformity of the law to the constitution when this will influence their decision in a particular case. This form of review may be extended to all laws without exception, including, of course, the laws governing parliamentary elections.

Legal disputes on the constitutionality of the electoral law. It can be argued that at several points Greece's electoral system, even in its present form, does not satisfy the constitutional requirements of universality and equality of the vote. Indeed, this has been the burden of actions brought before both the electoral court and the Council of State.[32] The two bodies have issued concordant rulings, for which they have offered the same or analogous explanations (hardly surprising given their overlap in membership since 1952). Since all of the complaints have been judged groundless, their interest lies in the legal reasoning and general thinking behind them.

First it must be noted that neither the electoral court nor the Council of State has tried to avoid taking responsibility in this field; both have emphasized that complaints referring to the constitutionality of the electoral law or of any related executive act belonged to their jurisdiction. The Council of State even rejected explicitly the idea that the constitution concentrated in the electoral court all competence relating to the validity of elections—which would have excluded review by the Council of State of decrees implementing the electoral law.

Besides, the electoral court affirmed that Parliament must exercise its constitutional authority to define the electoral system and the constituencies in conformity with the directness and universality of the ballot and with the principle of equality of the vote.[33] It has also upheld the constitution's provision that "the number of members of

---

[32] The Council of State considers inadmissible and dismisses without examining its substance any application for invalidation raised against the decree dissolving Parliament and announcing elections (general or by-elections). Like the French Conseil d'Etat, it considers this "an act of exercise of political power" *(acte de gouvernement)* quite outside its jurisdiction (decisions 250/1930 and 1596/1951).
[33] Electoral court decisions 5, 7, 20, 21, 36/1956.

Parliament for each constituency is determined by law in proportion to its population."[34]

Both the electoral court and the Council of State have ruled that no constitutional principle is violated by the threshold requirements for participation of parties and coalitions in the second and third distributions. The court's arguments were essentially (1) that the constitution's requirement of directness and universality of the ballot is not infringed as long as the system does not institute indirect elections; and (2) that the unequal treatment of the parties according to their different electoral strength constitutes not a violation but an implementation of the principle of equality.[35] The electoral court also upheld the provision giving the party leaders as many preference votes as there are valid ballots cast for their ticket in their constituency, challenged on the ground that it creates a prerogative for certain candidates.

In addition, the Council of State upheld an apportionment announced by simple decree and drawn up on the basis not of the last census but of one ten years old, disregarding the extraordinary displacements of population and demographic changes that distorted it. The Council's argument hinged on a twofold distinction between the "numerical" and the "conceptual" definition of seats and between "actual" and "legal" population, as well as on the government's authority to set aside the most recent census as long as it has not been ratified.[36]

The most recent legal dispute over the constitutionality of a part of the electoral system concerned the state deputies, for whom no one votes directly. The existence of these members—who resemble peers of a sort, nominated by the leadership of each party—clearly is not

---

[34] See, among other decisions, electoral court 17/1962, noteworthy for the interpretation it gives afterwards to this constitutional demand.

[35] Council of State 1596 and 1789/1951. The second point is formulated as follows: "The . . . determined . . . percentages [at that time 17 and 20 percent] constitute the dividing line between the coalitions and parties achieving, and those not achieving, the necessary electoral strength to take part in the second distribution. Therefore the different treatment of the parties and coalitions participating in the elections depends on their difference in electoral strength. Subsequently the inequality with regard to the legislative treatment of those who are unequal constitutes simply the implementation of the provisions of article 3 of the constitution with regard to equality." According to this reasoning, if the electoral law treated all parties in the same way, the principle of equality would really be violated. In 1978 the SSC acting as an electoral court confirmed the rulings of 1950, 1951, and 1956 in a lengthy decision (number 48/1978).

[36] Council of State decisions 699 and 700/1956. Again in 1961 badly outdated census information was used as the basis for apportionment, and the electoral court had no objection (electoral court decision 17/1962).

consistent with either the equality or the universality of the ballot. Two aspects of this matter were discussed: (1) whether the transitional government of July 1974 had the authority to enact a provision derogating from the very constitution (1952) it had reinstated, to create a new category of deputy and (2) whether the law (65/1974) that limited the assignment of the seats reserved for these members to the parties participating in the second distribution conformed to the derogating provision, which spoke of "proportional" distribution without any other limitation. Both these questions were resolved in the affirmative by the electoral court and the Council of State, and the 1975 constitution included a new provision (article 54 para. 3) intended to safeguard this interpretation of the law.[37]

Conclusions on the Judicial Validation of Parliamentary Elections.

Whatever one may think of the courts' reasons for repeatedly consenting to hear, and then rejecting on their merits, cases turning on the charge that aspects of the electoral law were unconstitutional, it is important to note one fact that binds all these decisions together: the courts have avoided handing down decisions that would reverse the whole or a large part of an election result or vitiate a posteriori the basis of the election of the existing parliament. They have been unwilling to hand down decisions that would entail the removal of the entire parliament, stigmatize the electoral law as unconstitutional, and generally disrupt political life—exposing in the process the defects of the system of judicial validation itself.

This, I think, has been the underlying reason for the failure of court actions challenging provisions of the electoral system that appear to be inconsistent with the constitution. It would be altogether less artificial, I believe, and more consistent with the constitution itself for the courts to reject such challenges on grounds of lack of jurisdiction. The SSC should cite the restrictive enumeration of grounds for objection in the constitution (violations of the electoral procedure, counting errors, and lack of qualifications), while the Council of State could argue the concurrent and exclusive competence of the SSC established by the constitution.[38] This stance would not only

[37] The Council of State (decision 3700/1974) considered that the government formed after the fall of the dictatorship had had unlimited authority to modify and adjust the constitution of 1952 which it had reinstated. For my critical observations on this decision, see To Syntagma, vol. 1, nos. 1 and 3 (1975), pp. 65 and 516; see also, electoral court 1 and 3/1975.

[38] I elaborated on this view when commenting on the decisions of the Council of State 1596 and 1789/1951 at the time they were issued; Neon Dikaion (Athens), vol. 7 (1951), p. 199 ff.

relieve the courts of having to put forward interpretations of the fundamental principles of the representative system as embodied in the constitution. It would also have the merit, in my opinion, of not encouraging the legislators to manipulate the electoral system through provisions that do not find broad support from public opinion.

3

New Democracy:
The New Face of Conservatism

J. C. Loulis

The purpose of this chapter is not only to discuss the New Democracy party (ND) in relation to the 1977 elections but also to describe its background. After tracing developments within the conservative movement from the interwar years to 1974, when New Democracy was formed, we will focus on New Democracy's ideology and performance in government, its organization, and finally its electoral campaign.

From the People's Party to New Democracy

During the interwar years the conservative movement in Greece was represented mainly by the People's party, Laiko Komma. In order to understand this party's dominant ideological traits one has to see it in the context of the crisis of legitimacy that shook Greek parliamentary democracy to its foundations between the wars. Greek public opinion was divided into two camps, one supporting constitutional monarchy, the other opting for a republic. The People's party was at the forefront of the monarchist movement, while the Liberal party led the republicans. Whichever type of parliamentary democracy was established, the opposing camp challenged it, fueling a perpetual crisis of legitimacy. This development was inevitable, since every change of regime was brought about partly by force and followed up with a rigged referendum approving the change. Four out of the seven coups d'état that took place in interwar Greece sprang directly from the conflict between monarchists and republicans.[1] Within the context of this bitter division, the People's party was bound to for-

---

[1] See G. Daphnis, *Ta Ellinika Politika Kommata* [The Greek political parties] (Athens: Galaxias, 1961).

mulate a simplistic ideology grounded in its passionate monarchism and its violent opposition to Eleftherios Venizelos, the charismatic leader of the Liberal party.[2]

But the People's party not only lacked a sophisticated ideology. It also suffered from the organizational weakness that beset all the Greek parties except the Communists.[3] Much has been written about the fact that such parties' relationships to the mass of the electorate were based on patron-client structures built up by local politicians and on the personal qualities of their leaders;[4] many have noted that these personalistic parties were simply "convenient vehicles for activities of prominent politicians," their weak organizations acting mainly as a "mechanism for helping prospective supporters in their dealings with the state bureaucracy and other power structures."[5] While this is undoubtedly accurate, it fails to get to the root of the problem—which remained more or less unchanged even after the war.

The organizational backbone of the People's party (which may be taken as typical of the Greek political parties of the day) was not a network of local party organizations—none existed—but the local politician himself. The party's vote was a return on services the local politician had rendered to his "clients," not an indication of support for the party. In fact, a politician who had created a strong patron-client system could afford to change parties without losing his political power. This of course explains why all local politicians totally opposed the creation of a strong party structure, which would have both challenged their power on the local level and severed the tie that guaranteed them electoral success.

The lack of a grass-roots organization led invariably to a lack of party organization at the national level. In effect, the People's party consisted solely of a small number of notables, the party leaders and the local politicians. There were no organized party militants or members. The national leaders established their communication with the masses either directly or indirectly, through the local politicians. Both national and local leaders campaigned on a personal basis, holding mass rallies that relied more on charisma than on ideology, and

[2] P. Bakoyiannis, I Anatomia tis Ellinikis Politikis [Anatomy of Greek politics] (Athens: Papazisis, 1977), p. 101, talks of a "personalization of party ideologies."

[3] In D. G. Kousoulas, Revolution and Defeat: The Story of the Greek Communist Party (London: Oxford University Press, 1965). Little can be found on the organization of the Greek Communist party. I deal with this issue extensively in my Ph. D. dissertation, "The Greek Communist Party 1940-1944: Policies, Tactics, Organization" (Emmanuel College, Cambridge University, 1980).

[4] K. R. Legg, Politics in Modern Greece (Stanford: Stanford University Press, 1969), p. 129.

[5] D. G. Kousoulas, "Greek Politics," Balkan Studies, vol. 8, no. 2 (1967), p. 411.

the masses identified primarily with the leader rather than with the party at both national and local levels.[6] The strongest "cross pressure" a voter was ever likely to face was admiration for a national party leader when a local politician of another party had rendered him a personal favor.[7]

This, then, was the People's party that (usually in coalition with other right-wing parties) carried the elections of 1932 and 1933.[8] But the 1936 elections ended in deadlock. Neither the bloc headed by Eleftherios Venizelos's Liberal party nor the anti-Venizelist bloc headed by the People's party could govern on its own. The Greek Communist party, which had received 5.8 percent of the vote and fifteen seats, held the balance of power. On August 4, 1936, General Ioannis Metaxas, leader of a small right-wing party, staged a coup with King George's support and banned all political parties. His claim was that he had saved Greece from Communism—hardly convincing considering how small the KKE was at the time.[9] The People's party's primitive organization (together with that of all noncommunist parties) collapsed completely the moment the few party notables had been neutralized by the police.

The king's decision to opt for an authoritarian form of government despite the fact that most Greeks were solidly behind the parliamentary institutions proved extremely damaging to the People's party.[10] Lacking a coherent ideology of their own, the conservatives had always been closely associated with the monarchy's cause, and when the monarchy became vastly unpopular during the dictatorship and occupation,[11] the People's party's political fortunes suffered accordingly. Moreover, since Metaxas held right-wing views, opposition

[6] See Loulis, "The Greek Communist Party."

[7] On the theme of "cross pressures" see Seymour Martin Lipset, *Political Man* (London: Heineman Press, 1960), p. 206.

[8] Daphnis, *Ta Ellinika Politika Kommata*, pp. 179-190.

[9] Kousoulas, *Revolution and Defeat*, pp. 118-125, attempts to justify the dictatorship in a chapter with the characteristic title "The Alternatives: Dictatorship or Revolution."

[10] See W. H. McNeill, *The Greek Dilemma: War and Aftermath* (London: Victor Gollancz, Ltd., 1947), p. 30. Kousoulas, "Greek Politics," p. 407, notes that "the remarkable thing about Greece is how vigorous the democratic political ethos remains in spite of the manifold weaknesses of the political system." Dixon of the Southern Department of the Greek Foreign Office reached similar conclusions in the middle of 1941. See *Mystika Arheia: Foreign Office: Fakellos Ellas,* Secret Archives, File (Athens: Nea Synora, 1972), pp. 112-113. (This is a collection of Foreign Office cables during the war.)

[11] On November 14, 1943, Anthony Eden noted that 80 percent of the Greeks were against the king. *Foreign Office: Fakellos Ellas, p. 257.* A British *aide-mémoire* to the U.S. State Department noted on August 4, 1943, that the number

to his dictatorship was bound to create a wave of anticonservatism and a general shift to the left in Greek public opinion, a phenomenon which became apparent during the occupation.

The Metaxas dictatorship signaled the first major manifestation of the authoritarian right in Greece and represented a clear break with the People's party's commitment to parliamentary government. By the criteria put forward by Friedrich and Brzezinski, the Metaxas regime was certainly not totalitarian. But the ideology that Metaxas tried to develop, radical rather than conservative, and strongly antiparliamentarian, had a definite resemblance to fascist ideologies.[12]

The People's party, being in a state of total disorganization and disarray, played no active part during the German occupation (1941–1944). Thus it seemed doomed to insignificance in postwar Greece, with little hope of attracting anyone beyond the monarchy's few remaining supporters. Nevertheless, its political resurrection came rapidly after the liberation; it was primarily due to the Communists' aggressive policies both during and after the occupation. The KKE, which had grown into a considerable political power in the years 1940–1944, attempted to seize power by force in October 1943, then again shortly after the liberation in December 1944, and during the years 1946–1949.[13] Thus, between 1943 and 1949 *parliamentary institutions were threatened from the extreme left, rather than the extreme right,* and the Greeks switched their support en masse to the conservative movement which appeared to be best able to oppose the Communist threat.

Thus even before the events of December 1944 "fear of communism" appeared to be "reviving royalist sentiment."[14] In 1946 the

of "convinced royalists in Greece is at the present small"; *Foreign Relations of the United States Diplomatic Papers, 1943,* vol. 4 (Washington, D.C.: U.S. Government Printing Office, 1964), p. 140.

[12] C. J. Friedrich and Z. K. Brzezinski, *Totalitarian Dictatorship and Autocracy* (New York: Praeger, 1961), pp. 21-23. For a collection of Metaxas's speeches see I. Metaxas, *Logoi Trietias 4/8/1936-4/8/39* [Three years of speeches] (Athens: Ethniki Etaireia, n.d.). See also J. C. Loulis, "Oloklirotika Revmata stin Synhroni Ellada" [Totalitarian trends in modern Greece], *Dimokratikos Provlimatismos,* no. 6-7 (April-May 1977), pp. 13-14.

[13] On the December 1944 events see, among other works, Kousoulas, *Revolution and Defeat;* McNeill, *The Greek Dilemma;* G. Papandreou, *I Apeleftherosis tis Ellados* [The liberation of Greece] (Athens: n.p., 1948); L. S. Stavrianos, *Greece: American Dilemma and Opportunity* (Chicago: Regnery, 1952); C. M. Woodhouse, *The Struggle for Greece 1941-1949* (London: Hart-Davis, MacGibbon, 1976); J. O. Iatridis, *Revolt in Athens: The Greek Communist "Second Round," 1944-1945* (Princeton: Princeton University Press, 1972).

[14] A view expressed by George Papandreou, then premier of Greece and a prorepublican. *Foreign Relations of the United States, Diplomatic Papers, 1944,* vol. 5 (Washington, D.C.: U.S. Government Printing Office, 1965), p. 138.

People's party, together with other right-wing groups, formed the United Nationalist Front and captured 55.12 percent of the vote by campaigning on a simple anticommunist, ultranationalist platform, in an election supervised by the Allied Mission.[15] In the referendum held in September 1946 the monarchy received 69 percent of the votes: most Greeks had come to believe that the king was "their best guarantee against the installation of a Communist regime."[16]

In 1950, however, new parliamentary elections conveyed an important message to the conservatives. The People's party, while still the strongest, obtained a mere 18 percent of the vote. Thus, the moment the Communist threat ceased to be imminent and the Civil War was over, support for the People's party dwindled dangerously. The party's leadership still appealed to the population with outdated archconservative slogans. But broadminded conservatives realized that it was time their movement projected a new image, and under the charismatic General Alexandros Papagos who had won the war against the Communists in 1949, a new party was formed: the Greek Rally. In its ranks were found, together with those conservatives who disagreed with the leadership of the People's party, conservative Venizelists. This indicated that the Greek Rally was willing to put an end to the vicious Venizelist–anti-Venizelist feud which had divided the two largest noncommunist movements in Greece—the conservatives and the liberals—for more than twenty years.

In effect, the conservative movement split in 1951 into two groups, the "narrow right" and the "broad right." The latter attempted to widen its appeal by abandoning its anti-Venizelist stance and was the less emphatically anticommunist. The 1951, and even more the 1952, parliamentary elections were a triumph for the broad-right Greek Rally party, which obtained 36.5 percent and 49.2 percent of the vote in those two elections. The narrow right represented by the People's party, on the other hand, received only 6.6 and 1.05 percent of the vote respectively.[17] These results underlined the fact that conservative voters had never closely identified with the People's

---

[15] On the United Nationalist Front's campaign see McNeill, *The Greek Dilemma*, p. 191. For details of the electoral returns, see "Postwar Elections in Greece," mimeographed (Athens: General Secretariat for Press and Information, 1974), pp. 1-3. See also the Mission's *Report of the Allied Mission to Observe the Greek Elections*, April 10, 1946, Athens, Cmd. 6812 (London: H.M.S.O.), pp. 4-23. Comments on the elections can be found in "The Greek Elections," *Economist*, vol. 150, March 30, 1946, and "Populist Victory," *Economist*, vol. 150, April 6, 1946.

[16] D. Phillips, "The Greek Civil War," *History of the 20th Century*, A. J. P. Taylor and J. M. Roberts, eds. (London: Purnell, 1973), p. 2044.

[17] "Postwar Elections in Greece," pp. 7-9.

party. Instead they had identified with a vague conservative "cause," a combination of monarchism, anticommunism, and nationalism. As soon as a more "attractive" party headed by a charismatic leader— something the People's party lacked desperately after the war—laid claim to that cause, conservative voters abandoned the People's party en masse.

There is little doubt that where party identification is weak because of the lack of a well-defined ideological framework, personalities play a great part in attracting voters; this has been the case frequently in Greek politics in general and in the conservative movement in particular. The leadership of General Papagos was one key to the Greek Rally's success, and another was the People's party's organizational weakness. It would have been much more difficult for the newly founded Greek Rally to draw the mass of the conservatives into its ranks had the People's party built a powerful organization. As it was, the Greek Rally was able to rival the People's party's primitive organization in a matter of months.

The formation and victory of the Greek Rally pointed to another important fact: the Greek conservatives' ability to revamp their image to meet changing needs. Thus while in 1945 the main reason for the conservative revival had been an "external" factor, the Communist threat, in 1951 it was a purely "internal" factor, the conservatives' own success in rejuvenating their movement.

After Papagos's death in 1955, Constantine Karamanlis, the young and dynamic minister of transport, with the backing of the king who had appointed him premier, took over the leadership of the Greek Rally party. In an effort to legitimize his leadership, Karamanlis founded a new party, the National Radical Union (ERE), which included most members of the Greek Rally. It projected a rather more technocratic image than the Greek Rally and adopted a more radical stance on socioeconomic issues.[18]

Under Karamanlis for eight consecutive years the conservative movement provided Greece with unprecedented political and governmental stability and spectacular social and economic development. Between 1922 and 1936 Greece had experienced twenty-six major cabinet changes (almost two a year) and seventeen changes in effective executive (more than one a year); between 1946 and 1951 nine executive and cabinet changes had occurred. By contrast, from 1955

[18] G. Lyhnos, "I Alitheia peri ton Politikon Dynameon stin Ellada" [The truth about the political forces in Greece], in G. Lyhnos, O Ethnarhis Karamanlis [Karamanlis the national leader] (Athens: Giovanis, 1975), pp. 147-191. This is a critical response to Jean Meynaud, Politikes Dynameis stin Ellada [Political forces in Greece] (Athens: n.p., 1965).

to 1962 there were only two major cabinet reshuffles and one change in effective executive.[19] Under the governments of the broad right, gross national product per capita jumped from $79 in 1950 to $240 in 1955, $305 in 1957, and $478 in 1963.[20] This performance enabled the conservatives to associate their policies with dynamism, progress, and efficiency and thus win more electoral contests.

Despite this success in government, ERE as a party continued to suffer from exactly the kind of organizational and ideological weaknesses that had plagued its predecessors. ERE did not create a mass organization, and the clientelistic power base of the local party notables remained unchallenged. The party (in effect, the party notables and their close friends) was activated only during electoral periods. No modern electioneering methods were used, and there was no internal party democracy. All power rested in the hands of the party leader and his entourage. The party's ideology remained sketchy, and its appeal continued to be centered around Karamanlis's charismatic personality (his honesty, forcefulness, and efficiency), the party's success in government, and a simplistic anticommunism based on memories of the Civil War. This passionate anticommunism was behind some of the illiberal methods the ERE government used, mainly against the Communists but sometimes against the left generally. It was also the cause of the party's willingness to accept an ultra-right-wing M.P. like Constantine Maniadakis, minister of security under Metaxas, in its ranks. Furthermore, many leading ERE members and the vast majority of the conservative press came to view every party on their left as Communist fellow-travelers, making no exception for Center Union and its leader George Papandreou, who in 1944 had done more than any other Greek politician to counter the Communist challenge.[21]

ERE won the 1956 elections with 47.4 percent of the vote and the 1961 elections with 50.8 percent. In 1963 ERE fell to 39.4 percent of the vote and was defeated by the Center Union in elections called after Karamanlis's resignation following an argument with the king.[22]

[19] A. Banks, *Cross-Polity Time Series Data* (Cambridge, Mass.: MIT Press, 1971), p. 23. According to Banks's definition, a major cabinet change occurs when "effective control of the executive power changes hands. Such a change requires that the new executive be independent of his predecessor" (p. xxii). Between ERE's electoral defeat in 1963, and 1966, there were five major cabinet changes and five changes in effective executive.

[20] Ibid., pp. 259-260.

[21] See for example the daily *Imera* of July 22, 1965, in *O Ethnarhis Karamanlis*, p. 48. For other attacks on Papandreou see p. 199 in the same work.

[22] See *Postwar Elections in Greece*, pp. 11-12. The results of the Greek elections are published in volumes edited by the Greek Ministry of Interior (Electoral

The party's defeat not only signified the end of conservative rule, but also reflected the first open conflict between a conservative leader and the monarch. That same year a disillusioned Karamanlis left the country, and under Panayotis Kanellopoulos ERE was defeated even more soundly in 1964, falling three percentage points below the vote it had obtained in 1963.

It is entirely outside the scope of this chapter to analyze in detail the events leading to the coup of April 21, 1967, or their causes.[23] What should be stressed here is that the king's decision to force George Papandreou to resign in 1965 was not only a totally unjustified intervention in parliamentary politics, leading to a rapid rise in political tension, but also an act which seriously damaged ERE's political fortunes. Had the Center Union served out its four-year term, part of its support might have eroded naturally, giving ERE a chance to make a comeback in the forthcoming elections. Instead, with the monarch's intervention, Papandreou suddenly became very popular, rightly seen by the public as a victim of the king's whims. At the same time ERE appeared totally subservient to the king's wishes, backing, on his instructions, a center minority government composed of M.P.s who had left Papandreou's party.

The authoritarian right made its new appearance in 1967. The colonels justified their coup exactly as Metaxas had, by claiming (absurdly) that they had saved Greece from Communism. The colonels' regime was strictly authoritarian, their ideology conservative and populist.[24] Unlike Metaxas, they did not attack the parliamentary

---

Section) in both French and Greek. On Karamanlis's resignation see Lyhnos, *O Ethnarhis Karamanlis*, pp. 161-162.

[23] A journalistic but objective analysis of the developments which preceded the dictatorship, and of the dictatorship itself, can be found in "Athenian," *Inside the Colonels' Greece*, R. Clogg, trans. (London: Chatto and Windus, 1972). Other accounts, covering one or both topics, are Andreas Papandreou, *Democracy at Gunpoint: The Greek Front* (London: Andre Deutsch and Pelican, 1970); G. Giannopoulos and R. Clogg, eds., *Greece Under Military Rule* (New York: Basic Books, 1972), published in Greek as *I Ellada Kato apo Stratiotiko Zygo* (Athens: Papazisis, 1976); G. Rallis, *I Tehniki tis Vias* [The technique of violence] (Athens: Eneias, 1975); N. Poulanzas, *La Crise des Dictatures, Portugal, Grèce, Espagne* [The dictatorships in crisis: Portugal, Greece, Spain] (Paris: n.p., 1975); H. Korizis, *To Aftarhiko Kathestos 1967-1974* [The authoritarian regime 1967-1974] (Athens: Gutenberg, 1975); N. Mouzelis, "The Rise and Fall of the Greek Junta," *New Left Review*, no. 96 (March-April 1976); D. K. Katsoudas, "Pros tin 21 Apriliou: Ena Theoritiko Plisiasma se Tria Vasika Erotimata" [Toward April 21: a theoretical approach to three basic questions], *Epikentra*, December 1976.

[24] See R. Clogg, "I Ideologia tis Epanastaseos tis 21 Apriliou" [The ideology of the April 21 revolution] in, *I Ellada Kato apo Stratiotiko Zygo*, pp. 81-112; Loulis, "Oloklirotika Revmata stin Synhroni Ellada," p. 13; Katsoudas, "Pros tin 21 Apriliou," pp. 25-26; and Kroyzis, *To Aftarhiko Kathestos*, pp. 45-61.

institutions as such, but instead blamed "corrupt" politicians for the weaknesses in Greek democracy. Like Metaxas, they claimed that authoritarian methods were appropriate when the "nation" was in "danger."[25]

No organized resistance to the dictatorship could take shape under ERE's auspices, given the party's organizational weakness, but virtually all conservative politicians, individually, opposed the regime, issuing statements, appearing as witnesses at trials of dissidents, writing articles, and even participating in military conspiracies.[26] From abroad Karamanlis spoke out strongly against the junta, in effect urging Greek officers to overthrow the military regime.[27] Of the three noncommunist dailies that closed down voluntarily when the dictatorship was proclaimed, two were conservative (*Kathimerini* and *Mesimvrini* published by Helen Vlachos). Furthermore, one of the two most outspoken antiregime dailies was the conservative *Vradini*. Of course there were also some exceptions: the conservative *Eleftheros Kosmos* became a staunch proponent of the junta and *Estia* flirted with the dictators. But the years 1967–1974 made most Greek conservatives more certain than ever of their deep commitment to parliamentary democracy, as they struggled uncompromisingly against a right-wing dictatorship.

With the dictatorship's collapse in 1974 after the Cyprus debacle, one might have expected an uncontrollable surge of leftism of the kind that had occurred in 1941. That this did not happen—and instead a large conservative vote was cast in the 1974 elections—must surely be attributed to three factors: first, Karamanlis's charisma and the respect he commanded among most Greeks, who considered him the politician most capable of reestablishing parliamentary democracy; second, ERE's uncompromising antidictatorial stand during 1967–1974, which helped draw a clear dividing line between the democratic and the nondemocratic right; and third, Karamanlis's decision to give to his new party, the New Democracy, a center-right orientation, thus expanding its appeal considerably and demonstrating

[25] See the series of articles by S. Konstandopoulos, "Poios mas Kyverna ke pou mas Odigei" [Who governs us, and where does he lead us], in the projunta daily *Eleftheros Kosmos*, October-November 1972, which state: "We do not want the present status quo as a permanent regime . . . George Papadopoulos represents the only insurance that our country will move step-by-step to democracy, and will avoid a permanent dictatorship."

[26] Politicians like Kanellopoulos, Rallis (who edited an antijunta magazine), Papaligouras, Papakonstantinou, Stefanopoulos, and Averoff (who took part in the navy's revolt) engaged in resistance activities.

[27] Karamanlis's statements are quoted in Lyhnos, *O Ethnarhis Karamanlis*, pp. 315-316, 321-328, 333, and 344-347.

FIGURE 3–1

Ideological Trends in the Greek Conservative Movement and the Extreme Right, from the Interwar Years to 1977

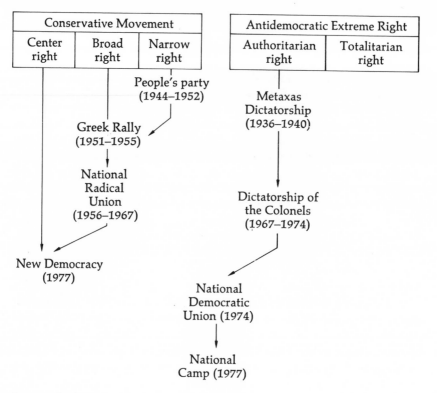

Source: Author.

once more the Greek conservatives' ability to meet challenging political developments dynamically.

New Democracy's shift to the "left" encouraged the extreme right-wing forces to fight the elections separately, as the National Democratic Union in 1974 and the National Camp in 1977. These parties in fact represented a coalition of exponents of the narrow right (obsessively anticommunist, anti-Venizelism being hardly an issue any longer) and the authoritarian right.

The ideological trends which have appeared within the conservative movement and the extreme (antidemocratic) right from the interwar years to the present day are summarized in figure 3–1. In the figure, as in the foregoing discussion, I have attempted to present an alternative to other, more simplistic interpretations of the development of the conservative movement in Greece[28] and to emphasize the distinction between parliamentary conservatism and right-wing authoritarianism, which some Greek authors, surprising as it may seem, choose to ignore.[29]

The New Democracy Party in Government:
Ideology and Performance

After his return to Greece on July 24, 1974, Constantine Karamanlis formed a broad government of national unity, and declared his aim of reestablishing democratic institutions and holding a referendum on the monarchy.[30] An August 2, Brigadier Dimitrios Ioannidis, leader of the second junta, who at the time was still quite powerful in the army, was suspended for six months. In October, George Papadopoulos, leader of the first junta, and all his close associates, were arrested.

On September 26, 1974, Karamanlis announced the formation of the New Democracy party. According to Panayiotis Papaligouras, minister of coordination in the ND governments between 1974 and 1977, Karamanlis had four objectives: to tackle the "national crisis" (that is, Turkish expansionism in Cyprus), to reestablish and solidify democratic rule, to give the country a strong government, and to make a powerful moderate party a force in Greek politics.[31]

Special emphasis was given to the fact that ND was a "new political movement"—not ERE under another name.[32] In fact ND had abandoned ERE's passionate and simplistic anticommunism, adopting at the same time a more radical socioeconomic policy, a more liberal attitude, and a generally more moderate approach to its political rivals. The conservative movement's rejuvenation was underlined also by the fact that the vast majority of its M.P.s (127) had run for office for the first time in 1974, while only a minority (68) had previously run as ERE or Greek Rally candidates and a mere 10 had run with the

[28] See for example Bakoyiannis's schema in *Ta Ellinika Politika Kommata*, p. 111.

[29] See Loulis, "Oloklirotika Revmata stin Synhroni Ellada," pp. 13-14, on the views expressed by four Greek Marxist scholars.

[30] For the cabinet's composition see *Une année de démocratie en Grèce* [One year of democracy in Greece] (Athens: Ministry of Press and Information, 1976), pp. 101-103, which also contains a brief chronology of the most important events from July 1974 to July 1975, pp. 120-125.

[31] See *16 Noemvriou 1974–16 Noemvriou 1975* (Athens: Nea Dimokratia, 1976), p. 10.

[32] *Oi Ideologikes Arhes tis Neas Dimokratias* [The ideological principles of New Democracy] (Athens: Nea Dimokratia, July 1975), p. 4.

Center Union. The influx of these new politicians undoubtedly helped give New Democracy a more broadminded, technocratic, and "centrist" outlook than its predecessors. It is important to note that 58.8 percent of ND's new M.P.s had done postgraduate studies abroad, compared with 31.5 percent of those who had run with ERE and the Greek Rally.[33]

The party's platform stressed ND's commitment to parliamentary procedures and its will to struggle against "every form of totalitarianism," its devotion to the "idea of the Greek Nation," respect for the individual, and the hope of achieving a balance of freedom and order.[34] In the field of foreign policy ND's pro-Western outlook and its belief in a united Europe were underlined.[35] The need for economic development and social justice were also stressed. In pursuing the latter, and despite its attachment to the principles of the "modern free economy," ND would not hesitate to "widen the economic sphere controlled by the state."[36] However, the limits of state intervention were never clarified.

Though otherwise ND's platform was relatively comprehensive, it remained evasive on a very important issue: the party's position in the political spectrum. The platform stated, "the labels 'right,' 'center,' and 'left' are misleading," but it did not specify what labels should be used instead.[37] A leading party member subsequently proposed differentiating between the parties on the basis of whether they were "democratic or antidemocratic," "modern or outmoded," and "Marxist or non-Marxist."[38] Another party leader, while stating clearly that ND was not a Marxist party, added that it would not "totally" accept "either solely the views of the Social Democrats, or solely the views of the other democratic parties in Europe."[39] Finally, yet another leader claimed that ND was "a progressive party of the center," "rightist" when tackling "national issues" and "leftist" when dealing with social issues.[40]

---

[33] Data in this paragraph are compiled from the curriculum vitae in *Oi Triakosioi tis Voulis ton Ellinon* [The three hundred of the Greek Parliament] (Athens: Kathimerini, 1976).

[34] *Oi Ideologikes Arhes tis Neas Dimokratias*, pp. 6-10.

[35] Ibid., pp. 12-13.

[36] Ibid., p. 7.

[37] Ibid., p. 5.

[38] K. M. Kallias, *I Ideologia tis Neas Dimokratias* [The ideology of New Democracy] (Athens: n.p., 1976), p. 84.

[39] Speech of P. Papaligouras, in *16 Noemvriou 1974–16 Noemvriou 1975*, pp. 11-12.

[40] Speech of Evangelos Averoff in Patras, *Kathimerini*, April 24, 1977, and interview with Averoff in *Apogevmatini*, October 15, 1977.

In an effort to clarify the basic principles of ND's ideology Karamanlis underlined six points in his speech to the party congress in April 1977.[41] The first of these was the party's belief in the "idea of the nation." This position, never really explained, was used to justify the view that ND was "outside and above the binding and misleading labels of right, center and left," since it had "as its single principle the nation's interests." Karamanlis seemed to claim that ND's belief in the "idea of the nation" set it "above" the other parties, which alone occupied the left-right spectrum—a view that was dangerously paternalistic and arbitrary.

ND's other principles were its belief in parliamentary democracy, social justice, a free democratic economy, and "peaceful coexistence." In connection with ND's economic policies Karamanlis stated: "A free economy exists when it combines justly and with measure individual and public welfare." He added that ND believed in the "creative zeal of the individual, free competition," but also in the necessity of state intervention in order to balance "social and economic conflicts and to reduce inequalities."[42] What Karamanlis did not make clear was whether his economic policy would be primarily free-market oriented or state interventionist. Particularly confusing was his description of a number of nationalizations as "daring" and positively "progressive." (The same confusion was reflected in the implementation of ND's overall economic strategy, which was frequently contradictory.)

Compared with ERE and the other vehicles of conservatism, ND undoubtedly presented a concrete platform and a rather more sophisticated ideological position. But in its efforts to broaden its appeal and to detach itself from "the past" (namely ERE) it refused to acknowledge that it belonged to the center-right.[43] Furthermore, it should be noted that ND has carefully avoided the use of the word "conservative," probably because it fears that the public will associate conservatism with "reactionary" rather than "progressive" policies— though Karamanlis himself endorsed the essence of conservative

---

[41] Constantine Karamanlis, "Oi Ideologikes Arhes tis Neas Dimokratias" [The ideological principles of New Democracy] in *Nea Dimokratia: A Prosynedrio tou Kommatos Praktika* [New Democracy, first party congress, minutes] vol. 1 (Athens: Nea Dimokratia, 1977), pp. 21-28.

[42] Ibid., pp. 25-26.

[43] See P. Gennimatas, "I Dialisi ton Psevdestiseon" [The evaporation of illusions], *Dimokratikos Provlimatismos*, no. 24-26 (December 1976), pp. 5-7 and 25-30; V. Valiliou, "I N.D. stin Evritero Horo tis Dexias ke tou Kendrou" [ND in the broader spectrum of the right and the center], *Vradyni*, February 20, 1976. Shortly after the 1977 elections party cadres started referring to ND as a center-right party.

philosophy when he stated that ND "retains and conserves from tradition only what time has proved to be correct and valuable."[44] Within the party there was little critical analysis of these ideological principles (at least until 1977) or discussion capable of giving them depth and scope. Instead, most party cadres appeared content simply to parrot Karamanlis and repeat simplistic party slogans.

In September 1974 Karamanlis announced, "All parties are free to develop their activities within the framework of the democratic institutions, without any discrimination . . . as long as they respect the country's laws."[45] This was the prelude to the legalization of the Communist party after twenty-seven years, a major political development which underlined the conservatives' new liberal approach toward Communism.

The November 1974 elections produced a landslide for New Democracy, which obtained 54.4 percent of the vote and could claim strong support all across the country. An urban/rural breakdown shows the following average share of the vote for New Democracy:[46]

District type	Average ND percentage
Urban	54.8
Semiurban	47.1
Semirural	57.2
Rural	56.6
Aegean Islands	52.6

The small extreme-right party, the National Democratic Union, which had an ultraconservative leadership and ran many projunta candidates, received only 1.2 percent.[47] This party, which had cam-

---

[44] *Politikes Theseis tou Konstandinou Karamanli. Apo Lougous ke Diloseis tou: Ioulios 1974–Maios 1976* [Political views of Constantine Karamanlis. From his speeches and statements: July 1974–May 1976] (Athens: Nea Dimokratia, 1977), p. 11.

[45] Ibid., p. 7.

[46] *Apotelesmata Apografis Plithismou-Katikion tis 14is Martiou 1971. Tomos III, Oikonomika Haraktiristika tou Plithismou* [Census of the population and dwellings] (Athens: Statistiki, Hypiresia, 1977). The district categories reflect the percentage of the population engaged in agriculture on the basis of the 1971 census: urban, up to 20 percent engaged in agriculture; semiurban, 20-40 percent; semirural, 40-60 percent; rural, 60 percent and more. The Ionian Islands are a separate category since the census does not differentiate between fishing and farming. Of course, by 1974, and even more by 1977, the percentage of people working in agrarian occupations had dropped considerably. Nevertheless, these broad categories can still be used as long as this qualification is borne in mind.

[47] On the electoral results, aside from those published by the Ministry of Interior, see *Elavon, Odigos Eklogon apo to 1961* [A guide to the elections since 1961] (Athens: Vergos, 1977).

paigned on an anticommunist platform and had demanded that the "purges" in the armed forces and security services cease, disappeared after the election. Opinion polls were used for the first time in a Greek election in 1974, but their findings related only to party choice.

On December 8, 1974, the referendum was held, with 69.2 percent voting for a republic and 30.8 percent for the monarchy (probably a solid conservative vote).[48] ND chose not to campaign for either cause, while all the parties to its left campaigned vigorously in favor of a republic. Karamanlis's decision to adopt a position of neutrality underlined one more extremely important change in the conservatives' outlook: the leadership of the conservative movement had ceased to be whole-hearted proponents of the monarchy, let alone, as before the dictatorship, totally subservient to the king. This decision, of course, caused grumblings within the party, and Spyros Theotokis, an archconservative M.P., resigned from Parliament. But apart from this isolated incident, the party was able to ride out the storm under Karamanlis's firm leadership. Parliament ratified the new constitution on June 11, then proceeded to elect Constantine Tsatsos, an eminent academic and ND politician, Greece's first president of the republic.[49]

An extensive discussion of the constitution and the powers of the presidency is beyond the scope of this chapter.[50] Karamanlis's views on the constitution, however, should be stressed since it was drafted under his direction. Karamanlis's chief concern was that the executive power be competent to tackle economic and social developments swiftly in a period of rapid change, and to this end he advocated "the prudent reinforcement of the executive power," without, he added, "weakening the power of Parliament."[51]

The first ND cabinet was mainly composed of experienced M.P.s and a few nonelected personalities: the average age in the cabinet was fifty-five—higher than the overall average for ND M.P.s, which was fifty-one (very low by Greek standards). The four most important party leaders, Papaligouras, Rallis, Averoff, and Theofylaktis Papakonstandinou (all ex-ERE members), were minister of coordination, minister to the president, minister of defense, and president of Parliament respectively. The second cabinet had an average age of fifty

48 For details, see *Apotelesmata tou Dimopsifismatos tis 8is Dekemvriou 1974* [Electoral results of the referendum] (Athens: Ypourgeion Esoterikon, 1977).

49 The text of the constitution is published in *Politika Themata* (June 1975), pp. 27-48.

50 For articles discussing the constitution from various viewpoints see issues of *Politika Themata* (February 1975), pp. 24-25, 43; (April 1975), pp. 33-34; (June 1975), pp. 8-9.

51 *Politikes Theseis Karamanli*, pp. 12-13.

and included a considerable number of young undersecretaries.[52] Karamanlis was gradually moving younger people to positions of power. Another noteworthy change was George Rallis's appointment as minister of education; he would launch a bold educational reform with great success.

During its first three years in government, ND concentrated its attention on four fronts: strengthening democracy, achieving socio-economic progress, changing the basic structures of the educational system, and tackling foreign policy issues (mainly Greek-Turkish relations and the speeding up of Greece's entry into the European Community). In the first area Karamanlis aimed at creating a political climate within which moderate solutions to conflicts would be found. He believed that Greece's greatest problem was political, namely, "securing the smooth functioning of democracy, with a stable and efficient government of the country."[53] New Democracy surely contributed to the smooth functioning of democracy during 1974–1977, not only because it avoided arousing political passions, but also because it encouraged a new spirit of liberalism in Greek politics. In July 1977 the London *Times* was able to observe, "Today the Greeks enjoy more democracy than they have ever had. And for all the grumbling and complaining, which is the daily reminder that this cherished freedom exists, Greece has become an oasis of tranquility in a world plagued by conflict and coercion."[54]

But securing parliamentary democracy also meant taking steps to neutralize antiparliamentarian elements in the army and punishing leading officials of the junta. This task was performed by the Karamanlis government, notably Defense Minister Averoff, firmly but gradually. In July 1974 juntist strength in the army was still considerable, and juntist conspiracies were frequent; in February 1975 the "conspiracy of the thirty-nine" was uncovered.[55] By April that year, however, the officers responsible for the 1967 coup, the violence at the Athens Polytechnic Institute in 1973, and the torture of dis-

---

[52] For the government's composition see *Une année de démocratie*, pp. 103-105.

[53] *Politikes Theseis Karamanli*, pp. 6-7.

[54] Mario Modiano, "Constantine Caramanlis, Changing the Way Greeks Think," *Times* (London), July 25, 1977.

[55] General Pahedon Gizikis revealed the existence of such juntist conspiracies in his interview with Giannis Maris; see *Apogevmatini*, July 13-22, 1976. On the members of the "conspiracy of the thirty-nine" see "To Who is Who tis Tritis Houndas" [The Who is Who of the third junta], *Politika Themata*, March 1-7, 1975, pp. 14-16. According to Takis Lambrias, undersecretary for press and information, Karamanlis survived at least four plots to "eliminate" him in the first six months after the collapse of the junta. *Times* (London), July 26, 1976.

sidents had all been charged with various crimes, for which they received heavy sentences ranging up to life imprisonment for Papadopoulos, Ioannidis, and their close associates.[56] In March 1975 fourteen lieutenant generals, twenty brigadiers, and other officers were placed on the retiring list, and these were followed by a further sixty high-ranking officers a week later.[57]

ND's liberalism and its decision to combat communism with concrete arguments[58] (rather than relying, as in the past, on oppressive police measures), together with its antijuntist policies, drew violent criticism from the archconservatives and the extreme right. *Eleftheros Kosmos* and *Estia* accused the government of persecuting "patriotic" officers while at the same time appeasing communism, whose influence, they said, was spreading unopposed, especially in the universities.[59]

On the socioeconomic front ND faced grave problems. When it took power, the Greek economy was going through a severe crisis. Inflation was as high as 27 percent. An economic slump was also apparent in 1974 (gross national income was declining at a rate of 3.8 percent annually, investment at 25.6 percent, industrial production at 1.6 percent).[60] The balance-of-payments deficit that same year was $1,212 million.[61] Despite spending 6.5 percent of the national income per year for defense purposes,[62] the ND government succeeded in bringing inflation down to 13.3 percent on average during the years 1975–1976 and raising industrial production by 4.4 percent in 1975 and 10.6 percent in 1976. The balance-of-payments

---

56 The minutes of the junta's trials have been published in many places, for example, *I Diki tis Houndas, Pliri Praktika* [The junta trial, minutes], P. Rodakis, ed. (Athens: Dimokratikoi Kairoi, 1976).

57 Details in *Une année de démocratie*, pp. 58–61.

58 "We condemn anticommunist hysteria," Panayiotis Papaligouras claimed. "Communism," he added, "should be confronted with ideological weapons." *16 Noemvriou 1974–16 Noemvriou 1975*, p. 11. "Communism cannot be fought either with 'sterile anticommunism' or with police measures . . . but only with an organized ideological struggle." See G. Rallis, "Skepseis gia tin Dimokratia ke to Ethnos" [Some thoughts on democracy and the nation], *Dimokratikos Provlimatismos*, no. 15 (January 1977), p. 7.

59 See for example "Na Min Stenahorisoume to KKE" [Let us not upset the KKE] *Eleftheros Kosmos*, January 21, 1977; "Ohi Axiomatikoi eis tas Fylakas" [No officers should be in jail], *Eleftheros Kosmos*, January 10, 1977; "I Kommounistikopoiisis tis Ellinikis Neolaias" [The Communization of Greek youth], *Estia*, March 1, 1977.

60 *Apologismos tis Kyvernitikis Drastiriotitas, 1974-77* [Report on the Government's activities] (Athens: Nea Dimokratia, 1977), p. 30, hereafter cited as *Apologismos*.

61 See Papaligouras's speech in *Prosynedrio tou Kommatos*, p. 133.

62 *Apologismos*, p. 14.

deficit was also somehow narrowed, to $1,091 million in 1976.[63] Despite the fact that full economic recovery remained an uphill struggle, ND's initial achievements in the economic sphere could not be easily ignored.

Panayiotis Papaligouras, minister of coordination, also gave his attention to achieving a more equitable distribution of income, by adopting a new tax policy, which transferred 45 billion drachmas from the wealthier to the poorer classes between 1974 and 1977.[64] The government showed a great deal of interest in agriculture, which it financed heavily (in 1977, 180 billion drachmas, as opposed to 94 billion in 1974),[65] and from 1974 to 1977 it increased farmers' pensions by 150 percent.[66] But mainly because of bad weather, agricultural production increased only 3.6 percent in three years.[67]

Despite these successes, the ND government's excessive intervention in the economy, which led to an even more inflated bureaucracy, coupled with its lack of a coherent economic strategy (which was, of course, a direct consequence of its self-contradictory and incomplete political philosophy) had certain negative repercussions which became apparent mainly after the 1977 elections, as inflation rose (to 24 percent in 1972) and the balance-of-payments deficit widened dangerously. It should be noted that public expenditures, which represented 30.8 percent of GNP in 1974, had risen to 35.2 percent in 1978. Public investment constituted less than 25 percent of the total amount of public expenditures, while public current expenditures reached 60 percent (minus expenditures for defense), out of which 57.7 percent went for the salaries of the bureaucracy (minus the employees involved in defense). A reliable economic study pointed out that "supply cannot follow the rise in total demand, so that inflationary pressures become greater, whilst at the same time a rise in productivity is impaired. Such an outcome is a direct consequence of public sector policies which direct their efforts at restricting expenditure by cutting down on public investment, probably because they are incapable of controlling current expenditures in goods and services."[68] A study sponsored by the free-market-oriented Center for Political Research

[63] Ibid., pp. 30-31.

[64] See Papaligouras's speech to the ND congress, *Prosynedrio tou Kommatos,* vol. 1, p. 135.

[65] *Apologismos,* p. 42.

[66] See Nikos Devletoglou's views expressed in a panel discussion, *To Vima,* November 19, 1977.

[67] *Apologismos,* p. 42.

[68] Institouto Ikonomikonke Viomihanikon Ezevnon (IOVE), *Dimosies Depanes ke Plythorismos* [Public expenditure and inflation], Athens, November 1979, pp. 7-33.

and Information (KPEE) noted that Greece's main economic problems in 1980 appeared to be: inflation; the widening balance-of-payments deficit; the fact that the structure of the economy remained unchanged (that is, the construction sector, and mainly apartment-block construction, remained overdeveloped, the manufacturing sector underdeveloped); low investment in the manufacturing sector; the expansion of the public sector; and low productivity (mainly due to the widening of the public sector). The study also observed that lack of investment was due (among other reasons) to ND's "unstable economic policy" and to industrialists' caution after a policy which encouraged widespread nationalizations.[69]

In the field of education George Rallis (ND) instituted impressive reforms. First, demotic Greek, the language of the man in the street, became the official language, while the artificial and pompous *katharevousa* (which the dictatorship had favored) was abandoned. This measure was not popular with conservatives or the extreme right,[70] and it cost George Rallis a number of votes in 1977. Other measures were connected with the planning and promotion of technical education, the restructuring of general education, the modernization of school texts, the construction of a great number of schools, and the creation of the Center for Educational Training and Research (KEME).[71] ND also encouraged a new spirit of liberalism in the universities, thus provoking another outburst from the extreme right.[72]

Finally, in the field of foreign policy under Karamanlis's personal guidance, ND adopted a pro-Western stand. "We belong to the West," Karamanlis stated repeatedly.[73] Nevertheless, Greece withdrew from NATO's military wing in August 1974 on the grounds that NATO had "not only proved incapable of stopping the Turkish invasion of Cyprus, but also had tolerated such an action."[74] Karamanlis also believed that Greece should promote an "independent" but not "nonaligned" policy: Greece had to belong to an alliance, but one that would "promote policies serving its own interests."[75]

[69] K. Kolmer, N. Tsoris, and K. Christidis, *I Andimetopisi tuo Ikonomikou Provlimatos tis Horas: I Plevra tis Prosforas* [Tackling the country's economic problem: the supply side] (Athens: KPEE, 1980) 2d. ed., pp. 37-40.

[70] For example, see "I Glossiki Paradosis ke i 'Ekpaideftiki Metarrythmisis'" [The tradition of the language and the educational reform] *Estia*, January 1, 1977.

[71] See Rallis's speech, *Prosynedrio tou Kommatos*, vol. 1, pp. 145-154. Also *Nea Paideia* [New education] (Athens: Nea Dimokratia, 1977).

[72] See Rallis's discussion with members of the ND congress, *Prosynedrio tou Kommatos*, vol. 2, pp. 38-42, 44, 51-53.

[73] *Politikes Theseis Karamanli*, p. 23.

[74] Ibid., pp. 26-27.

[75] Ibid., p. 23.

Together with his efforts to keep Greece in the West, Karamanlis tried very hard to speed up Greece's entry into the European Community (EC). According to the ND leader, not only political and economic but also "national" considerations made this an urgent matter.[76] (Of the fifteen trips abroad he made in three years, nine were in EC countries.) In addition, Karamanlis steadily promoted Greece's relations with its Balkan neighbors, visiting three of them and inviting three Balkan presidents and four foreign ministers to Greece.[77]

Karamanlis indicated many times his willingness to improve Greco-Turkish relations, avoiding the temptation to adopt possibly popular ultranationalistic policies and slogans (as some of the opposition parties, especially PASOK, had done). "Greece," he claimed, "believes in Greek-Turkish friendship," but "such a friendship . . . depends on whether Turkey will restore justice in Cyprus and will end its many provocations."[78] By "provocations" Karamanlis meant mainly the Aegean seabed dispute, which reached a peak in August 1976 when the Turkish survey ship *Sesmik I* explored seabed areas claimed by Greece without regard to the consequences. The Greeks' decision to appeal to the United Nations Security Council instead of using force was a clear manifestation of Karamanlis's moderate and responsible approach.[79] It is interesting to note that *Eleftheros Kosmos* and *Estia* attacked Karamanlis both for remaining outside NATO and for "appeasing" the Turks.[80]

The Organization and Structure of the New Democracy Party

After the 1974 elections had been won the ND leadership started its efforts to build up a strong party organization composed of a large number of active members. It did so in the face of great difficulties.

[76] Ibid., p. 26.

[77] See *Apologismos*, p. 20.

[78] *Politikes Theseis Karamanli*, p. 26.

[79] A *Time* editorial on August 8, 1976, urged Turkey to "call in her seismological research ship from the disputed areas." On the Greek government's reaction see *Times* (London), August 10-14, 1976. On the positions the Greek opposition adopted see J. C. Loulis, "Kommata tis Andipolitefsis ke Ageaki Krisi, Syngritiki Parousaisi ke Analysi ton Theseon tous" [Opposition parties and the Aegean crisis. Comparative presentation and analysis of their positions], *Epikentra* (October 1976), pp. 1-20. Also, "Vythiste to 'Hora' "! Mia Analysi tis Thesis tou PASOK" ["Sink the Hora!" An analysis of PASOK's position], *Epikentra* (September 1976), pp. 23-30.

[80] For example, see "I Politiki tou Katevnasmou ke Pote Katerrakothi" [The policy of appeasement and how it was reduced to rags], *Estia*, March 3, 1977; and "Pos 'Anikomen stin Dysi' ke Doulevoume Gia tin Anatoli" [How we "belong to the West" and work for the East], *Estia*, April 4, 1977.

On March 26 ND's Administrative Committee was formed; its twenty members included no M.P.s.[81] Seven of these members formed the Executive Committee, which met more frequently. The Administrative Committee's task was to design the party's organization, and its members—most of whom had not previously been involved in politics—brought many new ideas into the party. Precisely because of its composition, however, the Administrative Committee's actual power within the party remained minimal, particularly since the party leadership failed to provide it with the necessary leverage vis-à-vis the elected politicians. This could have been achieved had Karamanlis himself or one of his close associates regularly attended the committee's meetings and taken a personal interest in the implementation of its proposals.

Despite these problems, in September 1975 the first fifty regional organizations were formed, together with forty local organizations.[82] The regional committees were composed of members named by the ND M.P.s of each region, a provision that introduced rivalries between local politicians in many cases.

The most important development springing from the party's organizational efforts was the convening of a three-day congress on April 2, 1977, organized by ND's Administrative Committee, which assembled the party's M.P.s and notables along with 1,444 party members.[83] Actually this "preliminary" congress neither elected a party leader nor ratified the party charter (which was still provisional as of 1979).

The political importance of this meeting far exceeded the fact of its successful organization.[84] This was the first time that the members of a conservative party had been invited to play an active role in the party's internal affairs. In effect, they were allowed to speak on party matters; they questioned ministers closely and freely on issues concerning ND's governmental policies; and in sixty- to seventy-member committees, they discussed and amended the articles of the party's provisional charter and the other party statutes. I followed the proceedings closely, and I can attest to the spirit of liberalism that prevailed in all these discussions. Furthermore, the transcripts of the congress's proceedings were published in full, underlining both

---

[81] See *Politika Themata*, April 5-11, 1975, p. 19.

[82] *Prosynedrio tou Kommatos*, vol. 1, p. 31 (speech by ND's general director).

[83] Ibid., p. III.

[84] On the party congress see *To Vima*, April 13, 1977, and *Politika Themata*, April 9-15, 1977, vol. 1, pp. 11-20, 48-125, and vol. 2, pp. 9-158.

FIGURE 3–2
New Democracy's Organization under the Provisional Charter

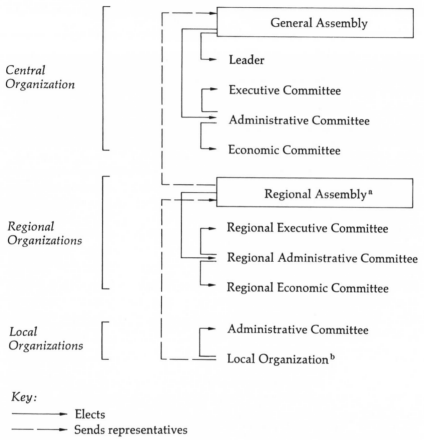

Central Organization

General Assembly

Leader

Executive Committee

Administrative Committee

Economic Committee

Regional Organizations

Regional Assembly[a]

Regional Executive Committee

Regional Administrative Committee

Regional Economic Committee

Local Organizations

Administrative Committee

Local Organization[b]

Key:

——————► Elects

— — ——► Sends representatives

[a] Sends to General Assembly representatives equaling number of parliamentary seats.
[b] Sends to Regional Assembly representatives doubling number of parliamentary seats.
Source: Author.

the existence of disagreements on some aspects of the government's policies and the cadres' firm demand for intraparty democracy.

According to the ND's provisional charter the party has three organizational tiers: central, regional, and local (see figure 3–2). The central organization includes the General Assembly, the leader, the Administrative Committee, the Economic Committee, and the parliamentary group. The regional organization coincides with the country's division into electoral districts, while the local organization is formed on the basis of smaller geographic entities, basically the community.[85] The General Assembly, which elects both the leader and the Administrative Committee, is composed of the leader, the elected M.P.s, candidates defeated in the last parliamentary elections, former M.P.s, representatives of the regional organizations in a number equaling the number of parliamentary seats (300), and, finally, representatives of the youth organization. The twenty-one-member Administrative Committee elects a seven-member Executive Committee and the Economic Committee. The regional organizations each contain an administrative, an executive, and an economic committee and convene a regional assembly whose membership parallels that of the General Assembly, together with the local organizations represented in numbers doubling the number of parliamentary seats in the region.

The two most important issues discussed at the party's congress concerned the number of representatives the Regional Assemblies would be entitled to send to the General Assembly and the regional organizations' power to influence candidate selection. The vast majority of those discussing the issue proposed that there be 600 regional representatives—twice the number of parliamentary seats— rather than 300. In connection with the second problem most party members appeared to favor the requirement that the party leader select a number of candidates from lists prepared by the regional organizations. These two proposals were indeed crucial if the party were to operate on a democratic basis.

Undoubtedly the preliminary congress was a major step in the ND's efforts to organize. But little else was done before the 1977 elections to provide ordinary members with actual power or the party with a final charter. By the time the party congress met, fifty-one regional organizations existed, and the number of local organizations had risen to 233.[86] Party membership, it was announced, was 20,000. Though these figures underlined the party's considerable efforts to recruit, they were hardly satisfactory. This becomes evident if one compares them with the equivalent figures for PASOK, the best organized noncommunist party. Several conclusions can be drawn from the figures in table 3–1 despite the fact that the figures refer to different dates. First, we may note that PASOK has one more

[85] The information in this paragraph and the next is from *Politika Themata*, April 9-15, 1977, vol. 2, pp. 82-88.

[86] See the speech of ND's general director, Yiannis Misailidis, in ibid., vol. 1, p. 32.

TABLE 3–1

ND and PASOK: Party Organization and Membership

	New Democracy		PASOK	
	Sept. 1975	April 1976	Sept. 1976	June 1977
Members	n.a.	20,000	n.a.	27,000
Regional organizations	50	51	61	61[a]
Local organizations	40	233	380	460
Cells	—	—	300	500

n.a.: not available.

Dash (—): not applicable.

[a] Author's estimate.

Source: "A Syndiaskepsi tou PASOK" [First congress of PASOK], *Exormisi*, July 15, 1977; P. Bakoyiannis, *I Anatomia tis Ellinikis Politikis* [Anatomy of Greek politics] (Athens: Papazisis, 1977), p. 206.

level of organization than ND, the cell, derived from the Communist organizational model. Second, ND's 20,000 members in 1976 represented only 0.74 percent of its 1974 vote, while PASOK's 27,000 members constituted 4.05 percent of its vote. Third, PASOK has distributed its membership through a much larger network of organizations than ND: with a membership total roughly one-third higher, PASOK had 1,021 organizational units, as opposed to ND's 284. Fourth, until the middle of 1976 ND did not have a regional organization for every electoral district (there were fifty-six electoral districts in 1974).

The slow and painful development of the ND's party organization during the years 1975–1977, its limited success in attracting new members, and, finally, the apathy and inactivity of most of these members[87] should be attributed to a single and most important factor: namely that *the party was far less significant as a mass organization than as a group of leaders and professional politicians.* This remained so because the party organizations were not given any real political power. They could influence neither the selection of the candidates for their regions nor the party's decision-making process. There was little incentive for ND supporters either to join organizations, without power or prestige, or to be active if they did join.

[87] See F. Hrimatopoulos, "Gia tin Politikopoiisi ton Opadon tis Parataxoes Mas" [For the politicization of our supporters], *Vradyni*, January 1, 1978.

Another serious repercussion was that most ND supporters were linked with the party not through its organization but—exactly as in the past—through the local M.P., who continued to distribute personal favors strengthening his patron-client ties. Efforts to preserve such relationships actually led some M.P.s to oppose the expansion of the party organizations in their electoral districts, in the hope of retaining personal control over contacts with prospective voters. Rivalries between M.P.s of the same electoral district continued within the party organizations, whose composition the politicians tried to influence. Most ND members owed their appointments in the party to powerful patrons, to whom they sacrificed their political independence.

Thus, despite ND's serious organizational efforts on the eve of the 1977 elections, all power still rested in the hands of the party leadership and the parliamentary group. The membership, limited in number, stood powerless and inactive on the sidelines.

New Democracy and the 1977 Elections: Campaign and Results

On September 20, 1977, the government announced that early elections would be held in November. In his letter to President Tsatsos, Prime Minister Karamanlis claimed, on the basis of article 41 of the constitution, that this decision was necessary because Greece faced grave "national problems"—the negotiations with the EC and the Greco-Turkish crisis. Since 1978 was expected to be a crucial year in both of these areas, Karamanlis believed that the government should enter 1978 with a fresh mandate.[88]

The strongest reaction to Karamanlis's decision came from the extreme right,[89] which denounced the ND leader for speeding up the elections in order to prevent the formation of a party to replace the National Democratic Union, which had disintegrated. Actually, serious efforts in this direction had started as early as January 1977 after a former ND M.P., the royalist Spyros Theotokis, had given an interview to a German weekly criticizing the government.[90] Theotokis and other archconservatives probably hesitated because they knew that had they formed a party, the authoritarian, projuntist right would be its main backers, giving it the dynamism and manpower it urgently needed. Furthermore, it was clear to them that the

[88] *Kathimerini*, September 21, 1977.

[89] See the editorials of the dailies *Eleftheros Kosmos*, September 21, 1977, and *Estia*, September 19, 1977.

[90] See the editorials in *Eleftheros Kosmos* urging Theotokis to form a new party, January 11 and 12, 1977, February 5, 1977, March 17 and 19, 1977, April 2 and 3, 1977.

only daily to support their cause openly would be the projuntist *Eleftheros Kosmos.*

Early in October Stefanos Stefanopoulos (ex-vice premier of the Greek Rally and of the Center Union, which he had left in 1965) and Spyros Theotokis took the plunge and announced the formation of the National Camp (EP). *Eleftheros Kosmos* tried to reassure the nation: "The nationalists do not long for the dictatorship."[91] EP's manifesto (probably drafted by Stefanopoulos himself) was essentially moderate. Though it endorsed the accusations *Eleftheros Kosmos* and *Estia* had made against the ND government, it used mild language and repeatedly stressed the party's commitment to parliamentary procedures.[92] It also underlined its monarchism, accusing Karamanlis of "betraying the king," in the hope of attracting a large portion of the promonarchist ND vote.[93] Gradually, however, under the pressure of projuntist hardliners, a harsher tone was adopted, and Theotokis soon proclaimed the need for amnesty for the imprisoned juntist leaders.[94] From this moment onward, the influence in EP of the authoritarian right could not be doubted. It came as no surprise when the EP list of candidates for Parliament included six politicians who had cooperated closely with the junta and another twenty-seven who had been associated with it.[95] Nikos Devletoglou, EP's chief economic spokesman, declared at the end of the campaign that the army's intervention on April 21, 1967, had been "totally justifiable."[96] Thus EP quickly assumed the form of a coalition of archconservatives obsessed with the fear of communism (what we have called the narrow right) and exponents of the authoritarian right. Despite its enthusiasm, fueled by fanaticism, such a party could not appeal to a broad conservative base and thus proved much less of a threat to ND than it had expected.

New Democracy started its electoral campaign with three trump cards: its considerable success in office, Karamanlis's charismatic personality, and its moderate ideology. Its main liability was its rather poor state of organization. The lack of a strong grass-roots organization contributed to the fact that ND could neither project efficiently

[91] *Eleftheros Kosmos*, October 4, 1977.

[92] Ibid., October 7, 1977.

[93] D. K. Katsoudas, "O Horos tis Extremistikis Dexias" [The extreme right] *Epikentra* (October 1977), pp. 15-19.

[94] *Eleftheros Kosmos*, October 10, 1977.

[95] Panos Gennimatas, "Symberasmata ek ton Meleton ton Syndyasmon tis EP" [Conclusions on the study of EP's electoral list], a brief unpublished study dated November 2, 1977, and written on behalf of KPEE's Research Department.

[96] Speech in Kilkis, *Eleftheros Kosmos*, November, 15, 1977.

the government's achievements at the local level nor keep itself well informed on important local problems and grievances that were bound to cost it votes if they were ignored. The channels for communication between the top of the party pyramid and its weak base either did not exist or, more often, were simply defective.

The chief liability of ND's electoral strategy was that *it appeared extremely static*. The party's main slogan, "ND: The Great Guarantee," stressed security. The secondary slogan should have been dynamic, should have promised some sort of change. Instead, it referred only to the past: "ND Found Chaos. It Created a State." This slogan (which did not even rhyme in Greek) reflected ND's whole electoral approach: to point to the party's achievements in government without offering a dynamic program for the future.

Another shortcoming of ND's electoral campaign was the party's failure to refute systematically and with solid arguments the views of its opponents.[97] PASOK, in its effort to project a moderate outlook, was forced either to become evasive about positions it had previously adopted or to modify them: it avoided stating that it was a Marxist party; it stressed only its short-term aims; its leader avoided the use of the word "socialism" in most of his speeches; party spokesmen adopted increasingly complex approaches on the EC, Greco-Turkish relations, and so on.[98] ND did not capitalize on these weaknesses, perhaps to demonstrate its confidence. Whatever the rationale, ND's passive campaign did not pay off. In particular, the party lost many votes to PASOK. It should be noted that according to an opinion poll conducted by KPEE in February 1980, 50 percent of PASOK's prospective voters viewed it as a "socialist non-Marxist party" and only 17 percent perceived it as a "Marxist party" in spite of its numerous pronouncements before 1977 that it was in fact Marxist.[99] This proves beyond any doubt that PASOK's electoral campaign (and its post-1977, "new," less militant approach) succeeded in projecting to the electorate a moderate image with little resistance from New Democracy.

In fact, only overconfidence can explain why ND scarcely made use of its second fifteen minutes of free TV time, an extremely valua-

[97] One ND official dismissed one of EDIK's leader's speeches as a "confused collection of accusations against the government." *Akropolis*, October 30, 1977.

[98] On PASOK's electoral strategy see chapter 5 in this book and J. C. Loulis, "Oi Treis Faseis tis Eklogikis Ekstratias tou PASOK" [The three phases of PASOK's electoral strategy], *Epikentra* (October 1977), pp. 1-14.

[99] On PASOK's brand of Marxism see J. C. Loulis, "I Politiki Philosophio tou PASOK. Marxistiki Methodologio, Sosialistikos Metashimatismos" [The political philosophy of PASOK. Marxist methodology, socialist transformation]. *Epikentra* no. 9 (July-August 1978), pp. 31-43.

TABLE 3–2
Support for ND, EDIK, and PASOK in Various
Socioeconomic Groups, 1980
(percent)

	Recalled Vote, 1977		
Group	ND	EDIK	PASOK
Sex			
Male	38.8	10.4	29.8
Female	46.9	10.7	27.3
Total	42.5	10.5	28.6
Age			
20–24	8.6	—	45.7
25–34	30.2	13.1	42.1
35–44	44.2	8.9	29.4
45–54	46.7	12.6	19.6
55–64	51.0	10.0	23.3
65–	49.6	5.4	24.8
Education			
Primary	42.2	11.2	27.2
Secondary	44.9	8.4	29.4
University	38.5	12.6	31.8
Socioeconomic group			
Upper-middle and middle classes	46.9	11.1	28.4
Lower-middle class	46.3	9.7	26.9
Skilled working class	46.5	11.8	25.8
Semiskilled & unskilled working class	36.8	9.5	31.9

Source: National survey conducted in February 1980 by the Center for Political Research and Information (KPEE).

ble campaign opportunity. Although Karamanlis had made a very impressive appearance in the first fifteen minutes allotted to ND, the party chose to use its second slot merely to broadcast parts of a Karamanlis speech that had already been published in the press. To all of these weaknesses one should add that the two opinion polls conducted on ND's behalf failed to pinpoint either the social background of ND's prospective voters or the issues that preoccupied the electorate. These polls were amateurish; no specialists were called in to help formulate the questionnaires.

A subsequent survey showed ND to be the strongest party in the following groups: women (46.9 percent), older voters (mainly over forty-five), the upper, middle, and lower-middle class, and the skilled working class (see table 3–2). It was particularly weak, however, in the younger age groups (below thirty-five), a development that could have an important impact on its electoral future if it should persist. Education appears less important than the other factors in differentiating ND's vote. PASOK's strength among younger voters and its more or less even support within the various socioeconomic and educational groups indicates beyond doubt that, more than any other factor, *age differentiated the voters of the two major parties in 1977.*[100]

ND's mistakes in the electoral campaign reflected not only errors in judgment but, more important, a defective organization. No modern methods were employed to test the major slogans; no systematic study of the other parties' views and the arguments that might be used against them was undertaken; opinion polls were used to inform the party on how the people would vote rather than to help it formulate its strategy. ND's organizational weaknesses became blatantly evident at its large rallies: crowds came, mainly to see Karamanlis, but they were undisciplined, and even party supporters interrupted the leader with inappropriate slogans at crucial moments of his speech. By contrast, at PASOK's equally large rallies there was excellent communication between leader and supporters, who knew exactly which slogan to shout at every pause.

Despite all these problems, the ND's showing on November 20— 41.85 percent of the vote—was not as disappointing as it appeared to ND officials at first glance. Under the circumstances of 1977, it was to be expected that ND would lose approximately 10 percent over its 1974 showing. First, the appearance of EP in 1977 stood to damage it much more than the National Democratic Union had done in 1974, since by 1977 it was clear that New Democracy had become a center-right party, alienating some of its archconservative voters; furthermore, EP had more appealing leaders than NDU. Second, ND should have expected some natural erosion of its support after three years in power. Finally, a small number of left-wingers who had voted for ND in 1974 in the belief that they were helping stabilize the parliamentary system were bound to withdraw their support in the different atmosphere of 1977.

Despite these reassuring thoughts, however, the electoral results also underlined some alarming developments: the erosion of ND's

[100] These conclusions are confirmed by surveys conducted by KPEE in July and October 1980.

TABLE 3–3

Urban/Rural Breakdown of the ND Vote, 1977, and Change since 1974

(percent; change in percentage points)

District Type	ND, 1977	Change 1974–1977		
		Decline in ND vote	ND loss to EP[a]	ND loss to left[b]
Urban	43.4	11.2	4.3	6.4
Semiurban	39.0	8.1	3.8	5.4
Semirural	43.3	13.9	6.6	7.3
Rural	41.2	15.4	8.0	8.2
Aegean Islands	47.2	5.3	1.6	3.8

Note: Districts are grouped according to the percentage of the population engaged in agriculture at the 1971 census as follows: urban, up to 20 percent; semiurban, 20-40 percent; semirural, 40-60 percent; rural, 60 percent or over. The Ionian Islands are a separate category since the census does not differentiate between fishing and farming.

[a] The percentage the National Democratic Union obtained in 1974 has been subtracted from the votes EP obtained in 1977, so as to bring out the percentage of ND's 1974 votes that EP probably attracted in 1977.

[b] To PASOK and the Communists.

Source: Compiled by the author from official returns.

support was quite large, reflecting considerable dissatisfaction with its policies; it appears that most of the ND defectors who moved to the left voted not for the Union of the Democratic Center (EDIK) but for PASOK (thus moving "two steps" to the left of ND); finally, PASOK succeeded in winning ND votes in traditionally conservative agrarian areas.

Table 3–3 shows ND's losses to both the right and the left. In order to estimate ND's loss to PASOK, we have subtracted EDIK's total losses from PASOK's gains. Since most of EDIK's losses probably went to PASOK, this remainder can be taken as an indication of the extent of ND defection to PASOK. These PASOK gains unexplained by EDIK's losses are (in percentage points):

Urban districts	3.3
Semiurban districts	3.1
Semirural districts	4.6
Rural districts	6.1
Aegean Islands	1.1

Before drawing conclusions from these data and those in table 3–3, we must note two qualifications: (1) the urban/rural breakdown has been devised on the basis of an outdated census (1971) and therefore has to be accepted cautiously (as noted in footnote 62); and (2) any switch of ND voters to PASOK that was cancelled out by a switch of EDIK voters to ND could not, of course, be detected from the data available; thus, the ND loss to PASOK may have been larger than our rough figure suggests. These points aside, several conclusions can be drawn. First, the ND lost more to the left than to EP; second, ND's electoral strength is no longer concentrated in rural areas, where the party lost heavily both to the left and to EP. In urban areas ND's losses were more modest and went mainly to the left. In the Aegean Islands the fear of a war is possibly the most important factor explaining ND's modest losses. Third, ND seems to have lost most heavily to PASOK in rural districts—and to have suffered an estimated two percentage-point loss to the Communists in these districts as well. In urban and semiurban areas, ND's loss to the Communists appears to have been approximately three percentage points, mainly made up of voters who—never strong ND supporters anyway—were switching back to the Communists.

ND's losses to the left in rural areas can be explained on the basis of dissatisfaction caused by crop failures; a variety of local grievances not effectively tackled by ND mainly because of its organizational weaknesses; and PASOK's torrent of promises of socioeconomic "change." There should be little doubt that ND's losses in rural areas were essentially a "protest vote"—rather than a sign of widespread conversion to socialism, let alone to PASOK's Marxism.

Postscript and Conclusions

In the first year after the elections the single most important development in relation to the New Democracy party was the convening of its first congress, which paved the way for the establishment of intraparty democracy,[101] ratified the party's charter, and articulated a more coherent political philosophy.

In fact the ND congress was the first to be convened by any non-Communist Greek party ever. Furthermore, it was the first to elect a party body (the ND's new fifty-member Administrative Committee), and, even more important, it was composed of party representatives who had all been elected by the party members. Of course, most of

[101] Recently, and for the first time in Greek party history, New Democracy selected its leader by democratic procedures; George P. Rallis beat Evangelos Averoff by four votes in an election held in the parliamentary group, as provided in ND's charter.

the 100,000 or so voters who had been mobilized (mainly by the M.P.s) to elect representatives to the congress were not active party members but merely supporters who had "joined" ND just before the congress simply in order to vote. Nonetheless the importance of the ND congress as a landmark in the democratization of the Greek parties cannot be ignored.[102]

Concerning the ND charter approved by the party congress, only a few points can be made. First, an article was included which stipulated that "the democratic structure and function of the party" was one of ND's "basic values." Intraparty democracy had become an important component of ND's philosophy.[103]

Second, it was stipulated that henceforth the Administrative Committee would be composed of seventy members, eighteen of them M.P.s elected by the parliamentary group. The party's president, vice-president, general secretary, and president of the Youth Organization are automatically members of the committee, and the rest are elected by the party congress. Its election will undoubtedly increase the prestige and power of the Administrative Committee. However, the ND charter finally adopted seems to have cut back the power given to the Administrative Committee in the provisional charter.[104] On the other hand, one should stress the increasing prestige of the party's ten-member Executive Committee, whose weekly sessions are attended by the party's vice premier and general secretary.[105] Also, it should be mentioned that party organizations on the local level have been given increased leverage in the nomination of the party's candidates for Parliament.[106]

Finally, the most important departure from the provisions laid down by the provisional charter was the one referring to the election

---

[102] On the importance of the ND congress see e.g., *Politika Themata*, no. 250 (May 1970), pp. 11-17. Also my comments in *Epikentra*, no. 7 (1979), pp. 2-4.

[103] *Ideologikes Arhes-Katastatiko*, article 1, part 2 (Athens: Nea Dimokratia, June 1979). It is interesting to note here that PASOK in a recent decision of its Central Committee stated that intraparty democracy was "not an ideological value or position" but simply "a means for the development of the function" (of the party). See this writer's comments in *Epikentra*, no. 7 (1979), p. 9.

[104] For example, the Administrative Committee now can neither prepare the party's program (article 7, para. (a) of the Provisional Charter versus article 7, para. (a), (b) of the ND charter) when organizing the congress nor "assist" the party leader in preparing the electoral lists (article 7, para. (e) of the Provisional Charter has not been included in the ND charter). See *Prosynedrio tou Kommatos*, vol. 2, p. 86, and *Ideologikes Arhes-Katastatiko*, pp. 23-24.

[105] *Ideologikes Arhes-Katastatiko*, p. 25.

[106] S. Stratigis, "To Katastatiko tis ND Themelio Dimokratikis Esocommatikis Diadikasias" [The ND charter, the foundation of intraparty democracy], *Epikentra*, no. 8 (May-June 1979), p. 45.

of the party leader. Under the new ND charter the body electing the leader is no longer the party congress but the parliamentary group.[107] The legalistic arguments advanced to justify this change were unconvincing, but the practical ones appeared much more reasonable—the claim, for example, that at this stage the party congress does not represent ND supporters as faithfully as the parliamentary group and that in case of a leadership crisis the convening of a congress is very cumbersome.[108] A proposal that the Administrative Committee should share this right with the parliamentary group was rejected.[109]

During the ND congress Premier Karamanlis made what was undoubtedly his most important and sophisticated speech on the party's philosophy. Thus in spite of his insistent rejection of any left-right classification of ND, he clearly stated for the first time that ND was indeed not a social democratic party. Avoiding the term "conservative," which has derogatory connotations in Greek politics, he explained that ND was a "radical liberal" party in European terms—a party whose views were somewhere in between "traditional liberalism and social democracy."[110]

This analysis has stressed both the successes and the weaknesses of the Greek conservative movement. Its achievements lie mainly in the field of government, where after the Civil War it succeeded in building a ravaged Greece into a prospering country with a dynamic economy. After the dictatorship, it not only tackled socioeconomic issues with relative efficiency (though certain serious errors in economic strategy cannot be ignored) but, more important, it secured a remarkably smooth transition to parliamentary democracy. Furthermore, it helped create an atmosphere of moderation, liberalism, and tolerance unprecedented in Greek political history.

Its weaknesses always lay in the fields of ideology and organization. A passionate monarchism, anti-Venizelism, and anticommunism plagued the conservative movement, preventing it from developing a sophisticated, liberal ideology, moderate in tone and affirmative in

---

[107] *Ideologikes Arhes-Katastatiko*, pp. 20, 21.

[108] See the minutes of the congress, *Proto Synedrio, Praktika* (Athens: ND, 1979), pp. 91-92. Also Stratigis, "To Katastatiko," p. 44.

[109] *Proto Synedrio*, p. 95.

[110] Ibid., p. 22. Before the ND congress, the Center for Political Research and Information (KPEE) published a large number of articles on the ideology of "neoconservatism" or "neoliberalism." Issue no. 6 of *Epikentra* (January-February 1979) is mainly devoted to "liberal conservatism." The issue includes articles by J. C. Loulis, A. Andrianopoulos, and P. Gennimatas. This was probably the first systematic attempt to tackle the problems related to the philosophy of the center-right. After the ND congress *Epikentra*, no. 8 (May-June 1979) analyzed Karamanlis's speech.

orientation. New Democracy is in fact the first Greek conservative party that has to a great extent cast aside these clichés and made a serious effort to develop a modern ideology. But that effort has been, as yet, inconclusive. Particularly during the post-1977 economic crisis, but also during the years 1974–1977, the Greek government, lacking a coherent philosophy, proved unable to structure a solid, concrete, overall economic policy. Instead it resorted to a number of supposedly "practical, nondogmatic" day-to-day measures, which were soon negated by a new set of contradictory measures.[111] Furthermore the party has never seemed sure where it stood on important questions of philosophical principle (individualism and the social good, equality and freedom, state intervention and private initiative, and so on). This has led New Democracy to project a hazy image which cannot attract solid and enthusiastic support for its ideas rather than its leaders, let alone create ideologically conscious followers. The term "radical liberalism" is also confusing. If by "radical" Karamanlis means to imply *extensive* state intervention, then one cannot clearly see the difference between his "liberalism" and social democracy. On the other hand, if the term is interpreted as connoting a radical departure from state interventionism, it is necessary to explain the difference between such liberalism and traditional liberalism or libertarianism. Finally, it should be noted that in spite of its adherence to liberalism (radical or otherwise), New Democracy's policies were very often particularly statist in many spheres of social life. State intervention in the private lives of the citizens was frequent, arbitrary, and above all regularly *paternalistic*.[112]

In the field of organization, ND, particularly after 1977, also made some significant progress under the guidance of the Executive Committee and through the efforts of the respected vice premier, Theofylaktos Papakonstandinou, and of the young and dynamic general secretary, Konstantine Stefanopoulos. The convening of the ND's first congress was undoubtedly a major step in its democratization. However, we must note that the party still lacks a strong grass-roots organization, that the patronage system continues to obstruct the creation of such an organization, and that, consequently, the party leadership retains a disproportionate slice of power.

[111] See J. C. Loulis, "Eleftheri Oikonomia ke oi Kyvernitikoi Oikonomikoi Prosanatolismoi" [Free enterprise and the government's economic policies] *Epikentra*, no. 11 (November-December, 1979), pp. 18-20.

[112] Some examples are provided in J. C. Loulis, "O Fileleftherismos stin Politici Philosophia tis Neas Dimokratias" [Liberalism in ND's political philosophy], *Epikentra*, no. 8 (May-June 1979), pp. 34. See also his forthcoming "Neo-Fileleftherismos ke Paternalistikos Syndiritismos stin Ellada" [New liberalism and conservative paternalism in Greece] to appear shortly in *Epikentra*.

So what does the future look like for New Democracy? Will its newly created democratic mechanisms develop and prove strong, ensuring continuity after its charismatic leader has left the scene? Will the broad outline of its political philosophy prove capable of rallying its current supporters? There is little doubt that its organization has a long way to go before modernizing itself. And that its political philosophy has yet to be translated into a coherent set of "conservative liberal" or "neoconservative" principles and policies, casting aside statism and paternalistic conservatism. It is in these two directions that ND has to move boldly if it is to remain a strong political force in the future. However, since the Civil War, the conservative movement in Greece has shown an admirable ability to rejuvenate itself, proving that it is indeed a progressive, dynamic movement. It seems plausible, then, to hypothesize that it may eventually overcome its weaknesses. If it does not, the effect will be far reaching, since today—whether one likes it or not—the New Democracy party appears to be one of the strongest pillars of parliamentary democracy in Greece.

4

The Union of the Democratic Center

Thanos Veremis

On November 17, 1977, EDIK held a rally in Constitution Square in Athens. The assembled crowd listened with profound emotion to the recorded voice of the politician who is perhaps the most venerated by his followers of any in modern Greek history: Eleftherios Venizelos, founder and leader of the Liberal party from 1910 until 1936. Thus EDIK emphasized the continuity of the liberal tradition, which it claimed as the party's heritage. Although in the elections of 1977 continuity proved a poor substitute for charismatic leadership, members of EDIK took pride in tracing their party's antecedents as far back as the Greek War of Independence (1821–1827) and the emergence of the first embryonic political parties.

It has been argued that the Greek political parties of the nineteenth century were anything but successful imitations of their Western European prototypes.[1] Extreme familism and clientelism, as well as the backward condition of the country's economy, minimized their individuality as ideological entities and precluded their development along associational lines. Given that Greek parties have not been class-based, mass parties but rather formations of notables, their development has always borne the particular stamp of their leadership. In the nineteenth century and the first decade of the twentieth, certain political orientations began to differentiate themselves on issues such as attitudes toward the Western world or the desirable extent of authoritarianism or liberalism.[2] A conservative position, focusing on national ingenuity rather than foreign influence,

---

[1] J. A. Petropulos, *Politics and Statecraft in the Kingdom of Greece* (Princeton: Princeton University Press, 1968).

[2] Ibid., p. 62. See also Keith R. Legg, *Politics in Modern Greece* (Stanford, Calif.: Stanford University Press, 1969), pp. 123-129.

was discernible in the antiparliamentary populism of President John Kapodistrias (1823–1831),[3] the state paternalism of Alexander Koumoundouros (1865–1881), and the national populism of Theodore Deliyannis (1881–1905). Conversely, a liberal, European-model trend was represented by the foremost constitutionalist, Alexander Mavrocordatos (1821–1865), the leading reformer, Charilaos Tricoupis (1875–1895) who was responsible for strengthening the private sector of the economy, and his political heir, Georgios Theotokis (1899–1909).

Deliyannis's political successor, Kyriakoulis Mavromichalis, a politician of lesser status than Theotokis, was unable to retain his following, which in 1910–1911 trickled into the ranks of Eleftherios Venizelos's Liberal party.[4] What may be described as a disruption of ideological continuity occurred when the better organized party of Theotokis joined the opposition to Venizelos in 1910. In essence, the Liberal party borrowed from both political traditions, its repudiation of the "old" parties notwithstanding.

History of the Party

Venizelos's Liberal party stood for and furthered Tricoupis's state-propelled capitalism, while including in its ranks a variety of political views ranging from social democracy and republicanism to an equivalent of Whig liberalism. The clash in 1915–1917 between Venizelos and King Constantine I over foreign policy became part of the party's heritage.[5] With the expulsion of the monarchy by a predominantly Venizelist parliament in 1924, the Liberals became firmly associated with republicanism until the restoration of King George II and his establishment of the Metaxas dictatorship, which ruled from 1936 to 1941. The subsequent occupation of Greece by the Axis forces and the flight of the monarch and his government to Egypt divided the already fragmented Liberals over the issue of the future of the monarchy. It was only after the first clash between Communist and anti-Communist forces that the majority of the Liberal leaders decided, however reluctantly, to throw their weight on the side of a crowned democracy. The Civil War which raged between 1946 and 1949

[3] Dates in parentheses indicate years in office. Elsewhere in this paragraph dates in parentheses indicate years active in politics.

[4] N. Oikonomou, "The Political Will of T. Deliyannis," in *Istoria tou Ellinikou Ethnous* [History of the Hellenic world], vol. 14 (Athens: Ekdotiki Athinon, 1977), pp. 180-182.

[5] Venizelos supported Greece's entry into World War I on the side of the Triple Entente, while the king preferred neutrality.

brought the liberals and the conservatives together in emergency coalition governments.

The defeat of the Communists in 1949 and the right-wing ideology it gave rise to (and which continued to dominate Greek politics all through the following decade) precipitated an acute identity crisis for the Liberals. Although the Liberal governments of the interwar period had been associated with anticommunism, the postwar rise of the conservative parties placed the Liberals in the center of the political spectrum, where they were exposed to attacks from both extremes. With nationalist orthodoxy monopolized by the right-wing establishment[6] and serving as the foremost criterion of political legitimacy, the fragmented Liberals could make only feeble attempts at regrouping as a center coalition. These attempts were further undermined by the difficulties the Liberal notables encountered in keeping the loyalty of their followers in an increasingly polarized political environment.

Reconciliation on a national scale was attempted by the old liberal Nicolas Plastiras, founder of the National Progressive Union of the Center (EPEK) in 1950 and prime minister from September 1951 to November 1952 in a coalition government with the Liberal party. Plastiras's effort to dilute the enmity between right and left and to treat the defeated and outlawed members of the Communist party with leniency foundered on the 1952 electoral victory of Alexander Papagos, marshal of the government armed forces during the Civil War and founder of the Greek Rally party.

EDIK's immediate predecessor was the Center Union party under George Papandreou, a Liberal politician of the interwar period and the first prime minister after Greece's liberation from the German occupation. Founded in September 1961, the Center Union represented a merger of parties ranging from moderate right to noncommunist left. The object of so fragile an association was the electoral defeat of the right-wing party under Constantine Karamanlis, which had been in power since 1952.[7] The general program of the Center Union focused on the need to end political polarization, reform the outdated educational system, defend civil liberties, and further the democratization of Greek society.

---

[6] The right-wing establishment consisted of the throne, the army, the gendarmerie, and the conservative parties in Parliament.

[7] With the death of Papagos in 1955, the king appointed Karamanlis prime minister and therefore successor to the leadership of the Greek Rally. Karamanlis renamed it National Radical Union (ERE) and led it to victory at the polls in 1956, 1958, and 1961.

The plea for democratization was charged with the rising expectations of a society experiencing for the first time a significant improvement in its standard of living. Since the mid-1950s, economic growth had become the focal point of Karamanlis's programs, which his followers identified with postwar reconstruction. The Center Union introduced in its campaigns the issues of equitable distribution of the newly acquired prosperity, as well as improvement of the overall quality of life. It was widely considered that the right-wing governing party, with its spoils system and lethargic bureaucracy, as well as its authoritarian attitude toward civil liberties, was retarding modernization. The Center Union, furthermore, gained an eager audience in the growing urban centers, where anonymity weakened the power of clientelism and where collective social grievances were given increasingly forceful utterance.

Although the Center Union never formulated a comprehensive socialist program, the emotional impact of a vague rallying cry for social reform was amplified by the fact that the party was made up largely of personalities who could not be accused of Communist sympathies and might credibly carry out social reform unhindered. The Center Union platform did not, however, gain impetus until after the elections of 1961. George Papandreou refused to recognize this third victory of the National Radical Union and charged the caretaker government of the royalist General Constantine Dovas with having helped state officials to rig the polls.[8]

From 1961 until Karamanlis's resignation in June 1963, Papandreou conducted his "unrelenting struggle" against electoral manipulation, which succeeded in seriously undermining the credibility of the right and won him the laurels of a social crusader. The elections of November 1963 gave the Center Union 46 percent of the popular vote and a slim majority in Parliament. It was not until after the resignation of Karamanlis as leader of the National Radical Union and the elections of February 1964 that Papandreou's "unrelenting struggle" was finally rewarded by overwhelming success. His party won 53 percent of the vote and 171 out of 300 seats in Parliament, an absolute majority both in the country and in the House.[9]

The rise of the Center Union from 1961 to 1964 was accompanied by the corresponding decline of the United Democratic Left (EDA), which had attracted protest votes against Karamanlis as well as

---

[8] See the discussion of caretaker governments in chapter 2.

[9] Jean Meynaud, *Politikes Dynameis stin Ellada* [Political forces in Greece] (Athens: n.p., 1965), pp. 119 and 121; originally published in Lausanne in 1964 as *Les forces politiques en Grèce*.

syphoned off Communist votes. In 1964 it became clear that Papandreou, besides winning over the clientele of his allies, had succeeded in persuading supporters of the non-Communist left that he was both willing and able to put democratic social reforms into effect. Yet the "Old Man," as he was affectionately called by his followers (in 1961 he was already in his seventies), was the product of a prewar amalgam of republicanism and personalistic politics and had little understanding of or patience for modern mass-party organizations. A man of considerable charm and oratorical skill, he had served as an effective rallying standard against Karamanlis, as well as a generally acceptable leader of the uneasy alliance which constituted the Center Union, but he was ill-equipped to fulfill his party's promise of reform and change.

In any case, this promise was obstructed by the fact that the Center Union was not a true formation of the political center at all, but a hodge-podge of positions ranging from the conservatism of Stefanos Stefanopoulos, via the traditional liberalism of men such as Sophocles Venizelos, George Mavros, and Constantine Mitsotakis, to the socialism of Elias Tsirimokos. Even though the party was dominated by members of the liberal camp, it is questionable whether the Liberals really continued to represent the center in Greek politics from 1964 onward. Be that as it may, the centrifugal tendencies in the party were exacerbated by the rise of a new political figure: the son of George Papandreou, Andreas. As a professor of economics at Berkeley, Andreas Papandreou had initially expounded neo-Keynesian economic theory, but by the end of 1964 he was associated with antiestablishment intransigence and aroused the hostility of many Center Union notables, who realized that he was likely to be a formidable contender for his father's position.

The throne did not, however, give the Center Union the chance to disillusion its public. Typically overreacting to Andreas's alleged effort to mobilize a personal following in the army (which the king had considered his own exclusive realm), Constantine II forced George Papandreou to resign in the summer of 1965 and incidentally propelled him to new heights of popularity. The latter's "unrelenting struggle" was now directed against royal interference in politics—a loaded issue in Greece ever since the nineteenth century, though somewhat eclipsed just after the Civil War. This new struggle rejuvenated the Center Union by giving it a concrete objective, which remained its hallmark until the final expulsion of the monarchy through the referendum of November 1974.

In the wake of George Papandreou's forced resignation, forty deputies bolted from the party and supported the government appointed by the king. Center Union deputies who had remained loyal to George Papandreou dubbed them "the apostates." The catalytic role of Andreas—the focus for the center-left within his party—in the clash between his father and the throne gave the Center Union a populist image which made it look quite dangerously radical to the more conservative public.

It was in order to prevent George Papandreou from winning another election that the colonels staged their coup against the government of Panayotis Kanellopoulos, on April 21, 1967, forcing Greece into a seven-year dictatorship. The military junta which came to power included individuals with long-standing affiliations with secret organizations within the army itself, who thrived on the Communist threat, real or imagined, and expectations of professional advancement. Its determination to forestall a Papandreou government that would ease pressure on the left and cease to regard anticommunist fervor as the primary expression of loyalty to the nation was the clique's very raison d'être—and it regarded a possible rival organization led by Andreas as equally intolerable.

The majority of the Center Union M.P.s chose to resist the military regime by simply abstaining from public activity. Leading figures in the party were periodically arrested on various charges. The most prominent among them were Andreas Papandreou, who formed an antijunta movement in Europe after being expelled from Greece; John Zighdis, who was also arrested and later testified before the U.S. Congress against the dictatorship; Demetrios Papaspirou, who collaborated with Panayotis Kanellopoulos in sending information abroad concerning the misdeeds of the junta; and finally George Mavros, who was deported to the island prison of Yaros for his opposition to the regime.

The Elections of 1974

With the fall of the dictatorship, former deputies of the Center Union who had remained loyal to George Papandreou during the 1965 schism and had refrained from any contact with the military regime convened and declared their intention of recasting the party in the mold of European mass parties governed by principles rather than political bosses.[10] On September 21, members of the prejunta parliamentary group elected Mavros president of the party. The only serious con-

[10] *To Vima,* September 4, 1974.

tender, Zighdis, felt himself unable to cooperate with his former colleagues and ran unsuccessfully as an independent candidate in Rhodes.[11]

In view of the impending elections, the Center Union-New Forces party (EK-ND) was hastily put together in October 1974. The New Forces constituent, an improvised coalition of groupings whose members were almost exclusively without previous parliamentary experience and had a record of resistance to the junta, consisted of the following: (1) the Movement of the New Political Forces, whose members included university professors and public figures such as John Pesmazoglu, George Alexander Mangakis, Demetrios Tsatsos, and others, (2) members of the minute Social Democratic party of Greece (SDE) including Haralambos Protopapas, (3) the equally small Christian Democracy party led by Nikos Psaroudakis, and (4) a group in their early thirties made up of the Center Union youth of 1961–1966 who were working for the political monthly *Prosanatolismi*, which had begun in 1973 in guarded opposition to the military regime.

In its founding charter, the Movement of the New Political Forces condemned traditional personalistic politics, party bosses, and patronage networks and declared its affinity with the social democratic parties of Europe.[12] With regard to private property, the movement stated that this should be not merely guaranteed as a legal right, but made attainable for all citizens.[13] The joint declaration of the Center Union and the New Forces of October 20, 1974, included vague commitments to the reform of "political mentalities" and the democratization of the party mechanism to bring the EK-ND closer to its popular base. It also included the promise of a party congress, which would be invested with decisive authority emanating from a wide popular base. The promise of this congress kept the alliance together until 1976 under the leadership of the moderate Mavros and of a temporary governing body made up of five members of the Center Union and four of the New Forces.

The EK-ND plunged into the electoral race of the fall of 1974. It was reputed to have candidates of the highest caliber, who were convinced that the electorate, awakened from its seven-year slumber,

---

[11] Andreas Papandreou meanwhile had formed his own party, the Panhellenic Socialist Movement (PASOK).

[12] Interview with the editor of the monthly *Prosanatolismi*, Yannis Tzannetakos. See also "Founding Declaration of New Political Forces," September 26, 1974, p. 3.

[13] It was only the less influential *Prosanatolismi* group that made its preference for a socialist system explicit in its declaration of October 1, 1974.

would vote as it would have done in May 1967 if the coup had not aborted the elections. The tone of the EK-ND campaign, however, was set by several low-key party spokesmen and could not kindle anything like the enthusiasm that George Papandreou evoked during his public appearances. Furthermore, the extreme positions Andreas Papandreou was taking in his campaign for his own Panhellenic Socialist Movement sufficiently alarmed a significant number of traditional Center Union voters that they scuttled for the security of Karamanlis's New Democracy. The impression that Karamanlis's charismatic presence was the sole guarantee that the army would not react to the transfer of power from the dictatorship to a parliamentary regime was largely responsible for New Democracy's overwhelming victory at the polls. The elections of November 17 gave New Democracy 54.4 percent of the popular vote and 220 out of the 300 seats in Parliament. The Center Union-New Forces received 20.4 percent and 60 seats.

Ideological Orientation and Political Considerations. The party program formulated by Mavros in his campaign speech in Athens on November 12, 1974, did not significantly differ from that of New Democracy. If one discounts the high-flow verbiage concerning "participatory democracy," "the checks imposed on capital (Greek or foreign) by the people," "Greek social democracy," and so on, EK-ND and its successor, EDIK, differed from New Democracy only in certain aspects of foreign policy. Although Mavros was in accord with Karamanlis's positions on NATO, the EC, and the West in general, he urged the government to pay less heed to foreign pressures and act more independently. He also appeared to have been better informed and more alert than the governing party on the Cyprus issue and on the negotiations over the status of American bases in Greece which began in the fall of 1976.[14]

With the death of George Papandreou in 1968 and the departure of Andreas to PASOK, the party had lost its comprehensive appeal for both old and new supporters. The fact that New Democracy had managed to achieve some degree of liberalization while PASOK had laid claim to the noncommunist socialist promise left groups within EDIK striving unsuccessfully to embrace both options simultaneously.[15] The attempt to combine the two principles brought the

14 "I Krisi tis EDIK" [The crisis of EDIK], *To Vima*, March 25, 1978, p. 7. Also P. Bakoyiannis, *I Anatomia ton Ellinikon Politikon Kommaton* [Anatomy of Greek political parties] (Athens: Papazisis, 1977), pp. 166-68.

15 *Prosanatolismi*, no. 36 (October 1975), p. 46.

party a major identity crisis and led to a schism between traditional Liberals and the modernizing New Forces.

Furthermore, in the past the Liberal elements of the Center Union had been closely associated with the struggle against the throne. Between 1944 and 1952, however, the Liberals found themselves reluctantly aligned with the king in their joint battle against the Communists. This partnership blurred the party's antiroyalist image, which was revived during George Papandreou's "unrelenting struggle." But in 1974, the abolition of the monarchy after the referendum irrevocably deprived EDIK of a popular cause and an issue which had clearly defined its identity.

Between the Two Elections

The incompatibility of old and new elements on the one hand, and the remarkable staying power of political tradition on the other, were clearly demonstrated in the period following the 1974 elections. Since the majority of the party's votes had been won by old Liberal deputies with strong local followings—men like Angelos Angellousis, Andreas Kokevis, and Stylianos Houtas—the socialist tendencies in the ideology of EK-ND inevitably receded. In February 1976 the New Forces group forfeited the right to be represented in the party's name, which was changed to Union of the Democratic Center (EDIK). In April of that year its charter was finally drafted, in theory vesting the "Panhellenic Congress" with the highest authority. In practice, the leader and the parliamentary group remained the determining forces in the organization, undermining the original plan for the party's democratization.

According to the charter (conceived and approved by the parliamentary group), EDIK is organized on three levels, local, regional, and central (see table 4-1).[16] The preponderance of the central executive, the leader, and the parliamentary group is overwhelming. Power is concentrated at the top and authority flows from above. The Panhellenic Congress, on paper the supreme party organ, does not elect the leader. The base of the party, therefore, has no opportunity to express its will in this key decision. This traditional orientation of authority has stifled the efforts and minimized the significance of the modernizing forces within the party.

Furthermore, moves by two important members of the New Forces tarnished the image of incorruptibility which had conferred

[16] The charter has not been revised.

considerable prestige on the group. The haste with which Demetrios Tsatsos and George Alexander Mangakis ensured, through the intervention of Karamanlis himself, their legal right to maintain both their academic and their parliamentary positions disappointed some of their adherents, though the political favoritism involved was actually trivial. The strong initial thrust of the New Forces within the party was blunted by the grim realities of politics. When the high expectations associated with the resistance to the junta gave way to the practical pursuit of power, the influence of the New Forces waned. Tsatsos became the spearhead of opposition to the party's old guard which resisted internal reform. After clashing with the leadership repeatedly, he was expelled in July 1976, on Mavros's initiative, for violating party rules. In September 1976, George Alexander Mangakis, Anastasios Minis (a former air force officer who had been tortured by the junta for his resistance activities), and Protopapas left EDIK and, along with Tsatsos, formed the Initiative for Democracy and Socialism.[17] Thus the party once more reverted to tradition: the notables could determine its fate unhindered.

The Problem of Leadership. EDIK's internal conflicts were lost on the man in the street, but he knew that the party's leader, Mavros, was neither charismatic nor forceful. At a time when most Greek homes in urban centers and all the coffee houses in the villages possessed television sets, Mavros's tedious parliamentary speeches in formal Greek, badly punctuated and interrupted by nervous coughs, were no match for either Karamanlis's self-confidence or Andreas Papandreou's well-staged polemics. Whereas Karamanlis projected the familiar image of the Greek father who knows best and Papandreou that of the rebellious big brother who challenges paternal authority with the aid of his polished Western education, Mavros could only be cast as the respectable gentleman from across the street trying to interfere in a family feud.

Mavros, a successful lawyer, had begun his political career with the Liberal party and had never left it. In the Papandreou government he chose to remain outside the internecine quarrels of the Center Union by assuming the governorship of the National Bank of Greece in 1964. During most of the dictatorship he led a rather uneventful life, until the last year when he was arrested for his opposition to the junta and deported to the notorious island prison of Yaros.

Mavros became deputy prime minister and minister of foreign

---

[17] Minis later resigned from the group over a controversy involving Tsatsos.

TABLE 4-1
EDIK: PARTY ORGANIZATION

Body	Frequency of Sessions, Tenure	Membership	Functions
Local			
Local Assembly	Meets once a year	Local committee members	Organization, policy, finance; elects Local Committee; elects representatives to the Regional Assembly.
Local Committee	Meets once a month	5–9 members elected by Local Assembly	Summons the Local Assembly.
Regional			
Regional Conference	Meets once a year	Representatives of local organizations; deputies, ex-deputies, candidates	Organization, policy, finance; elects delegates to Panhellenic Congress (one out of every 20 representatives at the Regional Conference is sent to the congress).
Regional Committee	Meets once a month	15–31 members elected by Regional Conference	Summons extraordinary sessions of the Regional Conference; elects regional officials.
Central			
Panhellenic Congress	Meets every three years	Representatives of regional conferences; deputies, ex-deputies, candidates; representatives of party's youth movement	Decides on major issues of ideology and determines the party program. Theoretically, it is the highest organ of the party.

Parliamentary group	The parliament	Deputies currently in Parliament	
Leader	Indefinite tenure	Elected by the parliamentary group	Chief executive; presides over Central Committee.
Political Bureau	Two-year tenure	12 members: leader, secretary general, 6 deputies selected by parliamentary group, secretary of parliamentary group, 2 non-parliamentary members of the Central Committee elected by Central Committee, 1 representative of youth movement	Selects party candidates for national elections.
Central Committee	Meets once every three months	60 members elected by Congress, and 20 deputies alternating every six months	Responsible for the organization of the party. Elects 2 members of the Political Bureau. May set up bureaus and committees at its discretion.
Other			
General secretary	Not specified	Recommended by the leader and appointed by Political Bureau	Ensures that political decisions are put into practice, assists the leader.
Central Committee of Accounts	Not specified	Five members elected by Panhellenic Congress	Responsible for checking party accounts and economic matters.

(*Table continues on next page*)

EDIK: Party Organization (continued)

Body	Frequency of Sessions, Tenure	Membership	Functions
Organizational secretary	Not specified	Extraparliamentary member appointed by leader	Participates in the Central Committee, deals with organizational matters of the party.
Professional organizations of the party, youth movement	Not specified	Formed at the regional level by party members of similar professional background or age	Organizations representing corporate interests. Their function is to keep the party in touch with corporate demands.

Source: P. Bakoyiannis, *I Anatomia ton Ellinikon Politikon Kommaton* [Anatomy of Greek political parties] (Athens: Papazisis, 1977), pp. 147–62.

affairs in Karamanlis's government of national unity after the fall of the dictatorship—a position which gave Andreas Papandreou the opportunity to level unfair criticism against him. His well thought-out statements on Greek relations with the West, the Cyprus issue, and Greek-Turkish relations were the high point of his parliamentary career. His integrity on the issues of foreign policy was recognized even by his staunchest critics.

International developments, however, were not favorable to EDIK's stance vis-à-vis the Western world. Mavros's conviction that U.S. policy toward Greece and Cyprus during the Nixon and Ford administrations would be revised by a more "enlightened" presidency foundered on the February 1977 Clifford mission to Cyprus. It soon became abundantly clear that the Carter administration would request the lifting of the arms embargo which the U.S. Congress had imposed on Turkey after the forceful Turkish occupation of the island in 1974. The further decline of American popularity in Greece which followed the Clifford mission inevitably swept away the Center Union's distinction between a good America and a bad America.

Unlike Karamanlis and Andreas Papandreou, Mavros waged his political battles on two fronts: with New Democracy to his right, and PASOK to his left. From 1976 onward he had to deal with yet a third, internal front, the social democrats of his own party. In spite of his pronouncement that "a leadership system in which one single man decides all issues is incompatible with present-day realities," he failed to rid himself of the influence of the old-guard diehards who opposed any substantial change in the party structure.

The 1977 Campaign and Elections

Karamanlis's decision to take the electoral plunge ahead of the required date found EDIK totally unprepared. Since the beginning of 1976, the party's attention had been absorbed by its internal quarrels. Organization on the local and regional levels had not been implemented, and the youth movement (ESDIN) had all but disappeared.[18] Despite the initial disarray caused by the proclamation of the elections, EDIK soon regained its self-confidence and ruled out any collaboration with parties of the opposition. Either because Mavros believed that the removal by this time of the military threat would help his party recoup its rightful following, or because he counted on

[18] In the university elections of 1976, ESDIN received only 2.7 percent of the vote.

a postelection coalition with a significantly weakened New Democracy, EDIK concentrated its attack against PASOK.[19]

On October 9, Andreas Papandreou delivered a speech in Patras in which he accused Mavros of deliberately aiding New Democracy and charged EDIK with being a right-wing party. In the heated battle of words which ensued, Papandreou's chief accusations were: (1) EDIK had consistently supported the government on all basic issues, including Karamanlis's decision to take the dispute with Turkey over the continental shelf to the International Court of Justice at the Hague for arbitration. This decision had served as an indirect recognition of Turkey's claims in the Aegean Sea. (2) After the elections, a considerably weakened EDIK would form a coalition with New Democracy. And (3) EDIK's claim to be the direct heir of the Center Union and its "unrelenting struggle" was totally unfounded.[20]

In reply, Mavros charged that: (1) EDIK had been leveling constructive and therefore effective criticism at the government's foreign policy. (2) Opposition such as PASOK's to Greece's entry into the European Community could only serve the interests of the superpowers, which sought to isolate small nations and make them their easy prey. (3) Papandreou's extremism had driven the electorate to vote for New Democracy in 1974. His radical statements had given the right wing, especially the extraparliamentary right, advantages against the parliamentary regime. And (4) it was Andreas's absence from all national struggles including the "unrelenting struggle," and not his family name, that should be the determining factor in an evaluation of his credibility.[21]

Papandreou challenged Mavros to repudiate the allegation that EDIK would join forces with the ND,[22] but Mavros avoided any statement that would commit him, thus permitting considerable speculation concerning EDIK's future strategy. Foreign reporters tended to agree in their appraisals. Andrew Wilson of the *Observer* intimated that the Center Union would lose ground to PASOK and would therefore probably combine with a weakened New Democracy: "Throughout their campaigns, both parties (EDIK and Nea Dimokratia) abstained from statements that would exclude the possibility of future collaboration." Campbell Page of the *Guardian* pointed out

---

[19] G. Drossos, a ND candidate and writer for the daily *Kathimerini*, was one observer who concluded that EDIK had joined battle with PASOK. (See his article of October 31, 1977.)

[20] *Kathimerini*, October 11, 1977.

[21] Ibid.

[22] Papandreou's speech in Larissa on October 16, 1977.

the possibility of a center-right formation's emerging, with Karamanlis assuming the presidency and Mavros the position of premier.[23] The well-informed Mario Modiano of the London *Times* also predicted postelectoral developments along these lines.

In terms of campaign organization, EDIK was a latecomer. New Democracy published its list of candidates on October 13, EDIK not until October 18. Furthermore, its budget allowed only for a bare minimum of publicity. In the major cities, EDIK's orange-and-blue stickers and posters were practically lost in the deluge of blue, green, and red campaign material put out by the other parties. Its presence in towns and villages, which were generally dominated by PASOK's green posters and the ND's blue—in that order—was even less conspicuous. The EDIK slogan "For change with certainty" (or "with security"—in Greek, *Allagi me sigouria*) sought to combine what seemed to many voters to be incompatible goals. It certainly failed to capture the imagination of those who sought adventure with PASOK.

Andreas for his part actually toned down his rhetoric, aiming his campaigns at New Democracy and EDIK supporters rather than at voters to his left. Mavros failed to point out this opportunism and instead made personal attacks on Andreas which only enhanced the latter's image in his followers' eyes. In the final analysis, PASOK voters were attracted by the party leader's dynamism, while being reassured by his newly acquired moderation that no cataclysm would follow his accession to power.

Although the Phrygian cap of the republic, which EDIK had adopted as its symbol, was an allusion to the Center Union party of 1964–1967,[24] few people realized that the initials "D.S." on the cap stood for democratic socialism, yet another inconspicuous latecomer in the party's vocabulary. EDIK's campaign headquarters were situated at a busy intersection at Omonia Square, the arrival point for most villagers coming into Athens. Its loudspeakers were less noisy than those of other party headquarters, and, like the visitors earnestly conversing with members of the EDIK youth movement, they concentrated on various points of the party's manifesto. Whoever wished to contribute to the campaign could purchase a twenty, fifty, or hundred drachma voucher (top value approximately $2.70). Two large portraits dominated the main wall: one of Mavros and one of Eleftherios Venizelos. Little of the glamour of 1974 revived in the

---

[23] *Kathimerini*, November 15-16, 1977.

[24] Kostas Mitropoulos, the popular cartoonist of *To Vima*, used to present George Papandreou accompanied by a little girl—young Democracy—wearing the Phrygian cap.

campaign of 1977. Of the original resistance group, only Pesmazoglu, Virginia Tsouderou, and Constantine Alavanos remained; the late Alexander Panagoulis,[25] Mangakis, and Minis—all celebrated figures of the opposition to the junta—were gone from EDIK.

The most crucial difference between the platforms of EDIK and PASOK arose over Greece's position vis-à-vis the European Community (EC). A debate between two able scholars, Pesmazoglu for EDIK and Constantine Simitis for PASOK, proved that EDIK was well equipped to discuss the issue and to defend its position effectively.[26] Arguing in favor of Greece's entry into the EC, Pesmazoglu acknowledged the need to negotiate the terms rather than to beg for admission. Conversely, Simitis claimed that if Greece did become a member of the EC, the country would not only become economically more dependent on Western monopolies but also would forfeit the option of seeking out clients elsewhere. He considered the EC part of a larger system of alliances which would prove detrimental to Greece's interests. Pesmazoglu pointed out that belonging to the EC did not necessarily entail membership of NATO and vice versa. France, he argued, was a founding member of the EC but had withdrawn from NATO, while Norway (often cited by Andreas Papandreou as a country to be emulated) was a sterling member of NATO which chose to remain outside the EC. Pesmazoglu also mentioned that neither Socialist nor Communist parties in EC member-nations had opposed entry, choosing instead to fight for the improvement of the institution. Finally, Simitis had no convincing answer to Pesmazoglu's question about the fate of Greek agricultural production if the government were to withdraw Greece's application for membership in the EC.

The fact that EDIK could not get these legitimate arguments across to the electorate demonstrated the party's serious inadequacy at communicating with the public at large. Although the technical nature of the EC issue militated against its being easily assimilated by the masses, the absence of any electoral machinery for promoting the party's position proved fatal for EDIK in the 1977 elections. It was perhaps an overestimation of the electorate's interest in the EC which led EDIK to place the subject at the center of its platform. In

[25] Panagoulis was the popular hero of the resistance who had made an attempt on the life of dictator Papadopoulos. He was elected to Parliament as a Center Union-New Forces candidate in 1974 but left the party's ranks after quarreling with the leadership. He was killed in an automobile accident in 1976.

[26] The debate was published in the newspaper *Ta Nea* in four installments between November 14 and 17, 1977.

doing so it provided PASOK with the opportunity to point out the similarity between EDIK's foreign policy and that of the ruling party.

Mavros's two televised appearances did not improve his reputation as a public speaker, but the points he made were not without substance. His major thrust was an attack on the government, insisting that the Cyprus question was an international issue which merited the exclusive attention of the United Nations and should not have been treated as a mere Greco-Turkish dispute.[27] In his own televised speech of November 12, Karamanlis dismissed Mavros's criticism as politically unrealistic—to which Mavros replied at his successful rally in Lamia on November 13: "The New Democracy leader considers any disagreement with his views as lacking in realism, and furthermore as a personal affront." This was one of Mavros's rare personal attacks on Karamanlis, and it hit home. Yet the Lamia speech, although well constructed, again focused on foreign policy, which failed to attract wide electoral interest.

It was Papandreou's two rallies, in Thessaloniki and in Athens (on November 16) that most clearly showed up the inadequacy of EDIK's organization at the grass-roots level. Athens's huge Constitution Square, with the lighted Parliament building looming in the background, was transformed into a sea of swaying humanity, green with PASOK flags. Most of the crowd were between seventeen and fifty years old; they represented practically all strata of Greek society and all professional groups, including middle-class businessmen and the military, and Papandreou welcomed their support with open arms.

The EDIK rally the following evening was an anticlimax, no match for Papandreou's in either numbers or enthusiasm. Most of those who turned out were between forty and sixty, middle class in appearance, and rather reserved in their response to Mavros's promises. Only a few orange-and-blue flags were distributed by individual candidates, and the occasional chanting of slogans was feeble and uncoordinated. Although many EDIK supporters sought consolation in the fact that in 1974 the impressive PASOK rally in Athens had not been matched by the party's subsequent electoral performance, it was clear that the positive spirit that had dominated the Center Union-New Forces campaign in 1974 was irrevocably lost.

When the ballots were counted, EDIK was found to have suffered heavy losses in most parts of Greece. In the electoral pre-

[27] Speech of November 10, 1977. For an extensive account of Mavros's ideas on foreign policy see George Mavros, *Ethniki Kindyni* [National perils] (Athens: n.p., 1978). The book contains a summary of its major points in English.

cincts of Athens and Piraeus alone it lost ten deputies; in Rodopi it lost both its deputies, and its share of the vote dropped by 22.3 percentage points; and in Zanthe its loss was as high as 25 percentage points. With few exceptions, EDIK's losses coincided with gains for PASOK. EDIK attributed the success of its chief rival to a belated expression of the people's wish for spectacular change, which had been stifled in 1974 by fear of a relapse into dictatorship. Yet an equally if not more important factor contributing to EDIK's disaster was its lack of effective organization, particularly at the local and regional levels. Its few electoral gains were in precincts with no regional unity (Thesprotia, Grevena, Lefkada, and Xanthi) and thus may be attributed to the personalities and initiatives of individual candidates.[28]

Continuity and Change in the Make-up of the Center Party, 1936– 1977. Although there has never been much difference in the social and professional backgrounds of liberal and conservative deputies—in both parliamentary groups lawyers have predominated—the Liberals who were elected in 1936 came largely from the urban centers, territories unified with Greece after 1912, and refugee communities.[29] In the parliament of 1964, the territorial representation of the two major parties was more uniform, with deputies from urban centers, the "new" territories, and the refugee communities evenly distributed between right and center. Lawyers were again numerically dominant, with workers and farmers conspicuously absent on both sides of the House. Of the 107 right-wing coalition representatives elected in 1964, as many as 20 percent had begun their political careers in the Liberal camp, while only two of conservative origin joined the ranks of the Center Union.[30] In 1974, after the fall of the military regime, the center supplied New Democracy and PASOK with several of its former adherents.[31] EDIK's claim, therefore, that the Liberal camp was constantly renewing the ranks of other major parties is not without foundation.

The absence of working-class and peasant candidates in EDIK

[28] *To Vima*, November 27, 1977, p. 10. Also C. Georgantidis and H. Nikolakopoulos, "Metatopiseis Psiphon kai Metaboles tou Eklogikou Charti . . ." [Displacement of votes and changes in the electoral map . . .], *Synchrona Themata*, vol. 1 (May 1978), p. 52.

[29] D. Kitsikis, *Ellas kai Xenoi* [Greece and the foreign powers] (Athens: Kollaros, 1977), pp. 195-98.

[30] Ibid., pp. 206-15.

[31] Mainly dissidents ("apostates") of the rift of 1965 (Papaspyrou, Stephanakis, Tsouderos, Bakatselos, Rentis) and their sons.

persisted after the dictatorship, with lawyers continuing to form the largest professional group in Parliament. With the exception of the elections of 1977, when PASOK scooped up the EDIK following in the rural areas, party notables (from families with more than sixty years' tradition in politics) have tended to be reelected irrespective of the party's fortunes. Of the 142 Liberal representatives in 1936, 16 had come from families of local notables. In 1964, the figure was 20 out of 171, in 1974 it was 19 out of 61, and in 1977, 6 out of 15. In 1974, as many as 33 of the 61 EK-ND deputies wielded overwhelming influence in their constituencies, while in 1977 only the six local notables did. Despite the fact that many influential party members lost their seats in Parliament in 1977, party bosses in rural as well as urban centers usually tended to secure their local power.

In 1977 both the average age of deputies and the proportion of deputies over forty-five was higher for EDIK than for either New Democracy or PASOK. In 1974, fifteen out of the sixty-one EDIK representatives were under forty-five, but only two out of fifteen in 1977. New candidates, therefore, are at a disadvantage, especially when the party is suffering a severe setback.[32]

Postelection Developments. The predominant feeling in EDIK after the election of 1977 was that the party's downward trend could not be arrested while the existing leadership remained in charge. George Mavros was promptly replaced by John Zighdis, who had been readmitted to the party on the eve of the elections. The hope was that the more dynamic deputy from Rhodes would be able to restore EDIK's self-confidence and would confront Andreas effectively in Parliament. But Zighdis, whose ambitions for the leadership had been frustrated in 1974, charged into the party like a bull into a china shop. It was not long before the remainder of the New Forces elements, along with a few other deputies, had been either expelled or driven to declare independent status in Parliament, and further electoral setbacks produced shock waves that all but destroyed the party.[33]

At the beginning of May 1978, a prominent deputy and one-time minister of the Center Union party, Athanasios Kanellopoulos, went over to New Democracy and became minister of economics, amidst

---

[32] *Elavon* . . . [Electoral guide from 1961 onward] (Athens: n.p., 1977); and *I 300 tis Voulis* [The 300 of the Greek Parliament] (Athens: Kathimerini, 1978). I would also like to thank Mr. Nikos Oikonomou for his valuable guidance on electoral information.

[33] The author, who visited EDIK's headquarters shortly after the change of leadership, could find no trace of the party's history before Zighdis.

accusations orchestrated by the powerful Lambrakis newspaper complex which had once supported him. Others, mostly EDIK politicians who failed to secure reelection in 1977, also succumbed to the lure of the ruling party. Although the process of defection has been arrested, EDIK is at the present moment denuded of its most effective members.

In 1979 John Pesmazoglu was joined by Virginia Tsouderos, Constantine Alavanos, George Mylonas, Evangelos Protopapas (who left the expiring Socialist Initiative party), and several others to form the party for Democratic Socialism (Komma tou Dimokratikou Socialismou, KODISO). This party constitutes the most promising effort to salvage the center wing from oblivion and a hope for the future of centrist politics. Whatever the shape of things to come, EDIK, with its remaining four deputies, will have great difficulty surviving future elections.[34]

Conclusion. The sharp decline of EDIK's popular support may be attributed to several causes, the most important of which appear to be the following:

1. failure of its leadership to deliver the promised reform within the party

2. incompatibility of the old party notables with New Forces elements

3. absence of a charismatic leader

4. lack of an effective electoral machine and an organization to promote the party's position (including its deplorable financial situation)

5. concentration on foreign rather than domestic policy

6. an overall identity problem, aggravated by the fact that New Democracy and PASOK laid claim to the right and the left wings of EDIK respectively.

In the prejunta period, the Center Union had served as the sole alternative for voters who opposed the right-wing ERE government but could not bring themselves to vote for the left-wing EDA. Andreas Papandreou's PASOK dealt the center a heavy blow, especially when it softened its position on domestic and foreign issues during the election campaign of 1977. Sandwiched between this strong new presence on the left and the government party, EDIK could effectively compete with neither.

[34] The remaining four EDIK deputies are Nikitas Venizelos (grandson of the great Eleftherios Venizelos), Constantine Bandouvas, Menelaos Xylouris, and John Zighdis. Xylouris left in February 1981.

5

PASOK and the Elections of 1977: The Rise of the Populist Movement

Angelos Elephantis

On September 3, 1974, Andreas Papandreou together with his close associates of the predictatorship period and cadres of the resistance organizations Democratic Defense and the Panhellenic Liberation Movement (PAK) held a press conference to announce the foundation and Declaration of Principles of the Panhellenic Socialist Movement (PASOK). Even at that early time, there was hardly any doubt as to the significance the party would have in Greek politics. In fact, PASOK started off with a number of valuable political assets. Papandreou's personal popularity, impressively demonstrated a few days earlier when thousands of his supporters had hailed his arrival at the Athens airport, the existence of a strong, if uncertain, current of support for him within the predictatorship Center Union, and his international connections, particularly with Western European social democratic parties, were so many factors which gave PASOK a running start, ranking it immediately among the chief protagonists on the Greek political stage. By the time the party was founded a general consensus had developed that it was bound to become the most important pole of attraction of popular forces and the most serious opponent of Constantine Karamanlis's New Democracy.

The accuracy of such forecasts was proved during the ensuing months. PASOK showed spectacular organizational growth. Its influence expanded throughout the country. Grass-roots organizations of the movement mushroomed in all urban centers, even in large villages, in all trades and professions, in the trade unions and the student unions. It succeeded in rallying a significant number of politicians of the former Center Union and also cadres of the Com-

The analysis in this chapter is essentially that put forward by the author and Mike Kavouniaris in "PASOK: Populism or Socialism," which appeared in the monthly review *Politis*, no. 13 (November 1977).

munist left and the far left. It did the best job of mass mobilization of any party on the left and seemed to be in the mainstream of the political ferment that spread throughout the country immediately following the fall of the dictatorship. Such was the momentum of PASOK's rise that it seemed to overtake EDIK and to pose an immediate threat to New Democracy. PASOK's election rallies and Papandreou's public appearances were invariably occasions for mass demonstrations with pronounced youth participation.

Some pundits interpreted PASOK's disappointing election result in 1974 as evidence of slackening popular support for the movement. However, to the extent that this occurred, it was to be attributed mainly to purely conjunctural factors of the 1974 election. Nor did it signify an end to PASOK's growth. The movement continued to gain ground, to grow in organizational terms, to win new adherents to its side. It was, in fact, the main beneficiary of the inevitably growing popular disillusionment with the government, attracting in the process the bulk of the forces that had made up the center in the predictatorship period. But even so, PASOK's meteoric rise in the November 25, 1977, elections, from which it emerged as the main opposition party with ninety-three seats in Parliament, came as a major surprise. Very few had predicted so devastating a rout of EDIK and so massive a swing of the center vote to PASOK. It had been generally accepted that Papandreou's socialist proclamations, his extreme views, and above all the threat of political destabilization inherent in his program would not appeal to the petit bourgeois and middle strata, deemed more likely to be attracted by EDIK's moderate rhetoric. But this judgment failed to take into account the powerful forces pushing PASOK forward.

To give an intelligible account of PASOK's electoral performance it is necessary to isolate and analyze the political, ideological, and organizational features of the movement and the political philosophy of its leader that were responsible for its success among the electorate.

The Charismatic Leader

Any comparative study of the patterns of political forces in Greece before and after the dictatorship would bring out the impressive changes which occurred between 1966 and 1974. Not only did none of the traditional parties survive in its previous form, but the new parties diverged widely from their predecessors in structure, functioning, and program. But beyond these observations, a deeper question remains: whether the economic development of the country during the 1960s ushered in a new and stable class configuration, and whether the postdictatorship pattern of political parties will answer its needs.

The most impressive element of change is the emergence of PASOK. Judging by the party's programmatic principles, its membership, its social base, and its functioning, it cannot be considered a lineal descendant of either the predictatorship Center Union or the traditional Greek left. It is an entirely new political formation, substantially different from any other party in Greek political history. On the basis of its program and the convictions of its members (and opponents), we must classify it among left-wing Marxist socialist parties, more akin to the French Socialist party than to Western European social democracy. But it has no precedent in the history of the left in Greece, where the only formation of any consequence has been the Communist party. Nor does PASOK resemble any of the minor socialist parties which have appeared at various times.

The main difference between PASOK and traditional parties of the Greek left lies in the absolute domination of its leader over the party. It would be no exaggeration to say that PASOK is Andreas Papandreou—despite a party constitution that provides for collective leadership and collegiate organs with the Central Committee at the top, and a broad network of rank-and-file organizations and cells following the Communist model. According to its own estimates it had 27,000 members throughout Greece at the time of the first party conference, held July 8–10, 1977, and the figure must have increased since the electoral triumph of 1977.

Appearances notwithstanding, however, the party base does not participate in any direct or constitutive way in the formation of PASOK's political line, which is determined almost solely by Papandreou—his actions, his rhetoric, his decision making. It is as if the personality and prestige of the leader simply pass the organization by, leaving it to serve as the channel for a one-way flow of communication. Communication upward through the party structure is virtually nonexistent. Indeed, the essence of PASOK is precisely the primary and decisive part played by Papandreou in decision making. The leader's authority radiates through all the components and forces of the party, endowing them simultaneously with cohesion and homogeneity. That this is actually the case is demonstrated by the pattern of development and resolution of intraparty political crises.

The confrontation that took place within PASOK's Central Committee in the spring of 1975 was illustrative. Almost all the old resistance cadres who sat on the committee protested Papandreou's "personalistic" style of leadership and demanded a clarification of the party's ideological tenets and its organizational reconstitution with special provision for safeguarding the prerogatives of the party's governing bodies. Both demands threatened Papandreou directly. Their thrust was to repudiate charismatic leadership and subordinate personality to the rules of collegiate leadership. And the outcome of the confrontation was clear: the dissident members of the Central Committee were summarily expelled. They subsequently founded Socialist March, but PASOK itself was scarcely perturbed even though this movement included figures once prominent in PASOK whose political prestige reached far beyond the confines of the party. It would seem that in the consciousness of its members and followers, PASOK was identified with the words and deeds of Andreas Papandreou, not with the views of the party organs, the Central Committee included.

The primacy of Papandreou's role has been officially and expressly acknowledged by PASOK. The report of the Executive Secretariat to the first conference of the movement asserted that since its foundation on September 3, 1974, PASOK had been passing through "a stage in which political forces of divergent descent and mentality have been militantly seeking common points of reference which will allow them to operate as a unified group, whose connecting link is the President of the Movement and the September 3 Declaration of Principles." In another passage of the same report we read that the personality of Papandreou is a "crucial parameter of the existence and operation of PASOK and determines it as a unified organized movement, as a unitary political entity."[1]

The Myth of the Savior. To understand why Papandreou overshadows his entire party, why party followers accept him and not the organizational structure as the connecting link of the party, one must first know that the myth of "Andreas" antedates PASOK and grew out of the myth of the "Old Man."[2]

Andreas Papandreou's fame as an economist had attained mythical dimensions even before the dictatorship. His participation in Kennedy's technocratic braintrust and his criticism of certain magnates of American politics gave him a reputation for unequaled expertise in economic matters. He would be able to lead Greece out of its economic straits, people believed, to put things in order, to implement a definite plan. The fact that as a minister in his father's 1964 government he had been the main point of contention between the govern-

---

[1] See the report of the Executive Secretariat to the first conference of PASOK, *Exormisi*, September 15, 1977.

[2] The "Old Man" was a popular name for George Papandreou. The "old man," in the vernacular, also means "father."

ment and the king, precipitating the July coup and the fall of the Papandreou government, enhanced his reputation as an incorruptible, dynamic, intransigent politician. And during the military dictatorship, his contact with foreign political circles, his resistance acts and declarations, made headlines and kept his glamour alive. Andreas Papandreou was generally seen as the strongest candidate for leadership of a future progressive political formation in Greece.

Papandreou's assets paid off handsomely after the fall of the dictatorship. The support he won from well-known resistance cadres made it possible for him to "go to the people" as the recognized alternative and rival to Karamanlis. He was also greatly aided, especially after the foundation of PASOK, by the big newspaper groups. Dailies like *To Vima*, *Eleftherotypia*, and *Ta Nea* gave his activities and opinions far more coverage than objectivity required.

The charismatic leader is far from unknown in Greek political tradition. In the nineteenth and twentieth centuries, Greek politics has been dominated by charismatic personalities: Eleftherios Venizelos, King Constantine, General Nicolas Plastiras, the "Old Man," and Constantine Karamanlis have at various times played the role of Savior incarnate. Papandreou's case is novel in that it replaces the image of the "Father-Savior," the austere and inaccessible head of the nation, with the image of the "Son-Redeemer," familiar and amiable, the friend, even brother, called by his first name, suffering the same ills as his fellow man, like him betrayed, persecuted; yet also the brilliant scientist, the dynamic leader, the uncompromising visionary. But even this powerful new incarnation of the magical leader was not sufficient to sustain and nourish a political party in the concrete political conjuncture of 1974: it was imperative that the leader-follower relationship be given an organizational structure and ritual.

The Rank-and-File Organization and its Legitimizing Role. To maintain his glamour, the leader requires successes which, whether real or fictitious, must be seen as his own personal achievements. Moreover, they must be continuous: the fundamental leader-follower relationship must be renewed on a daily basis. On the other hand, this magical relationship is incompatible with mediation by a third party, either an individual or an organization, which would blunt its immediacy and eventually destroy it. In a populist personalistic context, real mediation would make the entire structure collapse; the organization, therefore, is assigned a secondary role, and the whole mission of its rank-and-file entities is to cultivate the leader's myth and strengthen the members' bonds with him.

PASOK goes in for intense organizational activism, partly because so many of its adherents are people whose previous political experience was in Stalinist-model organizations such as EAM, EDA, the Lambraki Youth Movement, and resistance groups during the dictatorship. The concept of organization was part of the political education of these people, and PASOK could not afford to ignore it. PASOK's formal structure and the corresponding jargon both reflect Communist organizational practice (the standard charges leveled against party dissidents, for example, are intellectualism, elitism, factionalism, sectarianism, antiparty activities, and so on). In fact, however, what binds followers to PASOK is not the organization but the glamour of the leader, who is the sole decision-maker in the party. The organization's main functions are to recruit new members and integrate them into the party so as to neutralize discordant elements and maximize practical results, to execute orders from on high, and to legitimize the supreme leader's decisions.

In this context the local party organization is indispensable to the cohesion and rationalization of the system. It provides the mechanism through which the absolute domination of the charismatic personality is preserved, enhancing the myth of the leader. It institutionalizes that myth and nourishes it with a series of successes, for which credit goes by definition to the leader.

In its particular combination of charismatic leadership and organizational activism, PASOK is a novelty, a constellation previously unknown in Greek politics. For the first time, the absolute domination of the leader, the myth of the redeemer, has been "incorporated" in the ritual of the organization; the power of the myth has been implanted in an organizational procedure, which articulates a system of moral rules—both exhortations and prohibitions—giving homogeneity and cohesion to popular participation.

Political Orientation

PASOK's political creed can be summed up in the motto "National Independence—Popular Sovereignty—Social Liberation," which has served as the guiding thread of its politics ever since the movement's inception. These three broad goals have provided a constant source of inspiration for the formulation of concrete policies, and together convey the essential meaning of the socialist promise as PASOK construes it: to attain them is to attain socialism. PASOK calls itself a socialist movement based on Marxist methodology and theory but resolutely rejects Leninist principles and the bureaucratic state socialism of the Eastern bloc.

Political Theory and Applications. According to PASOK, Greece is economically underdeveloped and politically subordinate. Greece belongs to the "capitalist periphery." Ever since the foundation of the modern Greek state in 1821, it has suffered exploitation and domination at the hands of the imperialist countries that have been its "protectors." In reality such "protection" has amounted to little short of colonial domination, culminating in the U.S. occupation after World War II, the attachment of Greece to NATO, and its effective utilization as a U.S. military base and bridgehead against the Soviet bloc, the Middle East, and Africa. As PASOK sees it, Greece is a dependent country with its national sovereignty severely curtailed, and the NATO forces on its soil are "an army of occupation."

The crucial issue, then, which will decide the fortunes of Greece is the attainment of national independence. On the other hand, a necessary condition for national independence is popular sovereignty. Up to the present, the indigenous ruling classes—and their political embodiment, the parties of the right—have imposed on the nation a reactionary state which, in conjunction with the "parastate" (the secret service, elements within the army, the CIA, junta supporters, and the reactionary politicians who control the state apparatus), functions through an oppressive political system against the interests of the Greek people. The Greek right and the native monopolies together with the forces of the parastate are the *instruments* of the foreign imperialists: they rule the country as the agents of foreign interests.

The cornerstone of Papandreou's theoretical edifice, which is essentially a sociological one, is the contrast between rich and poor as conceived by the antiplutocracy model. According to this view, the "rich," the native oligarchy, are not an economically and politically autonomous force but a parasitic comprador stratum. They are not a class constituted on the basis of the development of the capitalist mode of production. They become rich by acting as the agents of foreign interests, and they wield political power to the extent that they have the support of the imperialists. They are the puppets of foreign imperialism.

The affinity of terminology notwithstanding, this simplistic picture of modern Greek society, based on a bipolar structure of classes and interests, is alien to the Marxist concept of exploitation as inherent in the capitalist mode of production, which structurally determines class divisions. Despite certain contradictions, Papandreou's analyses leave no doubt as to their meaning: in societies such as Greek society which do not belong to the imperialist "metropolis"—that is, in the dependent, "peripheral" countries—"the capitalist mode of production does not tend to dominate, nor can it wipe out the pre-

111

capitalist mode of production."[3] That is to say, capitalist relations of production cannot develop autonomously, they cannot subordinate precapitalist relations and forms of production, nor can they give rise to and sustain capital accumulation and the development of productive forces. Of course, Papandreou does not deny the existence of capitalist sectors in the Greek economy, but he considers them "enclaves," imported from abroad. As for the bearers of this imported capitalism, they are just a handful of people, whom he calls the "privileged Greeks," making a living at the expense of the huge majority of the Greek people, the "nonprivileged Greeks."

The dichotomy between privileged and nonprivileged Greeks encompasses both the rich/poor dichotomy and the Greek/foreign dichotomy, which underlies PASOK's orientation toward national independence and produces arguments and slogans often with thinly disguised nationalistic overtones. Thus, according to PASOK, the people's struggles must be waged mainly against foreign dependence "so that Greece will cease belonging to the West and will belong to the Greeks."[4] The achievement of the two other fundamental goals, people's sovereignty and social liberation, in a sense follows and depends on the realization of this primary one. PASOK conceives the relation between these three fundamental goals as a linear succession of stages. Thus it declares that "national independence is a necessary precondition for the attainment of popular sovereignty. Popular sovereignty, in turn, is a necessary precondition for the realization of social liberation."[5]

Foreign Policy. PASOK's assessment of the international situation and of Greece's place in it derives from its wider political philosophy. In the international division of labor, according to PASOK, Greece is "a peripheral economy" and, like all such, "politically, economically, and militarily dependent." Thus, PASOK's model closely resembles "third-worldist" views.

According to Papandreou, the immense accumulation of capital in the imperialist metropolis is an outcome not of the inherent possibilities of the capitalist system in developed countries but of the pillage of the third world, which supplies the necessary cheap raw materials and labor; it is also an outcome of the mechanisms of unequal exchange operated by the rich countries at the expense of the poor ones. One of the conclusions drawn from this analysis is that

[3] Speech by Andreas Papandreou at the conference of the Socialist-Progressive parties of the Mediterranean, Malta, July 22-25, 1977, *Odigitis*, July 4, 1977.
[4] This has been a leitmotif of Andreas Papandreou's sloganeering.
[5] Declaration of September 3, 1974 (date of formation of PASOK).

the working class of the imperialist countries has been coopted by the bourgeoisie since it shares in the loot—the social surplus of the third world—and therefore participates in its exploitation. This is the reason why the imperialist working class has ceased to play an active role in the development of the international revolution. Today, the role of revolutionary vanguard has passed to the third world countries, with the rise of the great antiimperialist movements which are working to encircle the imperialist metropolis.

The practical conclusion Papandreou draws from this analysis is that PASOK must seek to "develop its cooperation with all progressive parties and with all movements which may be considered progressive," that is, "which are an expression of the popular movement and are part of the struggle for independence and self-determination."[6]

PASOK Alliances. On this basis, PASOK has established relations with the Union of Yugoslav Communists, the French Socialist party, the Italian Socialist party, the People's Socialist party of Spain, the Belgian Socialist party, and the Labor party of Malta. PASOK also maintains close relations with certain North African and Middle Eastern governments. On the other hand, Papandreou has consistently criticized German and Austrian social democracy and has denounced the Socialist International as an instrument of the "right wing and U.S.-oriented German social democracy, promoting the interests of contemporary monopoly capitalism."[7]

Papandreou has also criticized the European Communist parties, especially the so-called Eurocommunist parties of France, Spain, and Italy. According to Papandreou the "Common Program" of the French Communists and Socialists paved the way to social democracy. Similarly, Enrico Berlinguer's "historic compromise" in Italy was just another name for class collaboration between bosses and workers; and in Spain, the Communist party has complied with the establishment of a patronized bourgeois democracy.

On the contrary, Papandreou and PASOK make no secret of their sympathy for "the genuine antiimperialist forces of the Arab countries," in particular Libya, Iraq, Syria, Algeria, and the Palestine Liberation Organization (PLO) with which they maintain close relations. As PASOK puts it:

> In North Africa and the Middle East, Algeria, Libya, Iraq, and, of course, the Palestinian movement make up the pro-

[6] Speech of Andreas Papandreou at the meeting of the Central Committee of PASOK, *To Vima*, September 3, 1977.
[7] Ibid.

gressive antiimperialist front. Because in our era the
dominant form of class struggle is the struggle between the
capitalist metropolis and the periphery, i.e., the struggle
for national liberation, these countries are in the forefront
of the struggle against monopolies and imperialism. This
is a point not to be neglected by the European left, especially
the left in south European countries.[8]

Speaking at the conference of Socialist and Progressive parties of
Mediterranean countries (Malta, June 22–25, 1977), Papandreou
stressed that these parties must struggle for the overthrow of imperialist dependency, for a radical change in the international economic order, and for the formation of a Mediterranean community
which ought to play an important part in the development of the
North-South contradiction. For this reason, these parties must coordinate their activities and promote Mediterranean cooperation.

The Europe Question. PASOK holds categorically that Greece should
stay out of the European Community (EC). The EC and NATO are
just two sides of the same coin, aggravating the dependence of the
country, perpetuating the exploitation of the working people, ruth-
lessly intensifying the pilfering of the social product generated by
the peasants. In strict opposition to the policy of the Karamanlis
government, PASOK fights against Greece's entry into the EC. Instead, it proposes a new trade agreement with the EC, one that would
protect Greek industrial production and safeguard the independence
of the country. After Papandreou's visit to Yugoslavia in February
1978, PASOK maintained that, in addition, the trade agreement might
include clauses concerning capital movement and the right of establishment. The mere volume of Greece's imports from the EC, according to PASOK, is a very strong negotiating weapon that, if wielded
properly, could permit Greece to achieve favorable terms.

The Superpowers. Papandreou believes that in the post–World War
period, the superpowers have played a decisive role in the development of the international situation. On the other hand, the balance of
forces between the superpowers is not static or immutable. Since the
war it has passed through three distinct stages: (1) the cold war,
from President Roosevelt's death until the 1963 Moscow agreement,
(2) the stage of peaceful coexistence culminating in the Helsinki agreement, and (3) the stage of combative coexistence unfolding in the
post-Helsinki period. Judging that peaceful coexistence had basically

[8] Malta Conference, *To Vima*, July 6, 1977.

diminished the power of the West, the United States moved to counterattack in the third stage, deploying, as its main weapons, Carter's rhetoric on human rights, aimed at undermining the legitimacy of the political system of the Soviet bloc, and the campaign for the self-determination of nations, also aimed against Soviet-type societies. The same tactics underlay "the provocative Cyrus Vance proposals for control and reduction of nuclear weapons which could be accepted by the Soviet Union only if it were forced to accept second place in the international military power structure."[9]

According to Papandreou, within the framework of combative coexistence a complex scenario was in progress in the mid-1970s. Its main manifestations were the Arab-Israeli conflict, Israeli "subimperialism," Turkish intervention in Cyprus, Turkish expansionist policies in the Aegean Sea, the plan to turn Cyprus into a U.S.-NATO base, and the Soviet Union's determination to maintain free passage through the Turkish Straits.

In conclusion, it can be argued that whereas Papandreou is lucid and categorical on the role of American imperialism, his views on the Soviet Union remain considerably more elusive. In the stage of combative coexistence as he conceives it, the U.S.S.R. is neither identified with the world revolutionary forces nor committed to repressing them; it may help them if their development serves its interests. Especially in the case of the Middle East, Papandreou claims that "the conduct of the U.S.S.R. in this area has displayed such weakness as to arouse suspicions of tacit bargaining with the United States for the fortune of the eastern Mediterranean and of the Balkan peninsula."[10]

Electoral Tactics. During the last electoral campaign, PASOK's electoral propaganda developed along two main lines. First, the party took an ultranationalistic stand. PASOK propounded an intransigent position vis-à-vis Turkey in its expansionist policy, denouncing the government's "contradictory" policy which would gravely jeopardize the territorial integrity of the country, leading ultimately to the loss of the Aegean islands. It denounced U.S. policy in Greece in equally harsh terms, insisting that it constituted the main danger for the nation, and it deplored the prospect of Greece's entry into the EC, branding it as a sellout that would spell economic calamity. The second main thrust of PASOK's electoral appeal was the promise of an exceedingly generous social policy. PASOK pledged to redistribute wealth, punish tax evasion and tax exemptions, increase salaries and

[9] Ibid.
[10] Ibid.

pensions, raise the floors on agricultural prices, increase subsidies to small enterprises, maintain the stability of incomes, promote social security, provide special care for women and children, and improve education.

The manner in which Papandreou presented his social program was highly significant. He avoided connecting his party's promises for social justice to the prospect of a socialist transformation or even to a substantial curtailment of the prerogatives and activities of big capital. His anticapitalism was disguised behind vague sloganeering for the "socialization of monopolies." And he never failed to pledge that the road to change would be peaceful, parliamentary, and democratic, clearly with the aim of minimizing adverse reaction from the conservative middle strata and facilitating the detachment of these strata from the influence of EDIK and New Democracy. Papandreou's instructions to his party's cadres for the electoral campaign were to avoid propounding "Marxist or maximalist goals because the optimum is an enemy of good."[11]

PASOK's main concern during the election campaign was to project the image of a party ready to assume the responsibilities of government, alien to extremism or exaggeration, a party working to ameliorate the condition of working people, peasants, small businessmen—all "nonprivileged Greeks." Above all, it wanted to be seen as a party striving for the integrity of the country and for its rescue in a time of grave national peril. Papandreou carried this effort to the point of undisguised paternalism; always he was anxious to convince, to reassure. Even the word "socialism" was used less and less in the course of the campaign, until at PASOK's last huge rally in Athens, attended by at least 200,000 people, as well as in Papandreou's television appearance, it disappeared altogether. The president of PASOK also took steps to dispel the army's fears. Referring to the officers' conduct during the military dictatorship, he praised their national stand, contrasting it with the activities of the small group of "junta supporters" who were solely responsible for the seven-year tragedy of the Greek people.

The Ideology of Populism and its Social Roots

The preceding analysis of the organizational structure and political orientations of PASOK raises a further more general question: Why is it that this particular system of ideas and concomitant political practice appeals to the masses?

[11] Andreas Papandreou's final speech to the first conference of PASOK, *Exormisi*, September 15, 1977.

However strong, no personality can simply mold the masses in its own image and likeness. For the charismatic leader to rise, in my view, a number of factors must be present (although often in crude and primitive form). In particular, a certain ambiance must have already been established in the form of convictions or ideas shared by the people whom the outstanding personality seeks to enchant. PASOK's main ideological themes were not invented by Andreas Papandreou. They are the offspring of contemporary Greek society, of its political adventures, and to a certain extent they reflect the actual demands of the popular strata. Papandreou does not exert his influence in a vacuum. There is something like a predisposition in the air, a feeling ready to be given shape. Andreas captures this element, and from the height of his campaign rostrum he returns it to the crowd, almost unchanged in its essence but endowed with a political dimension. Thus in a sense, Papandreou acts as a mirror for popular demands—hazy and contradictory as they may be—but the process of reflection transmutes the inarticulate exclamation of the people into political organization, electoral strength, M.P.s, local government officials, trade unionists. By the same process, anointed by the people, Papandreou is transformed into a leader, the archetype for every M.P. and local official and trade unionist. In short, leaders there are when others desire to be led.

The Social Radicalism of the Masses. During the dictatorship and more clearly after its fall two apparently contradictory phenomena appeared in Greece. On the one hand, both bourgeois and socialist ideologies went through a stage of acute general crisis; on the other hand, the masses were radicalized and veered left.

The crisis of socialist ideology, though specific to Greece, was connected with the crisis of the Communist left on a world scale. It was manifest in the general disillusionment with and questioning of principles, ideas, and persons consecrated in the course of decades, the split of the Communist party of Greece, the emergence of "groupuscules," many of which survived as tiny political formations, the general unreliability of the traditional parties of the left, and scores of other phenomena of cultural and political life.

Signs of an acute ideological crisis were also prevalent in the opposite camp. The military dictatorship was in itself the culminating symptom of the ideological crisis of the bourgeoisie, and in the final analysis it signified a crisis of legitimacy of the political forces which for decades had maintained the unity of the state, the state apparatus, and a bourgeois society. The mere fact that the dictatorship lasted for seven years underlined this protracted crisis of legitimation.

At the same time, the suspension of open political life imposed by the dictatorship created an ideological melting pot where traditional bonds and allegiances were ruptured without being replaced by stable new ones. Such situations are characteristic of societies passing through great transformations, whether they be progressive or retrogressive.

I cannot touch here on the crucial issue whether, apart from its strictly political and ideological causes, this political and ideological crisis was also due to the economic takeoff of the early 1960s. At this point, I can only urge the need for a deeper analysis that would take this side of the matter seriously into consideration. One thing is certain, however. During and after the military dictatorship, the fluid middle layers of Greek society were being agitated by the dissolution of formerly rigid ideological structures, simultaneously affecting the left and the right, the bourgeoisie and the working class, especially the crowded lower and middle strata of the cities and the countryside.

I have already stated that the ideological crisis was accompanied by the radicalization of the masses. The reasons are manifold and I will simply enumerate them: the oppression of the military dictatorship, the blatant adventures of imperialism (notably "genocide" in Vietnam), the conspiracies against the independence of Cyprus culminating in the Turkish invasion, the specter of economic distress and inflation during the last two years of the dictatorship, and the consciousness of new needs and problems created by the development of capitalism and by urbanization (pollution, the degradation of city life, ecological problems, education, the woman question, cultural needs). All these factors fed a potentially explosive social climate which, under the dictatorship, was obstructed from expressing itself overtly and from assuming appropriate political forms. The absence of open political activity and parties and the lack of communication blocked the channels through which the new problems would normally have been expressed; as a result, they were experienced as repression, and as political and ideological deprivation.

The lid was blown off the gas-tank with the fall of the dictatorship, and radicalization showed its face in public. Among other things, the haziness of its features was distinctly perceived for the first time. Simultaneously, a great many desired ends ranging from wage increases to national independence were hastily christened *socialism*. In the midst of the events and actions of the period immediately following the fall of the junta, there emerged a vague representation of society, a simplistic notion of history, a bipolar view of social conflict, an adulation of the achievements of the popular culture of the past, a romantic quest for the national roots, an equally utopian expectation of radical change, and a general messianic feeling. Demands—some reasonable, some wildly unrealistic—were being raised everywhere. And all this commotion was *socialism*, for any other name sounded tradition-bound and conservative. Yet the fact of the matter is that a populist, not a socialist, ideology was emerging. A movement of populist ideology had surfaced.

The Populism of the People and the Populism of Andreas Papandreou. We have already seen how and why Papandreou found himself in a privileged position in the midst of these developments. There he was at the rostrum—and below, the masses, eager to listen to what he had to say, or to what they believed themselves. The masses wanted to hear their own voice. And, indeed, it was *their* voice that came from Papandreou's lips unchanged—contradictory, disjointed, vague, neither more nor less refined, but enormously amplified, like the echo of a voice in a canyon or an empty room. For the myth of the Savior always goes hand in hand with the myth of the People. The People are always right. They only need someone to tell them they are right. And thus the frenzied applause and cheers of the crowd muffled the contradictions and dissonances and made the flaws in PASOK's internal organization seem trivial.

A fluid social and ideological situation such as existed in Greece after the fall of the junta allows a movement of populist ideology to draw into its orbit individuals and groups of markedly different political views. Populist movements are based on the ideological figment of the People. They accept this figment at face value without ever questioning it or squarely examining the contradictions inherent in it, namely the more or less pronounced social differences of its component groups and the concomitant differences in their social goals and aspirations.

Populism operates with a fragmentary and, by the same token, fraudulent image of the people. It can be effective only to the extent that it succeeds in masking the contradictions among the people through the pursuit of goals that seem to be the common denominator of otherwise divergent interests. As long as these common (and more often than not commonplace) goals remain abstract—as long as they are slogans, not concrete programs—they may be invoked without cost, or envisioned in moments of utopian trance. Moreover, a populist movement can be effective, can rally the masses, only as long as it is in opposition. Being in opposition, it can incorporate and eclectically articulate all sorts of demands that lack internal cohesion. It is only when the need arises to propose, and above all to enforce,

119

specific measures meeting specific social demands that the contradictions begin to break out: the satisfaction of one group entails the dissatisfaction of another. To put it differently, populism is made up of fragments of socialist and bourgeois ideology and, in the case of PASOK, of fragments of political wisdom garnered from the right, the left, the center, the far left, the Communists and the social democrats, from both popular and bourgeois political and ideological trends. As long as it does not have to enforce a specific policy, and ideological confrontation with rival political forces does not compel it to make its position clear, it can go on touting socialism, and the fluttering banners will veil its contradictions. Depending on the general ideology underlying the slogans and on the political forces acting as levers of social change in their pursuit, National Independence may easily come to signify nationalism, Popular Sovereignty can take on any meaning, and Social Liberation may boil down to antiplutocratic ravings.

PASOK's Social Base. Though, as we have seen, accumulated social problems helped to radicalize the masses, it would be wrong to imply that the masses were undergoing pauperization. As a result of rapid economic growth, especially since 1960, per capita income in Greece had increased significantly—from $380 in 1960 to $2,390 in 1975. Although the lion's share of growth was captured by the big bourgeoisie, the petit-bourgeois and peasant strata also benefited from economic progress. The inflow of foreign exchange from tourism, real estate development of peasant property (mainly due to tourism), the easing of unemployment through emigration to Western Europe, the regular receipt of emigrants' remittances by their relatives back home—these were so many factors improving economic welfare and ameliorating social problems. The overall standard of living had improved substantially.

However, advanced capitalism with its frenzied drive toward the continuous expansion of consumption creates new needs which, when not satisfied, induce feelings of deprivation.[12] In this respect, relative impoverishment, far from being uncommon in Greece, is actually the rule for the lower strata of the population. At the same time, the unevenness of capitalist development allows for the preservation and expansion of a very broad sector of simple commodity production, consisting of economic units of low productivity, inferior (or even obsolete) technology, and limited capital accumulation, engaging in manufacturing, trade, or brokerage. The maintenance of a

[12] See Nikos Mouzelis, "Thoughts on PASOK's Rise," *To Vima*, March 15, 1978.

large simple commodity production sector constantly renews the petit-bourgeois classes: small industrialists, handicraftsmen, merchants, middlemen.

These classes are being squeezed by competition from the advanced capitalist sectors and face acute problems ranging from sheer subsistence to the struggle to rise. The chief fact of social life for them is insecurity—fertile ground for discontent, antiplutocratic attitudes, and radicalism, often activated independently of the individual's personal welfare. To this traditional petit-bourgeois sector we should add the middle class, which has expanded significantly in Greece in the last decade and a half as a consequence of the development of the capitalist division of labor. Its members, though wage earners, either are involved in production (engineers, scientists, intellectuals) or belong to the huge mass of public servants, the functionaries of a monstrously overgrown bureaucratic state apparatus. Together, these peasants, lower and middle bourgeois strata, public servants, private-sector clerical workers, engineers and technicians, scientists, merchants, and handicraftsmen constitute a very broad social group unsure of its status in society.

PASOK gained ground mainly among this group. It began to spread at a time when the traditional center had entered a decline and its successor party, EDIK, was wavering between a hesitant anti-government stand and fundamental agreement with the government's reforms; a time, moreover, when the Communist left was plagued by a very deep ideological and organizational crisis. With its eclectic program, its paternalistic style, its populism conveniently catering to the needs and expectations of the popular strata, and its pronounced nationalism which helped simplify the complexities of the situation, PASOK was able to rally these strata behind its banner, offering them the hope of change, a vision of the redistribution of social wealth, the promise of social justice and political participation.

From a political point of view, PASOK seemed to be a real contender for power. The fact that it did not bear the "stigma of communism" was a guarantee that it would not provoke a violent reaction from the army or foreign powers. Thus it achieved the glamour of a party with a chance of wresting power from the right by parliamentary means and proceeding with the deep social and political transformations it deemed necessary for "the welfare of this country."[13] Naturally enough, the rise of PASOK was seen as analogous to the electoral triumph of George Papandreou in 1963 and 1964.

[13] Another of Papandreou's recurring themes.

Andreas lived up to popular expectations. His electoral victory on November 25, 1977, was largely due to the orientation he gave PASOK, to the way he appealed to the masses, to the way he handled centrifugal forces on the inside and the attacks of opponents on the outside of his party.

The Organizational Structure of PASOK

The fundamental fact about PASOK's organization is that it serves as a medium through which Papandreou maintains complete control of the party's political course. Thus, although the party constitution extols at great length the virtues of democratic procedures, in practice members are essentially excluded from participation in decision making. Two basic differences apart, the organizational structure of PASOK is almost identical to that of Communist parties. The differences concern the role of the party president and the role of the parliamentary party.

The supreme body is the party congress, which comprises delegates elected by the local and sectoral organizations, the members of the outgoing Central Committee and Disciplinary Board, and members of the parliamentary party. The congress assesses the overall activity of the Central Committee and determines the main policy lines of the movement within the spirit of the September 3 Declaration of Principles. Also, it elects the nine-member Disciplinary Board and sixty of the eighty members of the Central Committee.[14]

Despite its alleged supremacy, however, the first congress of PASOK has yet to be convened. According to PASOK statements, plans were made for 1980, by which time PASOK would have existed for six years and its character would have crystallized in one way or another. But 1980 ended without a congress. Thus, the sovereignty of the congress remains, for the time being at least, entirely theoretical.

The Central Committee, the highest organ according to the constitution, is composed of eighty members, sixty of whom are elected by the party congress while the remaining twenty are members of the parliamentary party. The Central Committee elects the Executive Bureau and the Committee of Financial Control. The Executive Bureau is composed of nine members including the president of the party. It is the highest executive organ of the party, and for all practical purposes it is dominated by the president.

The nine members of the Executive Bureau must be members of the Central Committee which elects them. The Executive Bureau

[14] Information on the organizational structure of PASOK is from the periodical *Anti*, December 31, 1977.

"supervises and checks the enforcement of decisions made and deals with all current organizational and political problems of the movement, within the framework of the general political and ideological guidelines set by the Central Committee." The Executive Bureau has set up twenty committees and working bureaus composed of members of the Central Committee and other party cadres. These committees deal with such matters as organizational, trade union, cultural, propaganda, and youth issues. For their coordination with the Executive Bureau, a Coordinating Council has been set up, composed of the first and second secretary of each committee and bureau (about forty persons in all). It sits about once a month. There is also an eight-member coordinating Secretariat of the Coordinating Council, which sits twice a week.

At the level of the prefecture the highest coordinating body is the Prefecture Assembly. This assembly expresses the views of the appropriate local and sectoral organizations on political and organizational issues affecting the prefecture. The executive organ of the Prefecture Assembly is the Prefecture Committee, which consists of eleven to fifteen members elected for an eighteen-month term. (Exceptionally, in the Athens prefecture there are four Prefecture Committees—three for electoral district B and one for electoral district A; and there are two Prefecture Committees for Piraeus and two for Salonica, Cyclades, and Dodecanese.)

PASOK's basic organizational unit is the local organization, composed of not more than eighty party members who live or work in the same place. Where no local organization exists, five members of PASOK may set up an organizational cell which may become a local organization.

The members of the local organization form the assembly of the local organization, which is convened once a month. The assembly elects the Coordinating Committee of the local organization for a one-year term. In addition to local organizations, PASOK has sectoral organizations, composed of party members with the same or similar occupations. The sectoral organizations function in essentially the same way as the local organizations.

PASOK has also been concerned with providing its parliamentary party with an organizational structure, including the following collective organs:

- *Parliamentary Work Sections.* These sections are oriented toward the functions of particular ministries. Each section is composed of the PASOK M.P.s who are members of the appropriate parliamentary committee.

• *Committee for Analysis and Programming.* This committee's task is to coordinate the functions of the entire parliamentary party.
• *The Commission for Parliamentary Control and Documentation.*

This, then, is PASOK's formal organization chart. As I have already indicated, the variety of party bodies, the competence and prerogatives of each, the exercise of parallel and multiple checks, are in reality all subject to Papandreou's control, and his personality is the real explanation for the party's ideological cohesion. From an organizational point of view, however, the matter is more complicated. PASOK's organizational system operates along two main axes: on the one hand, the charismatic personality of the leader provides the connecting tissue of the party, thanks to the unreserved allegiance to him of the party's members and followers and their deep belief in his supreme and irreplaceable qualities. This allows Papandreou to intervene in party affairs and make personal arrangements almost at will. On the other hand, he may choose to appoint to the higher organs of the party persons who have his absolute trust; once anointed by the president of the movement, these cadres may, in turn, act in his name without regard to constitutional formalities.

The crucial point, however, remains control of the parliamentary party. Papandreou himself confesses that "it is difficult to establish and operate effective collective organs in Parliament because the whole climate there favors individual performance."[15] Papandreou personally chooses the party's candidates and decides which are to receive party support. Even so, centrifugal tendencies cannot be precluded, especially in times of great tension.

The integration of the parliamentary party in the party apparatus (twenty of its members sit on the Central Committee) aims precisely at tightening the bonds between these two bodies. At the same time, PASOK's M.P.s have been assigned to various party committees and each operates in an allotted area of government policy. On the whole, it is a relatively easy matter for Papandreou to control the party's M.P.s as long as they depend almost exclusively on him for their nomination.

PASOK's Organizational Links with the Masses. PASOK seeks to integrate popular forces in its activities not only through Papandreou's direct communication with the masses but also through the Grass-Roots Development Committees. As far as we know, the most representative testimony of PASOK's organizational philosophy is Papan-

[15] *To Vima,* February 28, 1978.

dreou's address to the first conference of the movement.[16] According to Papandreou the traditional organizational pyramid had failed in Greece because the projected base of the pyramid, the "organizations at the level of town and village" had never materialized. He proposed to overcome this difficulty and enforce "democratic procedures in programming" by creating Grass-Roots Development Committees. These would "guarantee, at the level of village and town and in close cooperation with hierarchically higher organizations, not only the promotion of local aspirations and goals but also the genuine expression of popular opinion on general development targets and on the national-political options of our country."

As Papandreou conceived them, these committees would be part and parcel of the process of planning, particularly for local government. Thus, their membership should not be limited to PASOK members, though the party's local organizations and sectoral organizations would aim to recruit new members through them. In January 1978, Papandreou called on scientists and artists to join the development committees, which were under the control of PASOK Regional Development Committees. The aims of the Grass-Roots Development Committees were stated as:

> 1. The study of regional and local problems which will allow us to complete in a still more responsible way our social and economic development program.
> 2. Systematic mass contact between the people and the scientific and artistic forces of our country so that intellectuals come to serve our people directly.

Clearly the projected character and compass of the Grass-Roots Development Committees were narrowly partisan. Like the Regional Development Committees, they would be part of a concerted effort to broaden the organizational base and enhance the image of the movement.

According to the policy statement issued by the Central Committee at the end of its second session, a substantial increase in PASOK membership would be brought about by means of:

- The mobilization of organized members.
- An open broad campaign of recruitment of new members by the local and sectoral organizations.
- Forging links with the friends and followers of the movement and engaging them in regular functions.

[16] It appeared in the newspaper *To Vima*, August 19, 1977.

- Representation and expression of the demands of various social strata.
- Ideological and political instruction and education of members and cadres.
- Correct deployment and distribution of our forces for better and more responsible involvement with the people and their problems.
- Testing enrichment, and popularization of our political line.

PASOK as the Main Opposition Party

The foregoing remarks have been aimed at bringing out the factors responsible for PASOK's success in the November 25, 1977, parliamentary elections and its accession to the position of main opposition party. This brief analysis can now be rounded off with an outline of PASOK's election results, which will also provide a more accurate picture of its influence in social and geographical terms.

At the time of the 1974 elections, PASOK was only two months old. Its organizations were still rudimentary, its program vague and poorly understood. In addition, its candidates did not, as a rule, belong to the old and established political order, whose representatives had the advantage of manifold bonds with the electorates of the various districts. Despite this—and despite the adverse political conjuncture of the 1974 elections, in which the great majority of the electorate opted for Karamanlis's New Democracy, considering it the only political force capable of normalizing the political situation after the seven-year dictatorship—PASOK won third place, taking 13.6 percent of the vote and thirteen seats. In subsequent by-elections, it won two more seats, bringing its total to fifteen.

Going through the results of the 1974 elections, we see that in only six (Dodecanese, Lasithi, Hiraclion, Rethymnon, Patras, and Corfu) of the fifty-six electoral districts did the PASOK vote exceed 20 percent of the total figure. In fact, PASOK managed to poll a relatively high percentage only in districts which had been traditional bastions of opposition to right-wing parties.

The 1977 Elections. Between the 1974 and 1977 elections, PASOK built up its strength. The factors working in the party's favor had time to make their influence felt. Thus, in the 1977 elections the picture was very different.

PASOK fell below the 20 percent mark in only nine constituencies, most of which were one- or two-seat districts. In only one of them did PASOK fall below 10 percent. In some constituencies, it increased its vote more than 100 percent over the 1974 figure. In the entire country its vote increased by 87 percent, at the expense of EDIK in Fokida, Zanthe, Lesbos, Chania, Rethymnon, Hiraclion, and Lasithi and at the expense of both New Democracy and EDIK in Arta, Thesprotia, Florina, Xanthi, Helia, Arkadia, Evritania, Larissa, Trikala, Patras, Ioannina, and the Cyclades. Comparing the results of the 1964, 1974, and 1977 elections, one may conclude that PASOK did not manage to win over any significant percentage of the "traditional" Communist vote. In 1977, the two Communist-dominated formations (the Communist party of Greece and the Alliance of Left and Progressive Forces, dominated by the Communist party of Greece-Interior) together polled 12.4 percent of the vote (9.7 percent and 2.7 percent respectively), which is slightly below the percentage polled by EDA (then the only party of the left) in 1963 and 1964. This also indicates that in a period of fifteen years, between 1963 and 1978, the Communist left in Greece was essentially stagnant.

A final note on PASOK's electoral results. In 1977 the party's vote in most constituencies was between 20 and 30 percent of the total ballot. Thus, its strength was evenly spread throughout the country. It was not a locally based party, whose performance fluctuated wildly between regions. This also indicates that throughout the country PASOK had managed to win over the social strata that were its potential social base. The few departures from this rule can be easily accounted for by the presence either of a strong Communist influence (Lefkada and Samos) or of powerful EDIK candidates (Chios and Grevena).

PASOK's Members of Parliament. In the 1977 elections, PASOK won ninety-three parliamentary seats. Seventy-three of its M.P.s were elected for the first time, and another six had entered Parliament for the first time in 1974 on the PASOK ticket. Thus the rise of PASOK brought about a substantial turnover of parliamentary personnel. (A similar phenomenon had occurred in the 1950 elections, with the rise of EPEK, headed by General Nicolas Plastiras, and in the 1958 election, when EDA won second place.) Of the seventy-three PASOK freshmen, forty-nine had run unsuccessfully in 1974. We may conclude that, for the most part, PASOK's political personnel is being recruited and shaped from within its ranks: they are creatures of the party and owe their emergence into public life to the rise and progress of PASOK. This is patently true in rural constituencies, where forty of PASOK's fifty M.P.s had run on the PASOK ticket in the previous elections and did not belong to the political aristocracy of the pre-dictatorship era.

A closer look at the origin of PASOK's M.P.s reveals that the bulk of them came from the left wing of the former Center Union, especially the Center Union Youth Organization (EDIN), which had begun to rally around Papandreou even before the dictatorship. In this connection, it is worth noting a phenomenon relating to the discontinuity in the political life of the country induced by the military dictatorship. Most of the established families with long political pedigrees, which for decades had wielded immense power and influence locally, were not able to survive in the conditions prevailing after 1974. In the political void created by the dictatorship, their manifold bonds with their electorates were broken and they were driven from political life. Very few managed to resume their careers. Although this trend affected all parties, it was especially pronounced in the case of PASOK, as the age-pyramid of the party's M.P.s reveals: sixty-one out of ninety-three were under fifty, and twenty-seven of them were under forty years of age.

A similar point can be made concerning the previous party allegiance of the PASOK M.P.s. Very few had been prominent cadres of the Center Union or more generally of the center. In fact, the old Center Union cadres were divided between New Democracy and EDIK after the dictatorship. Only a handful of them joined PASOK. This suggests not only that PASOK's novel slogans could have no appeal to traditional politicians but also that, to the extent that they appealed to the masses, they could only be brandished by leaders who were not identified with any of the old parties.

However, in terms of social and professional status PASOK's M.P.s were far from reflecting the party's following, which was essentially popular. Indeed, the classes from which PASOK derived its main support and whose aspirations it claimed to express were hardly represented in the PASOK parliamentary party. It is true, of course, that the professional and social status of PASOK M.P.s is not the only or the decisive element of the party's social and political orientation. It is, nonetheless, important. Of the ninety-three PASOK M.P.s, forty-five were lawyers (many of them elected in rural constituencies), ten were physicians, seven engineers, and seven principals of private secondary schools and teachers. Further down were one craftsman, three peasants, and three retired army officers. To conclude, though the provenance of PASOK's M.P.s elected in 1977 can be traced neither to the established political order nor to big business, the group was almost exclusively middle class, in sharp contrast to PASOK's following, dominated by the petit-bourgeois, worker, and peasant strata.

After the Election. Immediately after its electoral success and its accession to the opposition, PASOK started shifting toward more moderate positions. To begin with, it attempted to cast off its "third-worldist" character. For this purpose, it repeatedly praised the French Socialist party as an authentic, revitalized socialist party. In pursuing this tactic (which was in fact only an extension of its electoral tactics) PASOK hoped to make the most of the possibilities opened up by its favorable election results. Its main goal was to attract former supporters of the decimated EDIK, who were socially and politically more conservative than PASOK's main clientele. It was extremely careful, therefore, to avoid being stigmatized as Communist or sympathetic to communism. Thus despite Papandreou's repeated recognition of the need for cooperation between opposition forces, PASOK avoided concluding a general agreement with the Communist party of Greece, which would have substantiated the charge that PASOK was heading for a "popular front" with the KKE and—given the anti-Communist feeling surviving in Greece—would have affected PASOK adversely. On the other hand, PASOK was skeptical about whether a popular front type of alliance between opposition parties would bring forth the "cumulative dynamics of unity." It might merely add together the strength of PASOK, the KKE, the KKE-Interior, and possibly some other minor movements and personalities. Against this limited gain, the party had to weigh the possibility that an alliance would fall apart, given the pronounced political differences of these parties—their antithetical stand on the EC, for example, or the constant conflict between the KKE and the KKE-Interior. In short, this would be a fragile alliance, unable to challenge effectively the bloc of the right.

For all these reasons PASOK opted for bilateral cooperation with other opposition parties on an ad hoc basis. It also concentrated its energies on its own autonomous political and organizational growth, taking advantage of its status as official opposition, of the political weight of its ninety-three deputies, and of its image as the only viable alternative to Karamanlis. PASOK believed that rising popular discontent due to the creeping crisis, inflation, and acute national problems, as well as the inability of the right to maintain its cohesion should Karamanlis retire, foreshadowed its own rise to power in the not too distant future.

6

The Crisis in the Greek Left

Michalis Papayannakis

An analysis of the results of the Greek parliamentary elections of November 17, 1974, and November 20, 1977, suggests two broad conclusions about the evolution of the Greek left: first, relations within the Communist left became clearer in the mid-1970s; and second, the influence of the left in the electorate remained stagnant.

1. Clarification was imposed, in 1977, in the area of the Communist left by the net "victory" of the orthodox, pro-Soviet Communist party of Greece (KKE) over its rival, the "interior" or "inner" KKE, and its four allies: EDA (United Democratic Left), Sossialistiki Poreia (Socialist March), Sossialistiki Protovoulia (Socialist Initiative), and Christianiki Dimokratia (Christian Democracy).

The KKE-Interior was born after a split in the KKE in 1968. Its official political line was National Democratic Antidictatorial Unity, which covered among other things an effort to "renew" the Greek Communist movement and to adopt in Greece elements of a "Eurocommunist" position.[1]

The EDA was the only legal party of the left in Greece between the end of the Civil War (1946–1949) and the military coup d'etat of April 21, 1967. After 1958, it was the almost unique mode of expression in Greek politics of the outlawed KKE. During and after

---

[1] The party line known as National Democratic Antidictatorial Unity (EADE) is explained in numerous party publications. See for example: Babis Drakopoulos, "I Politiki tis EADE stis Simerines Sinthikes [The EADE in actual conditions], *Kommunistiki Theoria ke Politiki*, no. 3 (March 1975), pp. 5-20; Leonidas Kyrkos, "EADE ke Dimokratiki Synergassia" [EADE and democraic cooperation], *Kommunistiki Theoria ke Politiki*, no. 8 (January 1976), pp. 3-9; Kostas Filinis, "O Dimokratikos Dromos pros ton Sossialismo ke i EADE [The democratic road to socialism and the EADE], *Kommunistiki Theoria ke Politiki*, no. 10 (April 1976), pp. 57-59. (*Kommunistiki Theoria ke Politiki*—Communist theory and policies—is the theoretical review of the KKE-Interior).

the junta period, the EDA became badly split. The overwhelming majority of its members followed either the KKE or the KKE-Interior. Those remaining, along with a few new members, tried to build a new left party similar politically to the KKE-Interior but with different organizational principles. Socialist Initiative consisted of former members of the centrist EK-ND (Union of the Center–New Forces), who had left that party after the 1974 elections; opponents of the junta and intellectuals, they sought to create a large European-style socialist party.

Socialist March was born from a split in the Panhellenic Socialist Movement (PASOK) in 1975. It included former members of the resistance groups Democratic Defense and the Panhellenic Anti-Dictatorial Movement (PAK, a predecessor of PASOK) who objected to the organizational methods of PASOK's president, Andreas Papandreou. Its objective was to elaborate a left-socialist, Marxist-inspired policy.

Christian Democracy was composed of left-oriented Christian intellectuals who were trying to give political expression to Christianity's social message.

EDA and the KKE-Interior formed a coalition with the KKE, the United Left (EA), in the 1974 elections. In 1977, just two months before the elections, they joined with the three other movements mentioned above to found the Alliance of Left and Progressive Forces (SPAD), commonly known as the Alliance (Symmachia in Greek).

In 1977, the KKE, running alone, obtained 9.4 percent of the votes, equal to the share obtained by the EA in the 1974 elections. By contrast, the Alliance obtained only 2.7 percent of the votes, about two-thirds of which one could easily attribute to the KKE-Interior. Only one Communist-oriented voter out of six therefore decided to oppose the orthodox KKE, which represents, in fact, a victory for the latter.

2. Together, then, the two Communist camps did not exceed 12 percent of the votes, one of the lowest scores obtained by the left since the Second World War. By comparing these results with those of earlier elections, one could formulate a second conclusion in terms of regression or stagnation of the left's influence in the Greek electorate. Such a long-term comparison is especially difficult, because of the extremely turbulent character of Greek political life, particularly as it relates to the scores of the left. However, even in such conditions, one can compare some basic indications: before the Second World War, the KKE (which was practically identified with the notion of left) never took more than 6 or 7 percent of the vote. After the war, the KKE refused to take part in the 1946 elections, but many

observers consider that it could have received 20 to 30 percent of the vote. Just after the Civil War, EDA took 10 percent in a very adverse political environment. In the 1958 parliamentary elections, the All-Democratic and Peasant Front (PAME, that is, EDA plus the very small National Peasant party) took 25 percent of the vote, but it is not clear how many of these voters were former left-oriented ones coming back to the fold as the normalization of political life proceeded and how many were center or center-left identifiers disgusted with the lamentable situation and policies of the numerous small center parties. The rest of the electoral returns for the left are shown in table 6–1. One can easily contest the validity of the 1961 score: the elections that year took place in a climate of "violence and fraud" as George Papandreou, president of the Union of the Center (EK), pointed out. But subsequent elections have been more or less free and orderly. The regression of the left in 1964 is partly explained by the fact that EDA did not present candidates in all of the districts of Greece, in an effort to reinforce EK's victory, but the impact was marginal. The low percentage of 1974 can be explained partly by the dilemma imposed on the voters, as expressed by the composer Mikis Theodorakis (himself an EA candidate): "Either Karamanlis or the tanks." Even if this factor actually played some role, it was not really decisive.

Despite these provisos, it is fair to say that overall the left seems to have stagnated, or even lost ground, over the last two decades.

From a different perspective, however, both of the above conclusions would have to be rejected. In particular, the left would have to be considered the great winner of the elections if one ceased to identify it solely with the KKE and included PASOK, the party discussed in the last chapter. Together PASOK and the Communist left took 23 percent of the vote in 1974 and 37.4 percent in 1977. Even if these percentages were reduced (but how much?) to allow for the participation of significant numbers of former centrist or even right-wing voters absorbed by PASOK, this notion of the left, new for Greece, would still represent a considerable gain over the series of returns mentioned above.

As far as the "victory" of the KKE in the 1977 elections is concerned, it would then be considered a serious defeat for traditional Communist policies and leadership and their influence. Although the KKE apparatus still might be considered victorious over the heretical efforts to "renew" it, it is now clear for the first time in Greece that the left extends far beyond the confines of the Communist party. Moreover, the KKE is more and more challenged both in the broad

TABLE 6-1
Electoral Performance of the Left in Greece and in Selected Districts, 1961–1977

District	1961 PAME Votes	%	1963 EDA Votes	%	1964 EDA Votes	%	1974 EA Votes	%	1977 KKE Votes	%	1977 SPAD Votes	%	1977 KKE + SPAD Votes	%
GREECE—Total	675,867	14.63	669,267	14.34	542,865	11.80	464,787	9.47	480,188	9.36	139,762	2.72	619,950	12.08
Athens A	75,776	23.17	61,030	18.67	54,431	16.98	49,528	12.73	47,039	11.50	24,530	6.00	71,569	17.50
Athens B	104,088	31.90	93,719	27.37	83,584	24.64	83,336	17.82	82,361	16.10	26,678	5.20	109,039	21.30
Piraeus A	29,150	23.10	23,741	18.88	20,498	16.54	17,981	12.26	16,603	11.00	6,411	4.30	23,014	15.30
Piraeus B	43,226	44.51	39,020	37.44	35,052	33.83	31,433	23.14	27,826	19.40	7,456	5.20	35,282	24.60
Larissa	21,605	17.55	26,175	20.27	24,718	19.35	16,385	11.88	21,548	15.00	3,321	2.30	24,869	17.30
Volos	16,831	17.54	17,575	18.01	18,160	18.99	15,469	14.82	15,251	14.40	3,593	3.40	18,844	17.80
Thessaloniki A	51,993	28.66	49,081	27.46	43,850	24.76	32,698	15.87	26,074	12.00	11,988	5.50	38,062	17.50
Lesbos	22,556	25.41	26,768	31.02	24,662	29.57	18,268	24.54	17,645	24.30	1,676	2.30	19,321	26.60

NOTE: PAME, All-Democratic and Peasant Front (EDA + National Peasant party); EDA, United Democratic left; EA, United Left; KKE, Communist party of Greece; SPAD, Alliance of Left and Progressive Forces, commonly called the Alliance.

SOURCE: Elavon, Odigos Eklogon apo to 1961 [A guide to the elections since 1961] (Athens: Vergos Editions, 1977). The 1977 official results were published in all Greek newspapers.

framework of the left and in its own domain of traditional communism.[2]

Finally, the above operation would also tend to show that the "renewal" of the Greek left, so desired and so discussed by many, was accomplished through PASOK, while the "renewal" of the traditional Communist left was a failure, at least in the mind of the electorate.

The above analysis denotes an obviously serious crisis in the Greek left, at least in its traditional Communist-oriented guise. However, election results alone are insufficient for explaining the complexity of this crisis. Its roots go back to the birth of the organized left movement in Greece.

Aspects of KKE and Left History

Since 1918, the year of its emergence, the KKE has been identified solely with the left. The following points seem essential for an understanding of its political identity and its evolution until the war. Most of them contributed to a situation almost unique in Europe.

1. The KKE did not come out of a split within a preexisting more or less large, socially well-rooted, and popular socialist movement, as did most other European Communist parties. Instead it was born by the unification of some small left groups after the First World War and under the impact of the October Revolution in Russia, with which it almost immediately and directly linked its ideals and its historical project. It did not inherit, to any significant extent, the theoretical, political, trade union, and militant experience of a solid old "reformist" socialist movement, as did other European Communist parties. Neither did it spring from the profound and authentically historical discussions ranging over all domestic and international issues that led to the birth of many of those parties. Most of the latter came to radicalize the slow but real penetration of socialist ideas that was already going on in their countries, with more or less success. Even when they tried to break all links with their past and their socialist comrades, they maintained important relationships with their old common social base and their cultural background. On the contrary, the KKE had to create these relationships, not in terms of any his-

---

[2] This "victory" of the KKE is strongly contested by many other observers. See for example: Nikos Antonatos, "2.1 ke 10.1: Pos Synkaliftikan ta Provlimata tis Aristeras" [2.1 and 10.1: how the problems of the left were hidden], *Politis*, no. 15 (December 1977); Angelos Elephantis, "I Laiki Etymigoria ke i Epiveveossi ton Tasseon" [Popular vote and the confirmation of tendencies], *Politis*, no. 15 (December 1977).

torical continuity, but by applying more or less well assimilated theories, analyses, experiences, and models, which were already contradictory and controversial. It tried to do so in an (inevitably?) dogmatic manner, but never succeeded in producing any global, original, and authentically positive approach to its own role in Greek politics and the terms of its actual and future definition in relation to political power.[3]

2. Before the war, the KKE never really gained a national-level political audience or enough electoral support. Its electoral base was at best around 6 or 7 percent. This is, of course, partly explained by its insufficient spread over the country, particularly the rural regions where the great majority of Greek people lived, and by the severe state repression it suffered, increasing in intensity from 1927 until the war. However, one cannot ignore the unrealistic, superficial, and unpopular character of its political line and slogans during this period. Thus, the KKE fought the republican regime (1927) following the overthrow of King Constantine and did not support, indeed sabotaged, the efforts of republican army officers to prevent the return of the monarchy in 1935. It adhered, for unknown or incomprehensible reasons, to the slogan "Independent Macedonia and Thrace" (that is, to their separation from the Greek national territory), and by the early 1930s it had adopted the political line of the "general political strike" and the "armed invasion of towns by peasants." Nevertheless, its political and social influence was not negligible, both because its strength was concentrated in a few zones where urban or rural workers were numerous and because its members were combative and zealous in a period characterized by strong social and political unrest.

3. The KKE was a member of the Communist International and naturally adhered to its famous Twenty-one Points. This gave the KKE the classic highly centralized structure of all Communist parties and the International the right to intervene in the party's affairs. Because the party's structure resulted in an extremely powerful and stable leadership, the question of its formation became very crucial for the KKE. There had been sufficient discussion and quarreling during the 1920s and it had seemed that the party might produce an indigenous and homogeneous leadership rooted in Greek political and

---

[3] Concerning the early history of the Communist movement: Angelos Elephantis, *I Epanghelia tis Adynatis Epquastassis* [The promise of the impossible revolution] (Athens: Olkos, 1975); Pavlos Nefeludis, *Stis Pighes tis Kakodemonias* [Back to the sources of misfortune] (Athens: Gutenberg, 1974); Antonio Solaro, *Istoria ton Kommunistikou Kommatos Elladas* [A history of the Communist party of Greece] (Athens: Pleias, 1975).

social reality, in spite of the enormous lack of experience mentioned above. This development was interrupted at a relatively early stage of the party's history by the Communist International, which nominated a whole new leadership in 1931. This was the most important foreign intervention before the war (but not the last in the party's history, as we shall see). The new leadership, self-perpetuated in various ways, governed the KKE throughout its history until 1956 at least, and many would say still does. Anyhow, it contributed decisively to giving the party, as Lefteris Apostolou has written,

> all the characteristics that transformed it into a 100 percent Stalinist-type party, servile toward the Communist party of the Soviet Union. Those characteristics would progressively lead the party to ruin in the years of 1943–1949. In the KKE, monolithism, cult of personality, and hostility to any dissidence . . . grew to the highest point. . . . The party's members and supporters, ready at any moment to give up even their life for the party, progressively became accustomed to think, to accept, that the leadership would think for them, to consider it their permanent and highest duty to wait while the leadership determined their policies and then to execute them in an exemplary manner, whatever they might be. . . .[4]

The KKE's high dependence on the famous "foreign center" deserves further emphasis. In the conditions of the early 1920s, one could hardly criticize a revolutionary Communist party for being a member of the International, although the principles of the latter were too dependent on Russian experience, and too quickly generalized and theorized by its sponsors. Socialist parties and other political or professional organizations were, and still are, affiliated to international organizations. And insofar as the Communist International's decisions related to common issues and interests, no serious objections could be raised, except, of course, by its enemies. But very soon interventions by the International multiplied everywhere, without anybody being able to distinguish (and the question has never been seriously asked in Greece) whether they were made for the sake of "proletarian internationalism" or indirectly in the name of the state interests of the U.S.S.R. and, later, of "brother" governing parties. While some strong and experienced European Communist parties could negotiate and deal with the Soviet leadership, the Greek Com-

[4] Lefteris Apostolou, "Ya ena Pragmatiko, Ischyro Komma tis Ellinkis Sossialistikis ke Kommunistikis Ananeossis" [For a genuine powerful party of Greek communist and socialist renewal], Avghi, February 26, 1978, p. 7.

munists never ceased to confuse internationalism with pro-Soviet devotion, never feared an eventual contradiction between these two notions or eventual conflicts between their own action or strategy, if any, and Soviet ones, never questioned any particular point of the latter. This orientation has been maintained throughout the history of the KKE. It was essential to the 1968 split and still perpetuates it.

These features of the KKE—its unusual development in the country, the absence of any other credible challenger or ally on the left, foreign-imposed and increasingly Stalinist leadership, the lack of a specific "political project" well adapted to its own national social and political environment—contributed to the party's weakness up to the war and, given the historical continuity of its structure, have influenced its evolution since. The points stressed above are still at the center of the intra-Communist and intra-left debate, whose results, if any, will determine the immediate future and shape of this political area.

From Triumph to Defeat. The KKE stepped into the immediate post-war period invested with enormous prestige and holding more than one winning card in the game that could determine the basic character of the new Greek political system. Indeed, it had accomplished a rare exploit: in the few years of Greece's occupation by German, Italian, and Bulgarian forces it had moved from virtual nonexistence to almost complete military and political domination in the country.

During the Metaxas dictatorship (which began on August 4, 1936), the party had faced unprecedented and very efficient repression. Torture, jailings, and exile, as well as police infiltration of the party organization sharply reduced its possibilities of expression and disrupted both its functioning and the confidence of its membership. By the time of the Italian invasion in 1940, the party was practically nonexistent. Some groups survived here and there, with almost no links or coordination between them; most of the leadership was in prison or exile, and only one or two thousand members remained.

By the end of 1944, the KKE was the main force leading and inspiring an enormous and decisive political resistance movement, the National Liberation Front (EAM), a real people's army, the National Popular Liberation Army (ELAS) tens of thousands strong, and a vigorous youth organization, the United Panhellenic Youth Organization (EPON), all mobilized to resist the occupation forces in the cities as well as in the countryside, large zones of which had already been liberated before the end of the war.

This miracle can surely be explained by the political vacuum which followed the prewar Greek regime. After successfully resisting the Italian invasion, and fighting desperately against the Germans, Greece had surrendered in 1941. Some members of the political elites of the former regime left the country, following the king to the Middle East: others collaborated with the occupation authorities or chose to stay out of any political or resistance activities. In such circumstances, resisting the enemy and preparing the conditions for a renewal of the socioeconomic, political, and intellectual life of the country were obviously two absolute necessities. The Communists, those who were still free and those few who succeeded in escaping from prison and exile (a great number had been delivered to the occupation authorities and transferred to concentration camps, including KKE Secretary General Nicos Zachariadis, and many were executed on different occasions until 1944), were among the first to respond to this challenge. They had experience of organization and clandestine work, they had ideas, a willingness to fight, and devotion to their cause. Despite some fluctuations about priorities (national liberation or social revolution, urban mass movement or guerrilla warfare, reinforcement of the resistance movements as a whole or development of the party apparatus . . .), they held to a national liberation and socially progressive line during the war. They succeeded in building up around them a strong mass movement of the left, willing to work with them and sharing their perspectives. This movement spread over the whole country: it found sympathy among peasants and in liberal and nationalistic sectors of opinion, it penetrated the traditional army milieu, and it even aroused a certain sympathy or esteem among Greece's allies.

In this period, the early 1940s, the main decisions and orientations of the resistance and left movement cannot be separated from the KKE's own strategic and tactical decisions. Although a great deal is now known about these years, their general outlines are still not very clear. The KKE's successive evaluations since the war and the Civil War have not been very explicit and have not offered any satisfying political analysis. They are essentially catalogs of the party's "errors" in its estimations of the domestic and international situation. Even after the 1968 split, the KKE-Interior leadership did not proceed to a thorough analysis of this decisive period until 1949: the argument seemed to be that the party was not yet "mature" enough to discuss these problems.[5]

[5] Ibid.

The question here is how the Communist and the left movement came, in the few years following the end of the war, to be defeated and strategically destroyed by a discredited, self-exiled, and militarily and politically feeble coalition of monarchists, right-wing conservatives, and republican liberals, even if they enjoyed massive and efficient foreign aid in men, arms, organization, and funding.

In the 1940s the KKE seems to have been caught up in an extremely complicated set of domestic and international contradictions and rapid changes, which it could not master. "Error" could be defined only in reference to an established line of action, and it seems that no single line was ever established or that more than one line was applied, which amounts to the same thing. No clear choice was ever made about domestic perspectives, about the extent, the nature, and the duration of the alliances built through the resistance movement. No clear and permanent policy evolved vis-à-vis other resistance organizations, exiled political forces, or allied governments. Instead of a sound analysis and estimation of the changes occurring in international power relations, there were generalities. No information was obtained about the evolution of perspectives and contradictions in the Balkans or in Soviet policies. The list could go on. All these deficiencies can be linked directly to the nature and evolution of the party leadership itself, and not merely attributed to "objective" factors and to the conspiracies of the Greek right and its allies.

There is no reason to think that the KKE and the resistance left associated with it could not have made another choice during the war, as did Tito for example, or after the war, as did the Western European Communist parties and left movements. They were probably tempted by both types of action and, for some time, looked seriously for a third possibility—Soviet and Eastern European help.

The left and the Communist resistance movement was thus involved in internal contradictions during the occupation and engaged in armed conflict with the British a few days after the liberation (1944). The Communists tried legal existence (1944–1947) but, at the same time, refused to participate in the first postwar parliamentary elections (1946). Subsequently, the movement reversed its policy and decided to participate in the 1947 referendum on the monarchy (which won in very irregular conditions) and again talked about insurrection without proceeding to any serious preparation for long precious months. When it did launch the second armed insurrection in 1947, the Communist movement was largely isolated and could not count on any would-be active or passive allies. On the contrary, the state was on the way to reconstruction, the government had

139

powerful allies (American intervention in the name of the Truman Doctrine, 1947), and a large part of the territory and the population was under its control.

The KKE leadership managed the war even worse than "a professional sergeant of the army"[6] and lost it. Finally, the KKE leadership failed to consolidate, in the given domestic and international context, a solid and permanent left-wing movement able to affect the political and social evolution of the country. It had aimed for both less and much more. By 1949 the Communist and left movement had lost, for a long time, any credible chance of seizing power or even of influencing people's ideas and expectations.

A New Start in the 1950s. The KKE was outlawed by the Greek government in 1947. At the end of the Civil War, its essential forces consisted of Greek refugees in various East European countries, particularly in the U.S.S.R. (Tashkent), and a few members in Greece operating under cover. To ensure the legal expression of left ideas in Greece, the clandestine KKE, as advised by Stalin himself,[7] helped in the formation of a new party, the United Democratic Left (EDA). The EDA was organized with some left socialist-oriented groups and persons, among whom was the EDA president, Yannis Passalidis. However, Communists were predominant in its leadership. The EDA represented itself as a front of different tendencies and espoused a rather moderate program.

Not all Communists adhered to the new party, however, since the KKE wanted to maintain its clandestine organization. This policy changed in 1958 when all Communists were asked to become full members of EDA and to dissolve their party sections. They had not realized any significant activity up to that year.

The rebirth of the left and Communist movement in Greece took place in a catastrophic situation. The country was ruined by the war and the movement itself virtually destroyed. The Civil War alone left 50,000 dead. Court martials sentenced to death 6,500 Communists. Another 40,000 were sent to prisons and concentration camps, while 60,000 fled to the Eastern European countries. An impressive array of legal and paralegal measures were taken to eliminate all Communist or leftist influence in the state apparatus and in the political, social, and economic life of the country. Under public law 509, all Communist or associated activities were forbidden. Under public law 375, Communists were practically identified

---

[6] Ibid.

[7] Solaro, *Istoria tou KKE*, p. 200.

as spies and, as such, were subject to the death penalty. Strict military or paramilitary control was imposed on most of the countryside and possession of a "certificate of social loyalty" administered by the police was required to hold any public job and many private ones, to obtain a hunting license, a driver's license, a passport, the right to take university entrance examinations, and so on.

Repression was particularly harsh in the early years. People were executed or exiled, for example, for collecting signatures for the Stockholm Peace Appeal. In this environment, EDA took 10 percent of the votes in the first election in which it participated, and after this exploit it achieved other political and electoral successes. It successfully reentered "normal" and legal political life by participating in the democratic opposition bloc in the 1956 elections. This bloc gained a majority of the popular votes but a very small percentage of the seats because of the working of the electoral system. The EDA reached its peak in the 1958 parliamentary elections, when practically alone it won 25 percent of the votes and 80 out of 300 deputies. The situation was unusual in that the centrist parties were divided and some of their factions openly supported the government's new electoral system designed to "put the left aside." This system favored the two parties with the most votes in the elections, but the weak centrist coalition took fewer votes than EDA.

Even while the left appeared to be growing, however, a number of factors were working to check its progress. From the beginning, relations between the EDA and the KKE had been ambiguous and somehow contradictory. The EDA's leadership was in touch with the political and social reality in the country and had to make its way under very difficult conditions. The KKE's leadership was essentially based abroad. It was still feeling the impact of defeat in the Civil War and was deeply involved in the enormous questions which arose during this period. Its character had not altered and its short- and long-term interests increasingly diverged from the interests of the Communist and leftist militants who had stayed in the field. In the first elections in which it could have been influential (1951), it chose a strategy that was contrary to what many Greek Communists and leftists thought necessary. It chose to attack both the right led by Marshal Papagos and the centrist republican bloc, under General Plastiras, with the slogan "Papagos equals Plastiras."

The case of the KKE leadership has been extraordinary. Not only did it survive the Civil War defeat, but it succeeded in keeping control even during the troubled period of de-Stalinization. As in many other Communist parties the world over, there was growing criticism and dispute in the ranks of the KKE after Stalin's death; but not enough to alter the party's overcentralized structure. Dissidents were persecuted, even violently, as in Tashkent, where in 1956 they underwent a real pogrom, in which the Soviet police and army were called in.

Again a change in KKE leadership was effected by foreign intervention. An international commission composed of six members representing six "brother" parties convoked the Central Committee of the KKE in 1956 and "explained" to its members, in the absence of their secretary general, their long series of errors and irregularities since the war. The report, presented by Rumanian leader G. G. Dej, "suggested" changes in the leadership of the KKE. The representatives of the six foreign parties (those of the Soviet Union, Rumania, Czechoslovakia, Hungary, Poland, and Bulgaria) even took part in the election of a new seven-member Bureau of the Central Committee, whose president was Apostolos Grozos and secretary general Kostas Koliyannis.[8]

New arrangements at the top did not change much of the party's methods and policies. Certainly its internal functioning did not become more democratic, and no autonomous thinking and analysis developed out of the foreign imposed changes in leadership. Relations with the EDA continued to be one-sided. Communist members of EDA had no access to the KKE's leadership and the EDA itself was accused by Soviet sympathizers of "parliamentarism" and fondness for the "Italian road to socialism."

In 1958 at the eighth plenum of the Central Committee of the KKE the decision was made to ask all Communists to dissolve their clandestine organizations and become members of the EDA. They should not organize "fractions" or other autonomous groups inside EDA, they were told, but Communist members of EDA's leadership would be members of the KKE's Central Committee inside Greece. This arrangement might allow for EDA's more autonomous development as a left party associated with the KKE and open avenues for the ulterior legal development of the latter. The above decision of the KKE never received unanimous consent from the party's leadership. It was discussed again in 1963 and 1965. A majority in the KKE's Political Bureau wanted the Communist members of EDA to organize autonomous and parallel groups at all levels of the EDA's structure, but this was strongly opposed by the minority and by EDA's leader-

---

[8] Ibid., p. 209. Nefeludis, *Stis Pighes*, p. 307. Dej's report to the Central Committee is published in *I Diaspassi tou KKE* [The split in the KKE], vol. 2, collection of documents edited by Panos Dimitriou (Athens: Politika Provlimata, 1975), pp. 557-582.

ship. In 1965 it was decided, finally, that EDA should cease to be a united party and become again, as it had been before 1956–1958, a front, within which the Communists would develop their own organizations and through which they would seek to obtain legal recognition for the KKE. There was a long and serious dispute about this decision; again the opinion of the Soviet party was asked. But the colonels came to power before the quarrel had been settled.

It is clear that a fundamental conflict was developing about control of the Communist and left movement in Greece. Its "interior" and "exterior" protagonists were progressing toward divergent solutions in both organizational and political terms. The political content of the dispute grew in importance.

The KKE's leadership had long fought any redefinition of the party's policies vis-à-vis other left and centrist forces. They stressed the necessity to combat "social-reformists" (1950)[9] and continually suspected the EDA of seeking "openings" to its "right." In the late 1950s and early 1960s, particularly after the creation of the Union of the Center (EK) in 1961, many KKE and EDA members believed they should help this center and center-left party gain access to the government in order to consolidate parliamentary democracy in Greece. The KKE leadership strongly opposed this analysis and promoted a "pure and hard" line, trying to keep tight control even over a strictly left formation such as EDA. Some "help" was given by EDA to the EK in the 1963 and 1964 elections, but it was probably very marginal. Nevertheless, KKE's leadership appeared in this period increasingly unable to think how to open new, credible, and progressive perspectives for the democratic and left movement in Greece. They had undisputed control over tens of thousands of Greek Communists in the Eastern European countries, and something like a "Greek socialist republic," without territory but with a government and some hybrid state structures. They had, or tried to have, similar control over Communists and supporters of the left in Greece.

The organizational and political credibility of the left could not grow in such conditions. On the contrary, with the emergence of the EK in 1961 it could only decline. The political campaign of "uncompromising struggle" which the EK carried throughout the country to contest the validity of the 1961 elections (those Papandreou had denounced for "violence and fraud") had direct impact on the Greek left and Communist movement. Above all it set the stage for the development of a noncommunist left, united behind a major centrist

9 Solaro, *Istoria tou KKE*, p. 205.

candidate—and in the process further isolated the Communist left and reduced its political credibility and influence.

Two unanswered questions related to the coup d'état of 1967 emerge from these conditions. The first is whether a strong left movement following a revolutionary line (clandestine organizations, carefully orchestrated demonstrations, popular uprisings, and so on) could have thwarted the coup. The second is whether strong left-wing support, rather than undermining the EK's policies, could have led to the same result by enhancing the EK's credibility as a "responsible" and peaceful administrator of a state after the Civil War.

Anyhow, by the end of this period, the left had not been defeated strategically by the coup. It had "only" proved its inability to imagine new and specific ways for democratizing Greek political life. In the years that followed, an increasing number of left-oriented people began to speak of a "traditional" left, in which they included the KKE, and to seek new solutions to an old, and quite new, problem hindering Greece's future evolution.

From the Military Coup to the Split of the KKE. The military coup d'état of April 21, 1967, was a "divine surprise" for everybody in Greece, including the left. The EDA leaders and press, of course, had long denounced the "dark projects" of the so-called parastate organizations and their links with the royal palace, the government, and the army. Even the identity of the principal leader of the military conspiracy, George Papadopoulos, had been publicized by the leader of the EDA parliamentary group, Ilias Iliou. Nevertheless, no appropriate policies, either legal or illegal, were elaborated by the party. Virtually the entire EDA leadership and apparatus membership were arrested "in their beds." The complete success of the coup meant the defeat not only of the peaceful and legal line of the party, but also of any "revolutionary" tendency inside or outside the EDA.

To justify the coup, the military junta invoked an imminent "Communist threat" and proceeded to arrest around 10,000 Communists or supposed Communists. Most were taken to the Athens hippodrome and subsequently sent to different prisons or into exile. In fact, the Communist threat was perfectly imaginary, and even the junta itself did not use this argument for long.

In reality, the coup was the culmination of a long political and institutional crisis. Following the EK's victory in the 1964 elections, the prime minister, George Papandreou, failed to establish confidence between the centrist government and the palace, the army leadership, and Greece's U.S. and NATO allies. In July 1965, King Constantine forced Papandreou's resignation and tried to form a new government composed of EK "turncoats." The right-wing National Radical Union (ERE) agreed to support such a government in Parliament. Three successive parliamentary attempts were necessary to achieve this operation. It provoked a situation just short of insurrection when EK and EDA organized huge mass rallies to denounce this decay of Greek political life. Later on, after some months of relative calm, ERE and EK agreed on a compromise which should have resulted in an election on May 29, 1967. All observers expected the EK to win, and the palace, the army, and the United States and NATO allies were increasingly anxious about the consequences: public sentiment against the monarchy was growing; the army's direct links with the palace and freedom from any real government control were being denounced; anti-American feeling was being encouraged by U.S. policies on Cyprus and vis-à-vis the EK and Papandreou. The EK itself was thought to be more "radical"—readier to introduce domestic reforms and independent positions in foreign affairs—than it really was. To many right-wing circles, stopping such an evolution was a matter of "national interest." It is almost certain that the palace was preparing a coup to forestall this development, but the colonels acted first. They received support from the palace, the army, and the allies, but they failed to gain any broad public support. People were tired and disappointed by the long political crisis but they did not seem eager to approve dictatorship.

From the time of the very first arrests (accompanied by torture, which Amnesty International and the Council of Europe repeatedly denounced), and as trials began to multiply during the summer of 1967, efforts were made to organize an effective resistance movement. At various times during these early years of dictatorship a "dynamic" resistance (as it was called, as opposed to "passive" or "mass" resistance) seemed to be taking off. This was true during the summer of 1968 (when there was an attempt on Papadopoulos's life) and at various times in 1969. But generally, most of the resistance during this period was not more than an extremely difficult clandestine political opposition, at least as far as the "traditional" and well-known Greek political forces were concerned. Most of them tried to survive by maintaining contact between leaders and members, exchanging information, signaling their existence by making statements to the foreign press, for example, or publishing books on "innocent" (that is, noncensored) issues, by creating legal, even if only barely tolerated, cultural and scientific associations or participating in existing ones, such as the Society for Studies on Greek Problems, the European Movement, the Greek American Union, and so on. Some parties or groups did more. The KKE, EDA, and later the KKE-Interior were among those that tried to organize clandestine party sections and to create or participate in a dynamic resistance movement. Finally, new directions began to emerge in many areas of the old political life. Some developed around former leaders and political lines, others in opposition to them—across the whole spectrum from the parliamentary right to the extreme left.

Among the first of these movements were the Patriotic Antidictatorial Front (PAM) created by EDA leaders and members; Democratic Defense (DA) founded by center-left and left-wing intellectuals, some of whom were old EK dissidents or members of political clubs close to it; Greek Resistance founded by EK members including Panagoulis, the man who had tried to kill Papadopoulos; Free Greeks, a right-wing group including some former military officers; and the Panhellenic Liberation Movement (PAK) founded in 1968 by Andreas Papandreou, son of the former prime minister and himself a former minister in the EK government from 1964 to 1965. A great number of smaller movements and parties (not all of them negligible) also appeared in this period of political and intellectual ferment—two or three Trotskyist groups, two Maoist ones, anarchists, Guevarists, and so on. Some of them had a real audience among students and were influential during the student unrest in 1973; two or three in fact were still strong in the student movement at the end of the 1970s.

What almost all the movements and individuals involved in dynamic resistance or illegal opposition to the junta had in common was the wish to "renew" both their own political sector and the political system in general. Left-wing ideas, both old and new, inspired a great many of these movements, a number of which established ties with one another. A PAM-DA agreement was signed very early in 1967. It was followed by long discussions between PAM-PAK and PAK-DA, and a tripartite agreement was prepared but never implemented. In 1970 a broader agreement was discussed by PAM, PAK, DA, and the Free Greeks. Finally, PAK refused to sign, and the three remaining organizations formed the National Resistance Council (EAS), which, again, never succeeded in defining any concrete political program or resistance plan.

This was a somewhat paradoxical and disappointing situation. Everything seemed to show that the time was ripe for a new takeoff of left-wing ideas and organizations. The coup d'état had shocked most people and destroyed many ideas, fears, beliefs, and myths. Psychologically and politically, the left won increasing sympathy, but the existing left-wing organizations could not benefit from this evolution and could not achieve a decisive breakthrough in Greek political life. New movements and groups were reluctant to cooperate closely with old ones. Various acts of opposition or protest were undertaken but no common strategies or programs were ever pursued and the various agreements that were reached always remained a dead letter. In particular the "traditional" Communist left was positively unable to mobilize around itself the political forces made "available" by the brutal military seizure of power. To the KKE's reduced credibility must be added the impact of the unprecedented split that occurred in 1968.

The KKE Split. The military coup d'état and the left's inability to resist it precipitated a necessary reexamination of the KKE's policies. Old questions, as we have seen, had already divided the party's leadership abroad and in Greece. The split took place when a majority of the KKE Political Bureau (four out of seven members) decided to convoke the twelfth plenum of the Central Committee. A heated dispute about procedural matters masked serious political problems. The plenum was to take place in Hungary in February 1968, without any significant participation from the party's "interior" members. Various discussions about the opportunity of this session and the issues to be examined led to confrontations over old policies and even references to contacts that this or that faction had had with the Communist Party of the Soviet Union. Finally the three minority members of the Political Bureau were accused of "opportunism" and "revisionism" and expelled from the party.[10]

For the first time in the party's history, the dispute was made public in broadcasts from the party's radio station in Bucharest, controlled by the dissidents. Moreover, the split spread to all levels. The Central Committee was divided into two equal camps. The one controlled by the official leadership was enlarged by the nomination of new members and held its own twelfth plenum. The other group, a majority of whom were inside Greece, organized an Interior Bureau of the KKE which later developed into a new party, the KKE-Interior. Soon every underground cell, every group of Communists in prison or in exile abroad, was divided. And the same was true of all organizations parallel to or controlled by the party: PAM, EDA, the youth organizations, and so on. The split was reinforced by the Soviet invasion of Czechoslovakia, which was approved by the KKE and condemned by the Interior Bureau and a significant number of former party members, particularly in exile, who had hesitated or refused to choose between the two camps.

---

[10] Materials on the issues have been published by the KKE-Interior in Dimitriou, ed., *I Diaspassi tou KKE.*

The split precipitated a new open debate of all the old questions as well as some more recent ones not only among Communists but also among all concerned citizens. It sought to examine and clarify the impeded de-Stalinization of the party, the role and extent of foreign intervention in its history, the causes and the real stakes of the Civil War, the party's prejunta policies, its organizational methods, the lack of any democratic processes inside the party or in its relations with its political base and environment, its ideology and political theory.

The KKE adopted a hard line against all dissidents. It accused them of anticommunism, anti-Sovietism, treachery, revisionism, liquidation of the movement, and so on. In prisons and among exiles, the orthodox tried to isolate and discredit any opposition or criticism. Abroad, in the Eastern European countries, supporters of the KKE-Interior or any other dissident line were similarly treated and faced more or less severe repression from the state or party authorities (except in Rumania, which favored the KKE-Interior). By contrast, among the dissidents, hesitation and irresolution prevailed. Many followed a prudent line, leaving some doors open, defending themselves against accusations and protesting undemocratic procedures, trying to prove their loyalty to "proletarian internationalism," seeking support and recognition from "brother parties." Some thought or hoped that reunification of the party could be achieved by dialogue and mutual criticism. Finally, disappointed and under pressure from the "base," they decided to hold a congress, which took place after the junta's fall, in 1975, as the First KKE-Interior Congress.

Other dissidents refused to choose sides, preferring to wait and see what would happen. Many of them kept in contact with each other and tried to formulate different positions on the problems of the left immediately after the junta's fall. They did not succeed in doing so, and most of them joined the KKE-Interior. Others joined the new postdictatorship EDA or other small groups. Finally, some of them quit any organized political activity and "went home."

The split within the Greek Communist party has been an important factor in the "traditional" left's paralysis and loss of prestige. It contributed to the left's inability to organize serious resistance to the junta, to mobilize large sectors of public opinion around its own perspectives, and to encourage smaller groups to work together.

The junta's fall cannot be attributed directly to acts of resistance. These were decisive, however, in November 1973 when thousands of students occupied the Polytechnic Institute in Athens and broadcast resistance slogans for several days. The movement gained a very large audience and popular solidarity; the junta, after some hestiation, sent in the army. Tanks entered the yard of the Institute, and during the shooting dozens of people were killed. This affair brought to a brutal end the "liberalization" of the regime that Papadopoulos had pursued for a few weeks, naming a prime minister, Spyzos Markezinis, and promising parliamentary elections. A new junta (headed by Ioannidis) seized power and returned to a hard line. It governed the country for some eight months and fell after the failure of its attempt to overthrow President Makarios and the subsequent Turkish invasion of Cyprus.

Thus, at the end of this period, the left, old and new, was neither defeated nor victorious. It was simply composed of an excessive number of parties, movements, groups, and individuals with divergent perspectives and interests. One more historic opportunity had been lost, mainly for the older ones among them—the KKE, the KKE-Interior, and the EDA.

Toward the 1974 Elections

A few days after the junta's fall and the inauguration of Constantine Karamanlis's "government of national unity," the Greek left entered legal public life. Many thought or hoped that the moment had come for real changes in its policies and structure—and for united action. But from the very beginning the differences were profound. Some of those who had participated in resistance movements agreed to become members of the new government, together with right-wing and centrist ministers, or to give it support without imposing any serious political conditions. Others refused to envisage cooperation and criticized the new government very strongly. This was the case of Democratic Defense, for example, which denounced its own political spokesman, George Mylonas, for accepting a job in the government and urged harsh measures against former members and supporters of the junta.

The KKE-Interior and the EDA adopted a position of critical and conditional tolerance vis-à-vis the new government, declining or simply not seeking closer cooperation with it. They clearly feared criticism from the KKE and from PAK's president, Andreas Papandreou. Indeed, the KKE and Andreas Papandreou had similar reactions: for them, there had been little change since the junta. The situation was "as broad as it was long," as the KKE put it—and according to Papandreou, just a changing of the "NATO guard" in Greece.

As far as unity of action was concerned, the first test would be the parliamentary elections to be held on November 17, 1974. For these elections, various groups formed during the resistance to the junta joined the old Union of the Center (EK) under the label "New Forces." The new formation took the name Union of the Center–New Forces (EK-ND) and was led by George Mavros. Equally or more important was the decision taken by Democratic Defense to join with PAK in forming the Panhellenic Socialist Movement (PASOK) with Andreas Papandreou as president. Democratic Defense was granted a considerable number of seats in the new party's governing bodies.

EDA and the KKE-Interior joined the KKE in an electoral alliance named the United Left (EA). This was a very curious decision indeed, later considered another error by most KKE-Interior members. Each party retained its complete autonomy but they ran joint lists. No serious mutual electoral commitments were agreed and no promises were made about the postelectoral political future. In fact, this was a good arrangement for the KKE. It succeeded in reestablishing contact with all Communist-oriented voters and in securing for itself—with its better organization, unscrupulous propaganda, and political work —most of the parliamentary seats won by the United Left.

The campaign developed on strictly political grounds. All of the parties had put together platforms addressing more or less the full range of socioeconomic and cultural problems facing Greece, but the main questions were political: the nature and evolution of postjunta political life, as well as foreign policy questions, namely solidarity with Cyprus, resistance to Turkey's threats there and in the Aegean Sea, and new relations with NATO and the United States.

The United Left parties advocated firm measures against former members of the junta (they coined the term "dejuntaization"), faster democratization, and an "antiimperialist" foreign policy (elimination of all foreign, that is NATO and U.S., military bases, internationalization of the Cyprus problem, strengthening of Greece's relations with the East and the third world, particularly in the Mediterranean, and so on). But there were no explicit, fundamental differences between these positions and those held by PASOK, EK-ND, and even, on many points, Karamanlis's New Democracy (ND). In fact, for the United Left parties, the main problem was to reconstruct their organization and influence and to deny Karamanlis absolute power, in both political and parliamentary terms. They had no thought, at this stage, of winning a majority.

PASOK, on the other hand, with almost the same policies but more emphasis on neutralism and nonalignment, claimed to be the only credible leftist alternative. Its famous slogan "Socialism for the 18th" (polling day was November 17) underlined among other things its determination to convince leftist voters that everything was possible now. It achieved real influence in the broad left electorate, taking 13.6 percent of the vote to the United Left's 9.5 percent. This was the first time the Communist movement had been successfully challenged for hegemony on the left. Moreover, the challenge came from a center or center-left movement, under noncommunist or even anticommunist leadership. This enlarged the potential limits of the left, opening it up to some who did not wish to be associated with communism. Otherwise, the 1974 elections showed no major novelties. New Democracy won an overwhelming majority (54.4 percent), and the centrist EK-ND (20.4 percent) ran far ahead of both PASOK and the Communist left. The latter had no significant audience outside the big urban centers.

The Greeks voted again in a referendum on the monarchy held on December 8, 1974, which was rejected by a majority of 69.2 percent, and in municipal elections in the spring of 1975. For the referendum the left appeared more united, forming a bloc against the monarchy, together with the Center (the ND endorsed neither side). For the municipal elections, things were much less clear. In most cases, all of the parties of the left agreed to present joint lists, and they won in the great majority of important Greek cities, including Athens, Piraeus, Thessaloniki, and Patras. But, in a few cases, each party acted for itself in concluding alliances with other forces; this was especially true of the KKE. After the elections internal disputes paralyzed many municipal governments.

Division and intraleft struggles grew up, too, in other fields, as each party or movement developed its own theoretical and political analysis. The KKE and PASOK, in accordance with their initial analysis of the new regime, maintained stern opposition to it along an "uncompromising" line: the government was an instrument of imperialist and domestic reaction. A popular movement and all "democratic forces" must oppose it in all fields. They expressed their opposition on every issue that arose, from the new constitution to Greece's demand for full membership in the EC. They adopted the same hard line in student and trade union elections. Meanwhile, they developed mutual criticism and competition for hegemony on the left. The KKE indicted PASOK for "petit-bourgeois" ideology and behavior, and PASOK accused the KKE of aligning itself with Soviet positions, particularly in the delicate Greek-Turkish dispute on Cyprus and in the Aegean Sea.

Even before the junta's fall the KKE-Interior had adopted the strategy known as National Democratic Antidictatorial Unity (EADE), which in fact was never understood in the same way by all of the leaders and members of the party. It implied unity of action among all left-wing parties and movements and at the same time a rejection of political "polarization." This meant that the "democratic" or "antidictatorial" right should not be excluded from common action in various fields of domestic and foreign policy. This line, it was thought, would help to consolidate parliamentary democracy in Greece and to implement the party's strategy, that is, "the democratic road to socialism." But actually to apply it was not a simple task. The KKE-Interior's proposals for unity of action sometimes seemed excessively conciliatory (for example in the trade union elections) or useless. Moreover, they were hardly welcomed by the left's popular base, which had suffered important political, economic, and social oppression under the junta. Finally, they were an excellent target for KKE and PASOK criticism. The KKE-Interior was denounced as a pawn of the bourgeoisie, seeking a "class truce" in Greece. Considerable pressure was exerted on the party and on its youth and labor organizations—which only reinforced the party's internal contradictions. Because of its more or less democratic internal administration, the KKE-Interior was especially vulnerable.

The left seemed to reach a crossroads late in 1976, when a new alignment of forces developed in almost all of the left and center movements. Unity was again the subject of the day, in prelude to the 1977 elections.

The 1977 Elections and Future Perspectives

The second parliamentary elections after the fall of the junta normally would have been held in 1978. They were moved up by the Karamanlis government on the grounds that a public sounding was needed on a certain number of very important issues that would come before the Greek government in 1978—negotiations with the NATO allies, matters relating to Cyprus, Greece's entry into the EC, and so on. Polling day was announced with two months' notice.

In fact, the campaign had begun months before. Many people, especially in the opposition, believed that the 1974 elections had not reflected the real desires and expectations of the electorate. The ND's huge parliamentary majority was hampered by internal contradictions and anxiety about its electoral future. A certain noncorrespondence between domestic political and economic problems and the government's capacity to respond was obvious. The opposition parties were gaining a larger audience and some, notably Papandreou's PASOK, were already calling for early elections. As a matter of fact, Papandreou and PASOK, together with Karamanlis and ND, were the only political forces interested in holding early elections. They were politically and organizationally ready, and they judged the moment propitious: PASOK's fortunes were rising, and ND's were descending no more than could have been predicted. It was time to capitalize on recent achievements before some new factor disturbed the political balance.

For the left, including PASOK, the year before the elections had been a time of discussion and confrontation over the crucial problem of unity or cooperation among the "democratic forces." Central to the discussion was the knowledge that no single party alone could hope to change the balance of political power in Greece. The centrist EDIK itself (which came out of EK-ND after four deputies left to found the Socialist Initiative group) advocated unity with PASOK and an effort to reconstruct the prejunta EK as an alternative to the ND government. This could have been a repetition of the 1961–1964 scenario.

On the traditional left, things were much less clear. Everyone talked about unity or cooperation, not only because nostalgia was strong among the left's electorate, but also because it seemed the only way to prove that the left had the will to offer an alternative route of access to political power. But in fact, deep differences existed not just about the terms of any program for unity but even about the objective itself. Moreover, the short- and long-term preoccupations of each party or movement were very often left in an opportune obscurity.

By the end of 1975 PASOK had developed an initiative for unity and cooperation among democratic forces, and a series of talks took place at PASOK's invitation. Unity around PASOK's own program was proposed, but after a while Papandreou put an end to the whole affair by accusing all of the other parties of seeking to minimize the national, political, and class contradictions in Greece. PASOK subsequently initiated its own political and electoral campaign in which it claimed to be the "only factor of change" in Greek politics.

The KKE had been one of the participants in the discussions with PASOK, the only party it considered a potential partner. When PASOK's initiative came to an end, the KKE rejected all overtures from other leftist movements. Indeed it remained adamant about the necessity to "crush the revisionists" of the KKE-Interior. This "isolationist" line seems to have been opposed inside the party, but no debate was ever made public.[11] In the end, the KKE decided, for the first time since the war, to run alone in the 1977 elections.

11 Yannis Tzannetakos, "KKE: Yati ti Merida ton Leontos?" [KKE: why did it get the lion's share?] *Politiko Kritirio*, no. 10 (January 1978), pp. 31-34.

The KKE-Interior was trying to apply the policy of National Democratic Antidictatorial Unity. It made an effort to build a coalition of different movements and groups in the broad framework of the left, rejecting, at the same time, clear-cut left-right political polarization. It is not sure that this approach was accepted by the party's four future allies: EDA, Socialist Initiative, Socialist March, and Christian Democracy. In any case, it provoked new criticism from the KKE. The KKE-Interior was denounced as the "Karamanlist left" or the "Karamanlist opposition" and its policy as "unity without principles." This last charge was not totally unjustified. Fear of criticism from their left prevented the various groups from stressing their own individuality and pushed them to vie with the KKE and PASOK for the most "uncompromising" vocabulary and combative spirit. Finally, their social and political base, though theoretically very broad, was fragile and shifting. The extent of the differences at the top was lost on the left electorate, which still dreamed of unity and believed that such differences could be resolved merely by the leadership's goodwill.

In conclusion, some weeks before election day (November 17, 1977), the situation in the left area was much clearer than in 1974. Political objectives were more or less well defined. The campaign was the last act of a year-long drama.

The Campaign. The KKE had rejected all appeals for unity from the other formations of the left. Its campaign was a limited and somehow nonpolitical one. It was plain that the party had chosen to address only the Communist-oriented electorate, and it made lavish use of symbols and reminders of the movement's past: a profusion of red flags bearing the hammer and sickle, revolutionary and resistance songs, constant references to the heroes of the resistance and the Civil War and to the international revolutionary and Communist movements. It also stressed labor's claims and struggles and antiimperialist themes, particularly opposition to NATO and the EC. Continual appeals were made to Communists and former Communists, be they supporters of the KKE or of any other Communist or leftist group. The thrust of the argument remained (as it had been since 1968) that "there is only one party" of and for the working class, namely the KKE. Both theory and practice excluded, according to KKE propaganda, the development of any other Communist party or organization. This meant war on the KKE-Interior, although its members were "effectively good and honest militants" who might eventually join the KKE. In a sense, the KKE did not conduct a really political campaign. It never set forth any concrete program for pursuing political power even in the long term. Its intention clearly was to count its supporters and their votes and to demonstrate its absolute predominance on the Communist left.

The KKE-Interior scored a victory with the conclusion of its Alliance with the EDA, Socialist Initiative, Socialist March, and Christian Democracy in the autumn of 1977. But the Alliance came too late, and its material and organizational resources were limited. Moreover, its main weakness was an excessive preoccupation with exact equality for the five groups as a means of forestalling the charge it was undemocratic or controlled by the KKE-Interior. The five always appeared together at rallies, and all took the floor at every meeting. Instead of conveying a sense of unity, this gave the impression that they did not trust one another. "Unity" was their slogan. They used it profusely, to the point that all other analyses and proposals they espoused became secondary to their audience. Stressing the "antiunity strategy" of PASOK or the KKE's "isolationism" was obviously not enough to convince the left electorate about the content of respective, and opposed, policies. The five raised some new and interesting issues: their short-term objective was a multiparty government after the elections, and this implied a united effort of the left and Communist forces to prevent the ND from gaining an absolute parliamentary majority. It also implied agreement of all concerned forces on such a line and, thus, a change in their "polarizing" policies and slogans. In a general sense, the first proposition seems positively realistic, but its implications for the other left forces were surely not. They meant, in fact, a complete revision of their lines and perspectives related to political power. The five could answer that this was the only way to justify their long-term objective —a decisive "renewal" of the left movement in Greece, be it communist, socialist, or whatever. Actually, their ideas and proposals were never explicit or convincing. Internal differences or divergences explain, to a large extent, this deficiency. Not all groups or individuals had adopted the way of "renewal." If they did so, it was not in the same or compatible terms. Being moderate and reasoned, though firm, concerning general policies was too easy for Socialist Initiative because of its origins, toilsome for the KKE-Interior because of its internal divergences, and almost impossible for Socialist March because of its neophyte (on the Marxist left) fervor. In the interests of avoiding open discord, the personality of each group tended then to disappear behind the sole slogan of unity. The question of Greece's entry into the EC is a significant illustration. The KKE-Interior, revising its policy, took a continuously favorable position. Socialist March, after long hesitation, adopted a very hostile stand. But during

155

the campaign, while the KKE and PASOK gave full play to their extreme anti-EC propaganda, the Alliance remained practically silent. The five seemed to adopt a "new style" in vain. Most of their public activities lacked imagination and looked drearily like their competitors': formally "uncompromising," even extremist, in their vocabulary and traditional, even banal, in their politics. The strong, clear-cut campaigns of the KKE and PASOK had already won the day.

PASOK's campaign to make itself the "sole factor of change" in Greek political life (which is analyzed in chapter 5) did not exclude, and even implied, increasing criticism of the KKE's "dogmatic," pro-Soviet positions and of the "ambiguous" and too "conciliatory" position of the Alliance. At the same time, it also meant a cautious overture toward nonleft voters and even former junta followers. PASOK judiciously combined, to this end, socialist claims and nationalistic intransigence ("Social Liberation" and "National Liberation").

The Outcome. The results of the elections were interpreted differently by the different political forces. They are still heatedly discussed in the context of the left. Several points relating to the left's performance must be stressed:

1. The election results and what they portend cannot be understood unless PASOK is included as an organic part of the left. This fact, though evident, seems to be neglected (whether deliberately or not) by most observers and analysts. PASOK's global result (25 percent of the vote) was spread over the entire country, even in districts where the Communist left had traditionally done best. In these districts, the KKE and the Alliance, taken together did slightly better than in 1974 but fell far short of EDA's scores in 1961, 1963, and 1964 (see table 6–1). A quite considerable part of the traditional left electorate seemed to find PASOK's program and style more congenial. There is no reason to think that in future elections a shift could be realized the other way around, to the same extent and with the same astonishing facility, unless major political rearrangements were to take place in this or that camp of the left.

2. The KKE won a victory over its Communist challengers and their allies. However, its performance denotes a very limited influence on the Greek electorate, including the left one. Its 9.36 percent of the vote, obtained in free and regular conditions, compares with the worst moments of the party's history when, though operating as a clandestine force, the KKE exerted a net predominance on the left and a real influence extending beyond the left. In fact, this was only a victory for the party apparatus, its organization, and its means, methods, and resources.

3. The Alliance met with a clear defeat. The smallest of the five groups were crushed. None of the four former deputies of the Socialist Initiative was elected, and EDA just saved its president, Ilias Iliou. More significant was the defeat of the KKE-Interior, the instigator and soul of the coalition. It obtained around 2 percent of the votes and one deputy. Its "message" was rejected by Communist voters. Its style and its concrete proposals were equally rejected. Its credibility dropped sharply in the broad left area.

4. The above developments led to the emergence of a new image of the left. What had once been a "left-controlled" left had become a broad and heterogeneous area without any common historical or political project. Nevertheless, in the aftermath of the 1977 elections the politics of the left were, indirectly but to a large extent, influenced by initiatives and developments within its right wing. Indeed, in the present situation, left policies of this or that tendency will only increase their chances of gaining access to, or participating in, political power if they can achieve some combination of unity, new social and intellectual initiatives, and "open door" policies toward nonleft political forces. Only PASOK, with its center and center-left origins, its unified and seemingly well-controlled organization, and its elastic and vague conceptions (uniting the "nonprivileged" Greeks against the "privileged" ones, and so forth) seems to show any promise of actually gaining access to political power for the left, although it pretends to engage in quite different tactics. Ironically, this way of enlarging the left's influence was an essential concept of the Alliance, which is no longer able to implement it politically.

The above factors have generated the present crisis of the left in its relation to the political process. Possible future trends are much less obvious. In a historical perspective, the Alliance's line of "socialism with freedom and democracy" and "nonpolarizing unity" seems the only realistic course, given the domestic and European context of Greek politics at the end of the 1970s. The loser is not always in the wrong. But such a line implies control over the political and social ground of the left. The Alliance failed to lay hold of such control and did not even succeed in integrating the so-called sixth party, that is, the numerous and unorganized left citizens who were looking for a new mode of expression in Greek political life, refusing to identify themselves with this or that apparatus. The challenge remains, and responses to it are a continuing topic of discussion.

Just after the elections, PASOK again spoke of the need for unity and cooperation among the "democratic forces," "responsible opposition work" in Parliament, and a "broad democratic union" for the municipal elections due in October 1978.

The KKE published its theses for its tenth congress in the spring of 1978. They suggested some "openings" to a "pacific way to socialism" and a somewhat neutral position vis-à-vis Eurocommunism (except its Greek version, which was vigorously condemned). However, no impressive novelties came out of this "discussion."

Discussion on similar topics went much deeper in the KKE-Interior, which held its congress in April 1978. The EADE line and the Alliance experience were at the center of the debate. The official position tended to be that these two fundamental lines of the party had been correct but their implementation was defective because of insufficient organizational capacity. Some groups, however, condemned the very principles of the EADE and Alliance lines and demanded a return to more classical orientations, be they more leftist-oriented or closer to the KKE's own conceptions.[12] Still others sought to maintain the Alliance scheme, to reject the EADE principle, and to "open" the party's action toward new problems and new fields, such as those concerning youth, women, the environment, culture, and "social and cultural minorities." In these fields, the "backwardness and conservatism of Greek society is a generalized phenomenon, including the whole area of the left, which is saturated with conservativism."[13]

In the EDA, finally, various contradictory tendencies were developing. Some sought greater cooperation with left-wing sectors of the center (which was badly fractionalized) and the creation of a socialist and social democratic formation. Others demanded an alliance with the KKE similar to that of the early 1960s. The EDA too held a conference in the spring of 1978, and these issues were on the agenda.[14]

Since the 1977 elections there has been quite a discussion of the future of the left. The problem, in a nutshell, is to know whether a new type of unity and further enlargement of this sector of Greek

[12] For a discussion of these tendencies, see: T. Romanos, "I Krissi tou KKE-Essoterikou ke to Etima tis Ananeossis tou Kommunistikou Kinimatos" [Crisis in the KKE-Interior and the search for renewal of the Communist movement], *Anti*, no. 89 (December 31, 1979), pp. 26-29.

[13] Kostas Zouraris, Makis Kavouriaris, Sophia Mappa, "KKE-Essoterikou: I Itta, i Ekdilossi tis Krissis, i Ananeossi" [KKE-Interior: the defeat, the manifestation of the crisis, the renewal], *Avghi*, March 2 and 3, 1978.

[14] For discussion of these issues, see: Manolis Glezos, "I EDA ke i Dyo Lysseis ya to Simerino Provlima" [EDA and the two solutions to the actual problem], *Anti*, no. 92 (February 2, 1978), pp. 10-12; Andreas Lendakis, "Mia Alli Apopsi ya to Provlima tis EDA" [Another point of view on the EDA's problem], *Anti*, no. 93 (February 25, 1978), pp. 16-18; Yuli Zitunaki, "I Triti Panelladiki Sindiaskepsi tis EDA" [EDA's Third Panhellenic Conference], *Anti*, no. 94 (March 11, 1978), pp. 12-14.

political life are possible. This is a very controversial matter indeed. Those who were entrusted by the left electorate with the direction of the movement seem, at the present moment, unable to achieve significant steps toward both more unity and further enlargement. PASOK could probably initiate expansion to its right or its left, but at the cost of much less unity on the actual left. In both cases, for the sake of credibility on its right or competition on its left, it has to combat the KKE and any effort to renew the KKE's base or leadership.

The KKE could make overtures to disappointed supporters or members of the KKE-Interior, especially those who are there by accident and who never truly adhered to the idea of a genuine renewal of the Communist left. It could also attract citizens of the "sixth party" of the Alliance mentioned above, who would be tempted to find at last a secure and stable "political roof," as they say in these milieus.

It is highly questionable, however, whether the KKE will be able to achieve a new breakthrough in the area of the broad left and, beyond it, among the so-called democratic forces. Its self-perpetuated leadership has not changed much since the 1950s; its doctrines are outmoded; its internal structure remains highly centralized and undemocratic; its behavior and mentality remain totalitarian; its pro-Soviet allegiance is almost unique in Western Europe. These same characteristics lie behind the long-term historical process that has progressively but constantly eroded the KKE's influence on the Greek left: it decreased in the early 1960s when the EK emerged; it missed an opportunity to make a new start during the junta period when it failed to integrate the new resistance and left forces; it further decreased after PASOK's development. Its inability to accept and to handle other noncommunist left forces condemns it to isolation. After having failed to bring revolutionary change in Greece during the 1940s, it is now failing to participate in a right-left rotation in political power under democratic conditions. If these are to be maintained, the KKE's actual line and behavior must be considered effectively nonpolitical by their solely negative nature.

Just after the results had been confirmed, the Alliance pronounced that the 1977 elections had not produced a democratic solution to the Greek political problem. What is more certain is that they produced no solution to the political problem of the Greek left. In this sense, the 1977 elections must be seen as part of an old political process, not the beginning of a new one. The conditions for such a new start are actually difficult, almost impossible, to imagine. If the lines along which it should move are more or less clear, the forces that could push in this direction are already in decline, or still in gestation.

7
Defining Greek Foreign Policy Objectives

Theodore A. Couloumbis

In dealing with the foreign policy of any state—whether large or small, developed or developing—the analyst must take into consideration both domestic and foreign factors. Greece (given its strategic location, small size, vulnerability from the sea, and numerous land borders to the north and the east) is exceptionally sensitive to external influences in the shaping of its foreign policy as well as the unfolding of its domestic politics.

The Legacy of the Nineteenth Century. The roots of the foreign policy of contemporary Greece can be traced, in part, to the historical experiences and the lingering, bitter memories of the nineteenth century.[1] The modern Greek state emerged in 1830, the product of an unequal revolutionary war pitting the Greeks against the Ottoman Empire. The birth of the small Greek state, however, was in large part a function of the competing interests of the Great Powers who were supervising the controlled and balanced dismantling of the Ottoman Empire. From its very birth the new Greek state was

---

A version of this chapter, which was written originally for this volume, has appeared with AEI's permission in Theodore A. Couloumbis and John O. Iatrides, eds., *Greek-American Relations: A Critical Review* (New York: Pella Publishing Co., 1980).

[1] For good short histories of modern Greece see C. M. Woodhouse, *Modern Greece: A Short History* (London: Faber and Faber, 1977) and Richard Clogg, *A Short History of Modern Greece* (Cambridge: Cambridge University Press, 1979). See also the overviews provided in John Campbell and Philip Sherrard, *Modern Greece* (London: Ernest Benn, 1968); Keith R. Legg, *Politics in Modern Greece* (Stanford: Stanford University Press, 1969); Jean Meynaud, *Les Forces Politiques en Grèce* [Political forces in Greece] (Lausanne: Etudes de Science Politique, 1965); and Constantine Tsoucalas, *The Greek Tragedy* (Harmondsworth: Penguin Books, 1969).

acutely aware of its dependency on the protecting powers—Britain, France, and Russia.

Three fundamental developments are central to nineteenth-century Greek history, and each has left a legacy that affects the state's foreign policies today. The first is the deep conceptual polarization that characterized Greek political parties and movements. Using contemporary terms, the two polar opposites may be referred to as "hawks" and "doves." The hawks were the traditional radical politicians whose energizing concept was the "Megali Idea"—that is, an irredentist reconstitution of a greater Greece incorporating the lands and peoples of the former Byzantine Empire. Their strategy called for continuous and unrelenting attacks on the disintegrating Ottoman Empire. They believed that heavy military costs and human sacrifice were justifiable in the name of freedom for the unredeemed Greeks (those under Ottoman occupation). Such nineteenth-century political figures as Ioannis Kolletis, Theodoros Deliyannis, and Alexandros Koumoundouros represented this hawkish orientation.

The "doves" also accepted the long-run objectives of the Megali Idea. Their immediate policy priorities, however, were the modernization and development of the young Greek state. State-building, they argued, was a prerequisite for successful external ventures and could not take place in times of continuous mobilization and warfare. Representatives of this orientation were such major nineteenth-century political figures as Alexandros Mavrokordatos and Charilaos Tricoupis.

By and large, politicians in the opposition tended to adopt hawkish and radical planks. With their assumption of power, however, they tended to adopt more moderate policies—if not more moderate rhetoric.[2]

The second major development of the nineteenth century is Great Power intervention in the foreign and domestic politics of Greece.[3] Reference has already been made to the decisive role played by the Great Powers during the Greek War of Independence. The

[2] It would be interesting to speculate as to whether this pattern is still applicable to Greek politics today. Andreas Papandreou and his PASOK opposition party are considerably more hawkish vis-à-vis Turkey than are Constantine Karamanlis and the Greek government. If the above "rule" were applicable, Papandreou could be expected to moderate his position considerably once he came to power.

[3] See John A. Petropulos, *Politics and Statecraft in the Kingdom of Greece, 1833-1843* (Princeton, N.J.: Princeton University Press, 1968); and Theodore Couloumbis, John A. Petropulos, and Harry J. Psomiades, *Foreign Interference in Greek Politics* (New York: Pella Publishing Co., 1976).

three powers retained the role of "protectors" of the Greek state throughout the nineteenth century. Acting either individually or in concert, they controlled both domestic political developments and the foreign policy initiatives of successive Greek governments. Intervention was facilitated by Greece's financial and military dependence on the Great Powers. Yet foreign interference was not a one-way street. Although the Great Powers sought to promote their own interests, the various Greek factions also solicited external support in the waging of their domestic political struggles. Greek domestic politics and Great Power interests were so totally interdependent that the first political factions to emerge in Greece in the 1830s and 1840s were formally referred to as the "English," the "French," and the "Russian" parties depending on which power each considered Greece's best protector. Present-day Greece's sensitivity about foreign interference in domestic affairs stems, in large part, from these experiences.

The third development is a combination of the previous two. It can best be described as a cultural division between secular "Westernizers" on the one hand and Orthodox traditionalists on the other. For the former, classical Greece serves as the main inspiration and is seen as the fount of the Western secular civilization. Slogans such as Karamanlis's "Greece belongs to the West" are contemporary manifestations of this orientation.

For the Orthodox traditionalist, Byzantium serves as the archetype of modern Greek society and culture. Greece is seen as a non-Western country upon which "alien" parliamentary and capitalist systems have been grafted by strong protectors. The Greeks (in terms of their tradition, culture, and personality) are seen as either a Balkan or a Mediterranean people rather than as Western Europeans. Contemporary variations of this basic orientation have been perhaps exhibited by the Panhellenic Socialist Movement and the Communist party of Greece, which have argued that Greece fits best with the states of the third world.

The Early Twentieth Century. In 1898 Greece rebounded from defeat at the hands of the Ottoman Empire thanks to the timely intervention of the Great Powers who kept the Ottomans in check and prevented what could have been a grave national disaster. The twentieth century, however, had in store for the small nation a new series of internal and external adventures. And once again, the situation was exacerbated by the underlying Greek political tendency toward strong and uncompromising polarization.

Twentieth-century Greek politics has been marked by (1) political polarization, first between the Venizelists (republicans) and the royalists in the period between the two world wars, then between Communist and anti-Communist forces in the post–World War II period, (2) continued Great Power interference in Greek politics, and (3) frequent intervention of the military.[4] Again, these three fundamental characteristics are intimately connected and mutually reinforcing. The division between royalism and Venizelism, for example, was a result of a foreign policy dispute. In 1915 Greece's charismatic prime minister Eleftherios Venizelos wanted to commit Greece to the war effort on the side of the Entente Powers, sensing their ultimate victory. The strong-willed King Constantine I, on the contrary, preferred a policy of benign neutrality favoring the Central Powers. The net effect was that Greece was split between two de facto governments in 1917, and both the Entente and Central Powers trampled on Greek sovereignty and independence.

During and shortly after World War II, a new and deep polarization developed in Greece. This pitted Communists against nationalists and again invited heavy intervention in Greek affairs by outside powers. Britain and the United States supported the nationalists while Bulgaria, Yugoslavia, and Albania as well as the Soviet Union backed the Communists.

All these political divisions have had a sad impact on twentieth-century Greece. Since the turn of the century, the nation has experienced five international wars, two civil wars (1917–1918 and 1946–1949), ten major military revolts, three periods of military/authoritarian rule, and two periods of foreign occupation, during World Wars I and II.

The United States in Greece: 1944–1974. Greece emerged from the tragic decade of the 1940s—the war, the occupation, and bitter civil conflict—a crippled state. The task of reconstruction and development was immense, and the psychological wounds of the 1940s were deep and difficult to heal.[5]

The governments that ran Greece in the early postwar period adopted an anti-Communist orientation internally and a pro-NATO

---

[4] For a useful recent study on this subject see S. Victor Papacosma, *The Military in Greek Politics: The 1909 Coup d'Etat* (Kent, Ohio: The Kent State University Press, 1977); see also Nikolaos A. Stavrou, *Allied Politics and Military Interventions: The Political Role of the Greek Military* (Athens: Papazisis, 1977).

[5] For some useful works dealing with the period of occupation, resistance, and the Civil War see John O. Iatrides, *Revolt in Athens: The Greek Communist "Second Round" 1944-1945* (Princeton, N.J.: Princeton University Press, 1972); D. George Kousoulas, *Revolution and Defeat: The Story of the Greek Communist Party* (London: Oxford University Press, 1965); and André Kedros, *La Résistance Grecque, 1940-1944* [The Greek resistance, 1940-1944] (Paris: Laffont, 1966).

and pro-United States orientation externally. In the 1950s there were no major cleavages among political parties on questions of foreign policy. The non-Communist political parties of the center and the right started from the same premise—that Greece had no option but to align itself with the major sea power that controlled the Mediterranean. Hence, an alliance with Britain, and later with the United States, was deemed not only advantageous but also inevitable. For Greek political strategists of the early 1950s life was, therefore, uncomplicated. The foe was world communism, and the threat came from the north (primarily through Bulgaria, which was closely aligned with the U.S.S.R.). NATO solidarity was perceived as Greece's only defense.

This clear-cut picture became clouded in the middle of the 1950s with the outbreak of the Cyprus conflict.[6] The political parties—especially those of the opposition—began to point out that the association with NATO called for sacrifices from Greece because the United States was tilting in favor of more "important" NATO allies such as Britain, and later Turkey. Moreover, according to the opposition (especially the left), Greece through its NATO association was burdened with a disproportionate share of defense-related costs. These parties, therefore, favored policies leading to détente and denuclearization and demilitarization in the Balkans. If successful, these plans would have relieved Greek governments of heavy defense expenditures and would have allowed the diversion of funds toward economic and social development programs.

The Zurich and London agreements negotiated between Britain, Greece, and Turkey in 1959–1960 led to a temporary resolution of the Cyprus dispute. Cyprus emerged as an independent state—a product of political compromise reflecting the balance of power within NATO. The Cyprus constitution, however, gave the Turkish minority community on the island disproportionate political power by permitting it to exercise a veto on important domestic and foreign policy questions. The arrangement was resented by the Greek-Cypriot majority, and attempts were made to revise the Cypriot constitution in 1963. This, in turn, precipitated the second major Cyprus crisis—one that has continued to the present time.

Greek-American relations were strained further in the 1960s. The economic and political development which was taking root in Greece in the 1960s and the climate of international détente resulted in re-

[6] There is a very large literature in English on the history and problems of Cyprus. A useful recent account, which contains careful references to the literature, is Kyriacos C. Markides, *The Rise and Fall of the Cyprus Republic* (New Haven: Yale University Press, 1977).

duced perceptions of a threat from the north. The smoldering Cyprus dispute only added to the frustration that had been building as a result of long years of American interference in Greek affairs.[7] A serious movement sprang up advocating Greek independence, an end to American interference, and the adoption of foreign policies that would no longer subordinate Greek national interests in Cyprus to NATO (that is, U.S.) interests. The most articulate exponent of this mood in the Greek political scene was Andreas Papandreou, who in the mid-1960s was a leading member of the Center Union party (headed by his father, George Papandreou).

The imposition of a seven-year right-wing military dictatorship in Greece temporarily covered up the deterioration in Greek-American relations. The dictatorship pursued an anticommunist and pro-NATO foreign policy. Throughout the junta period (1967–1974), U.S. foreign policy was supportive, by and large, of the military government. Thus, in the minds of the vast majority of Greeks, the United States was identified with a hateful authoritarian regime that mismanaged the country and oppressed the people. In July 1974, this regime perpetrated a mindless coup against the late President Makarios of Cyprus, thus furnishing Turkey with a perfect opportunity to invade and occupy northern Cyprus under a cloak of legality.

Greek Foreign Policy since 1974

The seven-year dictatorship—despite its right-wing orientation—tried to discredit Greek politicians, whether of the left or the right.[8] As a result, Greek political forces emerged from their seven-year ordeal with a deepened sense of unity. The essence of this new unity can be summarized as follows: With regard to external issues, the parties agreed that Greece should attain the maximum feasible independence from superpower tutelage. With regard to internal issues, a consensus emerged that sustaining democratic structures and processes over time served not only a specific party's interest but also the collective interest.

The transition from dictatorship to democracy was accomplished with a minimum of disorder and violence. As most Greeks saw it,

---

[7] See Theodore A. Couloumbis, *Greek Political Reaction to American and NATO Influences* (New Haven: Yale University Press, 1966).

[8] There is a great deal of literature on the dictatorship, though its quality is uneven. Two of the better books dealing with the dictatorship are Richard Clogg and George Yannopoulos, eds., *Greece Under Military Rule* (New York: Basic Books, 1972); and [Rodis Roufos], *Inside the Colonels' Greece* (New York: Norton, 1972).

Turkey posed the greatest and most immediate threat to Greece's territorial integrity. This perception helped keep both public and elite demands in check. And at the same time, it refocused the attention of the Greek military on its duties of external defense rather than internal involvement in the political process.

The disillusionment caused by seven years of authoritarian rule contributed also to the healing of the two central problems that had plagued Greece throughout the twentieth century. With the referendum of December 1974 the Greeks settled the volatile issue of the monarchy by opting more than two to one for a presidential parliamentary republic. Further, with the elections of November 1974 an important segment of the Greek political world was reintegrated into the parliamentary process. The KKE (after practically forty years of underground existence) was legalized and permitted to seek the votes of the Greek public. Thus, the year 1974 can be considered a milestone, marking the deemphasis of monarchism and communism as the two polarizing issues of Greek politics.

When Karamanlis, after eleven years of self-imposed exile in Paris, was called back to Athens to head the government of national unity, Greece was faced with two major new challenges: internally, to restore a viable democratic system, and externally, to redress the military balance vis-à-vis Turkey and settle the thorny Cyprus and Aegean disputes before they could degenerate into bloody and destructive conflict.

Foreign Policy Problems, 1974–1978. The Greek governments and opposition parties of the postjunta period were confronted with a number of serious problems. Beginning with the strategic (global) dimension, Greece had to take its bearings. Following Turkey's military action on Cyprus (especially the unprovoked August 14, 1974, operation which resulted in the occupation of the northern 40 percent of the small island), the Greek government was forced to reappraise its position in NATO. Britain, despite its status as guarantor of the Cypriot republic (together with Greece and Turkey), did not react substantively to the Turkish invasion. The United States, the leading power in NATO, sought to localize the Greek-Turkish confrontation on Cyprus and to prevent the conflict from spreading to the Aegean. But it also accepted the fait accompli of the Turkish invasion.[9] NATO

[9] For highly critical treatments of U.S. policies toward Greece see Laurence Stern, *The Wrong Horse: The Politics of Intervention and the Failure of American Diplomacy* (New York: New York Times Books, 1977); and Theodore A. Couloumbis and Sallie M. Hicks, eds., *U.S. Foreign Policy Toward Greece: The Clash of Principle and Pragmatism* (Washington, D.C.: Center for Mediterranean Studies, 1975).

as an organization, likewise, was caught without provision for settling territorial and jurisdictional disputes between member states. Its actions subsequent to the Turkish invasion were limited to general exhortations to the parties involved to resolve the dispute peacefully and to their mutual satisfaction. NATO, of course, was primarily concerned with restoring its seriously damaged southeastern flank.

The questions raised by these events were quite stark: Should Greece remain in NATO or withdraw from it? If it were to stay, under what conditions should it do so? Regarding bilateral relations, should the United States retain the military base privileges it had enjoyed since the early 1950s? What about Greece's arsenal—should it continue to be stocked primarily with U.S. weapons and equipment, or should alternative sources be sought?

In the global setting there was also the issue of Greece's contacts with the Soviet Union. Greek-Soviet relations had been unfriendly to cool throughout most of the post–World War II period. During the mid 1960s, however, there was a thaw in political relations and an even more rapid warming in the commercial, economic, and cultural spheres. The trend was slowed down somewhat (but not reversed) during the dictatorship. In 1974 the Soviet Union adopted a peculiar stand on the Cyprus issue. After strongly opposing the Ioannides-sponsored coup against Makarios, the U.S.S.R. quietly acquiesced to the fact of the Turkish invasion and occupation of northern Cyprus. After 1974, the U.S.S.R. supported "internationalization," rather than "NATOization," of the settlement process in accordance with United Nations resolutions (which among other things called for the removal of all foreign troops from Cyprus).

Turning to the regional setting, questions facing foreign policy makers in Greece involved the shaping of relationships with the European Community (EC), the Balkan countries, and the Mediterranean countries (especially the oil-producing states in the Middle East). Should Greece press forward its attempt to become the tenth member of the EC? Or, should it view itself primarily as a Mediterranean or Balkan country and opt for flexible policies that were economically and politically multidimensional?

The main factor complicating Greece's global and regional relations and policies was the country's relationship with its neighbor and NATO ally Turkey. Since 1974, Greece and Turkey had been on a war footing, involved in a costly and spiraling arms race. The two had also been waging a vigorous political battle for the sympathies and support not only of NATO allies (chiefly the United States) but also of nonaligned states and former adversaries (such as the U.S.S.R. and Eastern European countries).

The disputes between Greece and Turkey can be divided into those concerning Cyprus and those concerning the Aegean. Cyprus was placed under British colonial rule in 1878. The national fate of the small island did not become an issue until the 1950s when the Greek-Cypriot majority (80 percent of the population) began demanding decolonization and self-determination—that is, *enosis* (union) with Greece. In response, the Turkish-Cypriots, encouraged by Britain and Turkey, began demanding *taksim* (partition)—that is, the division of Cyprus between Turkey and Greece. A political compromise—the establishment in 1960 of an independent Cypriot Republic —was ultimately reached, and it reflected the strong NATO pressures in favor of a settlement. Since 1963, however, the young state has been in turmoil as internal and external parties have struggled to arrive at an acceptable constitutional formula clarifying the political relations of the two ethnic communities and specifying the role and prerogatives of "guarantor" powers such as Britain, Greece, and Turkey.

At the end of the 1970s, there appeared to be primarily two opposing viewpoints among those pondering the Cyprus problem. There were those who characterized Cyprus as a province disputed by Greece and Turkey and who believed in determining the status of the island through direct negotiations between the governments in Athens and Ankara. In contrast, there were those who viewed Cyprus as a new and troubled state, plagued by ethnic conflict and foreign interference, and who believed in maintaining and protecting the sovereignty of the island.

The Aegean question, according to many analysts in Greece, turns on the basic threat which Turkey poses to the security and territorial integrity of the Dodecanese and Aegean islands. Its chief components are as follows:

The air-space question. In 1952 the International Civil Aviation Organization (ICAO), with Turkish acquiescence, assigned Greece responsibility for controlling air traffic over the Aegean. On August 6, 1974, at the height of the Cyprus crisis, Turkey declared the Aegean air-space a "forbidden zone." Greece countered by declaring it a "dangerous zone." As a result, international commercial flights over the disputed area were discontinued. The situation was eased somewhat in the summer of 1980 when Turkey followed by Greece lifted their restrictive NOTAMs (Notices to Airmen), thus restoring commercial air traffic across the Aegean. But Turkey still argues that the eastern half of the Aegean air-space should fall under Turkish operational control within the NATO command structure. Greece counters that this would jeopardize the sovereignty and security of Greek Aegean and Dodecanese islands since, under such an arrangement, these islands would lie within Turkey's security zone.

The Aegean continental shelf. Greece and Turkey have advanced rival claims to the Aegean continental shelf. The Greek position is based on the Geneva Law of the Sea Convention (1958), ratified by Greece in 1972. This convention states, among other things, that inhabited islands are entitled to their continental shelf. Turkey claims that it is not bound by the Geneva convention, which it has not ratified. Further, it questions the "right" of islands to have a continental shelf, and it advances the view that the Aegean is an "open sea" characterized by "special circumstances." As in the case of air-space, Turkey argues for a median line in the Aegean, east of which Turkey would have sovereign control of the continental shelf. Greece has responded that such an arrangement not only is contrary to international law but also undermines the security of Greek islands lying near the western coast of Turkey. Such an arrangement would encourage Turkey to raise questions in the future about the sovereignty of Greek territory.

The limit of territorial waters. Currently, Greece claims a six-mile territorial waters zone around its mainland and islands. Should Greece enlarge this zone to twelve miles—which appears to be the new, generally accepted international norm—then the issues of air control and continental shelf delimitation automatically would be redefined. Given the number of Greek islands in the Cyclades, Aegean, and Dodecanese and the relative proximity of some of them to Turkey, much of the disputed area (whether for air control or continental shelf purposes) would fall under the territorial jurisdiction of Greece. Consequently, Turkey has asserted repeatedly that it will oppose with all available means a unilateral move to enlarge Greek territorial waters to a width of twelve miles.

The fortification of the Aegean and Dodecanese Islands. Following the 1974 Turkish invasion of Cyprus, Greece fortified the Aegean and Dodecanese islands. Turkey protested—pointing out that this action was contrary to the defortification provisions of the Lausanne Treaty (1923) in the case of the Aegean islands and the demilitarization provisions of the Greek-Italian Peace Treaty (1947) in the case of the Dodecanese.

The Greeks argued that the islands had been fortified according to the inalienable right of all countries to defend their territory, and that Turkey had also fortified some of its own islands contrary to

169

the Lausanne treaty. Greek officials claimed that the fortifications had been erected strictly for defensive purposes and were made necessary by a number of belligerent actions by Turkey. First, Turkey had pursued an expansionist policy on Cyprus. Second, Turkish officials had made many statements questioning the "Greekness" of the Dodecanese and Aegean islands. And third, a Turkish amphibious military force—ominously named "the Aegean Army" and backed by numerous land craft—had been stationed on the western coast of Asia Minor.

The issue of minorities. By the end of the 1970s the issue of minorities had not been forcefully raised by either the government of Greece or the government of Turkey. However, politicians and the press in both countries often returned to this question. Turkish concern centered on the status and the rights of the Turkish-speaking Muslims (over 100,000) located primarily in the region of Western Thrace. Greek concern focused on the status and rights of the 10,000 Greek-speaking Orthodox Christians remaining in the city of Istanbul and on the islands of Imbroz and Bozcaada. Both sides complained about treatment of these minorities. Greece also raised the issue of proportionality of the two minorities that was provided for in past treaties, which called for the maintenance over time of minority populations of approximately equal size in Eastern and Western Thrace.

An obvious question arises from the whole cluster of issues outlined above. Should the various issues be treated separately or linked together in a package settlement? The tendency in Greece has been to separate the Cyprus problem from the Aegean issues. The tendency in Turkey has been to link the two sets of issues. In the near cold-war atmosphere that has characterized Greek-Turkish relations since 1974, any one of the disputes could spark an all-out conflict between the two countries.

Political Parties and Their Foreign Policy Programs

A discussion of the Greek political parties' stands on foreign policy should begin with one important caveat. Political parties seek votes on the basis of planks covering domestic as well as foreign policy issues. The relative popularity of each party with the Greek electorate, therefore, does not necessarily reflect the popularity of its foreign policy position. In fact, since 1974, domestic issues (such as economic security, employment, strengthening of the democratic process, and "dejuntification") probably have weighed more heavily in the minds of voters than foreign policy issues. Moreover, there is consensus regarding Greek-Turkish relations. The shared feeling among all political parties and the public is that Turkey poses a major external threat and that Greece's best defense is the continuous modernization and strengthening of its armed forces.

Before proceeding with a comparative presentation of the parties' foreign policy positions (summarized in table 7–1), we must look briefly at the "trends" reflected in the two elections since 1974. As a review of electoral trends since World War II suggests, there is enough citizen support in Greece to sustain two large noncommunist (bourgeois) parties. The Greek Communist movement, normally commanding around 15 percent of the electorate, is divided between two splinter parties—one pro-Moscow and the other Eurocommunist in orientation. In addition, numerous other factions espouse variations of Marxism-Leninism.

The elections of 1977 and subsequent developments are beginning to clarify the political map of Greece. The National Camp has established itself as a party to the right of Karamanlis's New Democracy. In turn, since the early part of 1978, New Democracy has been trying to strengthen its image as a party of the center as well as the right. The disappointing electoral results in 1977 and the difficulties following the resignation of George Mavros as party leader seem to have seriously weakened the Union of the Democratic Center. At present, this centrist party is fragmented into a number of factions. The Panhellenic Socialist Movement, for its part, appears to be making moves toward the center—thus positioning itself as a party of the center-left. The left, as indicated above, is still split between the orthodox Communist party of Greece and a Eurocommunist movement, which includes the United Democratic Left and the Communist party-Interior. The balance within the left appears to be tilting in the direction of the orthodox camp. In the next election the center-left and the center-right can be expected to run a close race.

The Foreign Policy of New Democracy. The foreign policy of New Democracy (and hence the Greek government) begins with the assumption that the international system is unfortunately primitive, respecting neither legal nor moral restraints.[10] "Localized wars, civil

10 The foreign policy position of the New Democracy party (which has governed Greece since the November 1974 elections) has been stated repeatedly by Karamanlis in speeches to the electorate and the Greek Parliament. A full review of this policy can be found in his speech delivered to Parliament on December 14, 1977. The Athens daily *Vradini* is the Greek newspaper most closely associated with the New Democracy position. Other newspapers friendly toward the ruling party include *Apogevmatini* and *Acropolis*. *Kathimerini* is a fine conservative-to-moderate newspaper that maintains considerable objectivity and some distance vis-à-vis the entire Greek political spectrum.

TABLE 7-1
PARTIES' STANDS ON FOREIGN POLICY ISSUES

Issue	New Democracy (right-center)	PASOK (center-left)	EDIK (center)
NATO	Stay in politically. Special relationship militarily.	Sever or renegotiate favorably all relations with NATO.	Stay in politically. Strengthen European defense arrangements in and out of NATO.
U.S. bases in Greece	Keep those that are compatible with Greek national interest.	Should be removed from Greek territory.	Their presence should be linked to the improvement of conditions in Cyprus and the Aegean.
Membership in European Community	Highest priority.	Entry not advantageous. Greece should seek special agreements with EC.	Highest priority.
Military expenditures	Whatever is necessary to maintain balance of forces with Turkey.	Whatever is necessary to maintain balance of forces with Turkey.	Whatever is necessary to maintain balance of forces with Turkey.
Foreign nuclear weapons on Greek territory	Hypothetically only when compatible with Greek national interest.	No.	No position found on this subject.
Relations with the U.S.S.R.	Would like very good relations.	Would like very good relations.	Would like very good relations.
Balkan cooperation	Take initiative in promoting bilateral and multilateral cooperation.	Take initiative in promoting bilateral and multilateral cooperation.	Take initiative in promoting bilateral and multilateral cooperation.

Mediterranean cooperation	Good relations, especially with traditionally friendly Arab states.	Seek to develop a Mediterranean common market.	Continue good relations, especially with Arab states.
Cyprus	Support Cypriot government in its effort to restore the sovereignty and independence of state.	Support Cypriot government and avoid a bad settlement through NATO.	Support Cypriot government and avoid a bad settlement through NATO.
Greek-Turkish Aegean issues	Negotiate bilaterally on all issues. Submit differences to international adjudication.	Nothing to negotiate. Protect Greek sovereign rights against any encroachment.	Avoid further negotiations until the Turks show signs of serious interest in talks.
Attitude toward terrorism	Must be stopped by strong national and international measures.	Opposed to it. Especially sensitive to right-wing terrorism. Not opposed to revolutionary movements (for example, PLO).	Opposed to it in all of its manifestations.
Trade and foreign investment terms	Free trade and mutually advantageous foreign investment. Public sector assists in investment efforts.	Promote trade and investment subject to needs of national economic planning.	Free trade and mutually advantageous foreign investment. Public sector assists in investment efforts.
Defense equipment procurement	Continue procurement from Western sources. Augment domestic defense industries.	Diversify sources. Develop heavy defense industries.	Emphasis on integrating Greek defenses with those of independent Western Europe.
Relations with China	Cultivate good economic and other relations.	Continue improvement.	Continue improvement.
General cultural and political orientation	West.	Nonaligned.	Western European.

(Table continues on next page)

Issue	KKE (Marxist-Leninist left)	EP (far right)	KKE-Interior and EDA (Eurocommunist left)
NATO	Sever all ties with NATO.	Return to NATO fully. It was a mistake to leave.	Reduce political ties with NATO.
U.S. bases in Greece	Should be removed.	Useful to defense of Western world against communism.	Should be removed from Greek territory.
Membership in European Community	Greece should withdraw from EC.	Scrutinize and improve conditions of entry.	Seek alliances with progressive movements in Western Europe.
Military expenditures	Costs too great. Caught in trap of U.S.-induced arms race with Turkey.	Whatever is necessary to maintain balance of forces with Turkey.	Whatever is necessary to maintain balance of forces with Turkey.
Foreign nuclear weapons on Greek territory	No.	Only when compatible with Greek national interest.	No.
Relations with the U.S.S.R.	Close ties are the best guarantee for the growth of international socialism and world peace.	U.S.S.R. is always a threat to Western world. But pursue détente if possible.	Continued improvement.
Balkan cooperation	Take initiative in promoting bilateral and multilateral cooperation.	Détente if possible. But do not underestimate threat from north.	Take initiative in promoting bilateral and multilateral cooperation.

Issue			
Mediterranean cooperation	Continue good relations, especially with Arab states.	Continue good relations, especially with Arab states.	Good relations, especially with traditionally friendly Arab states.
Cyprus	Support Cypriot government plus avoid a bad settlement through NATO.	Support Cypriot government in a fair settlement within the Western setting.	Support Cypriot government and avoid a bad settlement through NATO.
Greek–Turkish Aegean issues	Internationalize issues. Expose Turkish chauvinism.	Negotiate bilaterally on all issues. Submit differences to international adjudication.	Negotiate bilaterally on all issues. Submit differences to international adjudication.
Attitude toward terrorism	Opposed to it—especially right-wing manifestations.	Opposed to it—especially left-wing manifestations.	Opposed to it—especially right-wing manifestations.
Trade and foreign investment terms	Trade and investment subject to needs of national economic planning. Improve exchanges with socialist countries.	Free trade and foreign investment key to continued economic development.	Trade and investment subject to needs of national economic planning.
Defense equipment procurement	Promote development of denuclearized and disarmament zones in Balkans.	From Western sources.	Diversify sources. Develop domestic defense industry.
Relations with China	Extremely suspect. China is a U.S. apologist.	Continue improvement.	Continue improvement.
General cultural and political orientation	Nonaligned. Friendly to U.S.S.R.	Friendly to West and U.S.	Western European.

SOURCE: Author's review of speeches of party spokesmen reported in Greek newspapers. See also the sources cited in the notes to this chapter.

wars, acute social and political conflicts and . . . multifaceted criminality" are the norm rather than the exception. This is obviously a dangerous system, and one that allows no room for "perilous acrobatics." [11]

In such an international setting Greece's fate by "tradition and necessity" lies with the democratic West, according to New Democracy. Greece maintains, and will continue to maintain, multiple links with the West in the political, economic, cultural, and security spheres. The securing and perpetuation of such multiple links has been the continuing policy of successive governments since the birth of the modern Greek state. Changing the Western orientation of Greece would, in effect, mean isolating the country from its natural allies. This, in turn, would increase even further the seriousness of the Turkish threat.

Therefore, according to New Democracy, the logical step was for Greece to seek entry into the European Community as soon as possible. By aligning itself with Western Europe, Greece will become a part of a "huge political power." At the same time, the country's democratic institutions will be strengthened and the rate of socioeconomic development will be accelerated. New Democracy strongly believed that Greece's application for EC membership, which predates those of Spain and Portugal, should have been uncoupled from those of other countries.

With Karamanlis at the helm, Greece withdrew from the military side of NATO in August 1974 as a sign of protest over the organization's inaction in the face of the Turkish invasion of Cyprus. Greece also withdrew in order to gain full control over its armed forces in the event of open conflict with Turkey. As of the late 1970s the New Democracy's policy called for arriving at a "special arrangement" with NATO whereby Greece would maintain control over its own armed forces during peacetime and only integrate them with the rest of NATO in case of generalized East-West warfare. In addition, following 1974 the government reduced the number of U.S. military bases on Greek soil from seven to four and placed them under Greek control. In the future, it was emphatically stated, the establishment of bases would be permitted only when such facilities were considered necessary to Greece's national interest.[12]

Beyond relations with the West, Greece initiated bilateral and multilateral contacts with its Balkan neighbors in order to encourage

[11] Karamanlis, in a speech to Parliament, December 14, 1977.

[12] By the end of 1980 a generally acceptable formula was found and Greece reentered the military structures of NATO. The status of U.S. bases in Greece remained a subject of Greek-American negotiations at the time of writing.

peaceful cooperation and strengthen security in the region. Greece also continued a policy of friendly and cooperative relations with its traditional friends in the Arab world. Finally, Greece planned to expand economic, cultural, and commercial relations with East European countries and the Soviet Union.

New Democracy's approach to the Cyprus and Aegean problems was clear and firm. Turkey, because it was attempting to change the legal status quo, was held responsible for both disputes. The situation on Cyprus (the Turkish occupation, the plight of refugees, and so forth) was considered morally reprehensible and logically inadmissible. Hence, Greece supported efforts toward settlement through talks between the two Cypriot communities held under U.N. auspices. Responsibility for reaching an acceptable agreement, of course, ultimately rested with the government of Cyprus. Greece, in other words, did not wish to dictate terms to the government of an independent country.

The position of New Democracy on the Aegean issue was to seek earnestly a peaceful settlement. The recommended sequence was as follows: (1) negotiate bilaterally with Turkey on the various Aegean questions (continental shelf, air control, and so on), (2) avoid situations that might give rise to aggressive unilateral acts in the interim period, and (3) submit points that cannot be agreed upon bilaterally to the adjudication of the International Court of Justice.

The New Democracy recognized that international disputes are usually solved through negotiations, arbitration, and war. Because war would be disastrous for the peoples of both Greece and Turkey, the first two options should be pursued vigorously. In the meantime, Greece should remain patient, safeguard its unity, and continuously reinforce its defensive capability.

Foreign Policy of the Panhellenic Socialist Movement. PASOK, according to its leader, Andreas Papandreou, has been described as Marxist but not Marxist-Leninist in orientation.[13] It advocates, therefore, the transformation of Greece into a genuinely socialist state but within the framework of a multiparty parliamentary system.

According to PASOK's conception of the global system, the world is polarized between the two superpowers—the United States

[13] For an early statement of PASOK foreign policy views see Andreas Papandreou's speech to PASOK membership in *Eleftherotypia*, September 20, 1977. For an English language version of Papandreou's views on world developments see his "Confrontation and Coexistence," *Monthly Review* (April 1978). The weekly newspaper *Exormisi* reflects the official views of PASOK. Other newspapers that offer sympathetic treatment to PASOK are *Ta Nea* and *Eleftherotypia*.

and the Soviet Union—locked together in a "combative coexistence." NATO and the Warsaw Pact are mechanisms through which the U.S. and the U.S.S.R. control the European area. PASOK has adopted, in this perilous global system, an antiimperialistic ideology. The metropolitan centers (the U.S. and the U.S.S.R.), the reasoning runs, use multinational monopolistic companies to control periphery-state (third world) economies and use defense equipment and foreign base complexes to perpetuate their political control. Thus, the long-term objective must be to end the dependence of periphery states on metropolitan centers of power. To this end, the party strongly supports cooperation among third world states in order to ensure the independence and self-determination of their peoples.

Western Europe, PASOK argues, is currently divided into an industrial north and an agrarian south. The United States works through the industrial north, and NATO and the EC are nothing more than coercive devices designed to accommodate the foreign policy of southern European states to the global strategy of American imperialism. In order to escape the tutelage of the industrial north (and by implication the United States) Greece must not remain a member of the EC and must remain outside NATO. All U.S. bases must also be removed eventually from Greek soil.[14]

According to PASOK, the capitalist nations of the West are reaching a state of economic and social crisis. Inflation, unemployment, and worsening income distribution are progressively afflicting the capitalist powers. The countries of the Mediterranean littoral (north and south) will be bound by a common fate as this situation becomes more and more acute. Hence, PASOK believed that countries such as Portugal, Spain, and Greece should stay out of the EC and NATO, while countries like France and Italy should withdraw from these organizations. Together, then, after adopting compatible political systems which will foster more progressive social and economic

---

[14] Since this chapter was written, Andreas Papandreou has softened his position on the European Community. In frequent statements reported in the press late in 1980 and early in 1981 he indicated that he now sees a shift in Western Europe which is leading it toward greater political independence from the United States. In a major speech delivered to the rank and file of PASOK on November 10, 1980, Papandreou expressed more moderate positions than he had before on the issues of European accession, NATO, and the U.S. bases. The tone of pragmatism pervading this speech opened a number of small windows toward the West. If, for example, better terms for Greece's participation in the EC and NATO were offered (such as a guarantee of Greece's existing boundaries with Turkey in the case of NATO), PASOK could find its way to accommodating continued participation in these organizations. In December 1980 during a visit to Britain, the PASOK leader reiterated and amplified these views in speeches at Oxford University and at Chatham House.

planning, all these Mediterranean countries should set common policies toward other parts of the world. Trade movements and investment conditions in the Mediterranean region should be high on their list of priorities. They should seek to improve the terms of trade and employ a common modus operandi in dealing with international economic institutions such as the World Bank and the International Monetary Fund.

Further, operating on the principle that "the only language that is understood [in international politics] is the language of power," PASOK has occasionally recommended the formation of a Mediterranean Economic Community. This community would act as a catalyst for the creation of a Europe of federated socialist states. It also would allow the Mediterranean sea to belong to the Mediterranean peoples—free of all foreign fleets and bases. In PASOK's view Turkey and Israel have been centers of American "subimperialism." Hence, the struggles of the Palestinian and the Cypriot peoples are manifestations of the greater struggle of all the Mediterranean states for independence.

Andreas Papandreou's policy with regard to Turkey in particular is *para bellum*. Greece will protect its national independence and territorial integrity by preparing for warfare and by not appeasing a revisionist and expansionist Turkey acting with the encouragement of the United States. PASOK, therefore, favors reaching a settlement on Cyprus in the spirit of the U.N. resolutions and outside the suffocating pressures of the "NATO family." PASOK has criticized Karamanlis and, since May 1980, George Rallis for their handling of the Aegean issues—especially the eagerness to negotiate on the continental shelf and air rights and the willingness to submit the issues to international adjudication. PASOK believes, on the contrary, that Greek sovereign rights are not negotiable. Accepting adjudication is an indirect way of admitting that Turkey has the right to contest Greece's sovereignty and territorial integrity.

To meet the immediate and major danger resulting from Turkey's subimperialist designs, Greece must expel foreign imperialists from its territory, arm itself comprehensively, build an arsenal that is diversified in source and in scope, develop a sizable domestic defense industry, and secure, if necessary, nuclear weapons for use as the ultimate deterrent of aggressive behavior.

In the economic sphere PASOK advocates developing and/or strengthening certain strategic industries such as defense, energy, and mining (exploitation as well as processing). The party strongly favors maintaining majority national control of foreign business ventures in order to avoid the corrosive and exploitive impact of monopolistic and oligopolistic multinational corporations. Thus, the best economic strategy for Greece is one that encourages small-scale, labor-intensive industries oriented toward the welfare of the worker.

Foreign Policy of the Greek Democratic Center. EDIK's conception of the international system as well as its political ideology and general foreign policy recommendations are similar to those of New Democracy.[15] According to EDIK, there exists a bipolar international system in which a semblance of order is maintained through the balance of nuclear terror. Greece's role in this system is and has been determined on the basis of historical and (especially) geographical criteria.

EDIK believes Greece's immediate and long-range economic and political interests are served by close association and involvement with the Western world and its institutions. Consequently, the cornerstone of the country's foreign policy should be full membership in the EC. EDIK advocates not only the economic but also the political unification of Western Europe. This, in turn, means the development of a strong Western European defense agreement—one that is independent of the United States and that can carry its weight in and out of NATO. Too often, in EDIK's view, the fate of Eastern and Western Europe has been the subject of a Soviet-American strategic dialogue that has excluded the Europeans themselves.

The future effectiveness and warmth of Greece's relations with NATO and with the United States (including the question of U.S. bases in Greece) should rest on the rule of reciprocal advantage. Turkey's invasion of Cyprus and its aggressiveness in the Aegean have met with indifference (if not encouragement) from NATO and the U.S. administration. This experience has been deeply disillusioning for Greece. How can Greeks consider NATO a credible security community if it fails to aid Greece when the country is seriously threatened by another NATO ally? Hence, EDIK relates normalization of Greek-American and Greek-NATO relations to fair and mutually acceptable settlements in Cyprus and the Aegean.

Like all the other major parties, EDIK advocates a strong, vigilant, and mobile Greek defense establishment in the face of the Turkish threat. Moreover, EDIK has proposed a moratorium on

---

[15] EDIK's foreign policy positions are best reflected in George Mavros's recent book *Ethnikoi Kindynoi* [National dangers] (Athens: Atlantis, April 1978). Mavros resigned shortly after EDIK's poor showing in the November 1977 elections. Since that time, the party has been in turmoil. Mavros and other key political figures have declared themselves independents. The party is currently (as of July 1978) headed by John G. Zighdis. Newspapers that have reported favorably on this party's activities are the dailies *To Vima* and *Ta Nea*.

Greek-Turkish negotiations given Turkey's apparent unwillingness to negotiate seriously on either the Cyprus or the Aegean issues. U.N. resolutions, the party believes, provide an adequate frame of reference for a just settlement, and the Cypriot state should negotiate with the occupying power—that is, Turkey. Greece, of course, should offer its full backing to the Cypriot government headed by President Spyros Kyprianou.

In EDIK's opinion, time is on the side of Greece. Turkey faces enormous economic and political difficulties. The Cyprus adventure has cost the Turkish people $3 billion from 1974 to 1978. Politically isolated and economically strained, Turkey cannot maintain the present state of affairs for long. Although militarily Turkey has the capacity to occupy all of Cyprus, politically it cannot justify such a flagrant move. At the same time, Turkey cannot afford a war with Greece. The continued arms race and the political and psychological warfare are costing both countries dearly. Of the two, however, Turkey is the less able to afford a protracted cold war; eventually it will be forced to enter genuine and meaningful negotiations. This process, EDIK believes, can be speeded up considerably by serious and substantive proddings from the United States and NATO. The arms embargo imposed on Turkey by the U.S. Congress has been a step in the right direction, and such pressure should be continued.[16]

Foreign Policy of the Greek Communist Party. The KKE adheres to a traditional Marxist-Leninist orientation and is clearly pro-Moscow in its policy approach as well as its political ideology. In 1977 the party registered a substantial gain in its share of popular vote—in contrast to its Eurocommunist rival. (In 1977 the KKE-Interior ran in coalition with EDA and three small center-left splinter parties.)

The KKE views itself as the vanguard of the working class— waging "a struggle against imperialism, for democracy free of monopoly controls, for a polity of the people enjoying national independence, democracy, and socialism." [17] Greece, under the tutelage of conserva-

---

[16] Between 1978 and 1980 the political forces contained in EDIK were subdivided at least six different ways. Some elements were absorbed by New Democracy and others by PASOK, John Pesmazoglu established his Social Democratic party (KODESO), Alexandros Baltatzis revamped his Agrarian party, and George Mavros, the old leader of EDIK, formed the Center's Array (Parataxis Kentrou). EDIK, considerably reduced in forces, continues under the leadership of John Zighdis. The EDIK positions described above are also broadly those of KODESO, the Agrarian party, and the Center's Array; there are no major foreign policy differences among these small parties.

[17] *Kommounistiki Epitheorisi* [Communist review], organ of the Central Committee of the KKE. The Greek daily *Rizospastis* reflects the views of the KKE.

tive governments, is seen as a country in transition from under-development to development. At present, it is an amalgam of capitalist medium-industrial and agricultural sectors.

According to the KKE's analysis, foreign monopoly capital combines and other structures of international imperialism have been assuming gradual control of the means of production. The growth of "state monopoly capital" in Greece and other transitional countries has only contributed further to this process. The KKE's objective is to bring about the revolutionary transformation of Greece. This will lead to national independence and popular sovereignty and will ensure the creation of an antiimperialist and antimonopolist society. However, to fulfill the prime objective—the transformation of society—the state first must be cleansed of all agents of international imperialism.

In general the KKE advocates what it calls an independent and peaceloving foreign policy. The party's specific priorities include the adoption of a new democratic constitution, the decoupling of Greece from NATO and the EC, the abrogation of treaties that violate the sovereign rights of Greece, the closing of foreign bases on Greek soil, and the nationalization of foreign monopolies and domestic monopolistic enterprises in sectors of national significance. Application of the above policies, it believes, will lead steadily to the evolution of a genuine socialist democracy.

Regarding the Greek-Turkish disputes, the KKE argues that both countries have been caught in a vicious trap set by the imperialist powers. By promoting chauvinistic elements in both Greece and Turkey, the imperialist centers have kept the two in a state of continuous conflict so that the imperialist military-industrial complexes could profit from the sale of arms to both countries. Hence, the proper Greek reaction should be the pursuit of policies that will eliminate dependency on foreign powers. In the case of Cyprus, Greece should follow a settlement strategy of internationalizing the problem and arriving at a solution through the U.N. (as also recommended by the U.S.S.R.). The Aegean disputes should be likewise settled outside of NATO and through negotiations between Greece and Turkey.

Foreign Policies of the National Camp. The EP is a coalition party of far right elements.[18]. It ran on a platform of "national reconciliation"—proposing amnesty for the former junta leaders who are serving long jail sentences. The party is nostalgic for firm and

---

[18] For favorable coverage of this party's views see pre- and postelection issues of *Eleftheros Kosmos*, an Athens daily.

anti-Communist policies and has advocated the return of the monarchy. Strongly anti-Soviet in orientation, EP has demanded strict and unyielding vigilance against both domestic and international communism. NATO and the United States are viewed as Greece's "natural protectors"; therefore, it is deemed essential to rebuild strong and friendly ties with both. At the same time, EP seeks some sort of NATO guarantee against any future Turkish aggression toward Greece.

Foreign Policy of the Greek Eurocommunist Movement. Five left-of-center parties (EDA, KKE-Interior, Socialist March, Socialist Initiative, and the Christian Socialist Movement) combined forces to form a Eurocommunist coalition similar to those of Spain and Italy.[19] Disillusioned with the imperialist behavior of both superpowers, the Greek Eurocommunists favor socialism for Greece and an alliance of Western European progressive movements of the left. Hence, this coalition of Greek parties approves of Greek membership in the EC.

Interestingly, however, the Eurocommunists have downplayed the issues of total withdrawal from NATO and the removal of American bases from Greek territory. They reason that it has been impossible to implement socialist domestic legislation because such legislation normally has been coupled with foreign policies that have challenged strategic superpower interests. The Greek Eurocommunists prefer to reverse policy priorities. They prefer to concentrate, in other words, on cultivating a socialist consciousness in the domestic setting without challenging the global superpower status quo. In this way, they believe they can avoid arousing the kind of adverse superpower reaction that might result in the internal destabilization of Greece.

After the 1977 elections (and because the Eurocommunists failed to capture a significant portion of the vote), parties such as EDA and KKE-Interior hardened their foreign policy positions. In the late 1970s, they were demanding that Greece sever all ties with NATO, oust the U.S. bases from Greek soil, reexamine the terms of entry into the European Community, and pursue the maximum feasible rapprochement with the U.S.S.R. and Eastern Europe.

Prospects

Greece emerged from seven years of dictatorship and from the tragedy of Cyprus a politically disillusioned country. Grave doubts regarding

[19] For views and coverage favorable to this movement's activities see *Avghi*, an Athens daily.

the Western world and its security structures were widespread among the public and political parties alike. Compared with the pre-1967 period, political opinion on domestic as well as foreign policies moved perceptibly to the left.

Despite the disillusionment and pervasive doubts, however, there is considerable reason for cautious optimism concerning the future of Greece. The traditional divisions between royalism and antiroyalism and between communism and anticommunism have been put to rest. Since 1974, Greek politics has evolved toward consensus rather than polarization—especially given the near universal perception of a Turkish threat. Moreover, the danger of military intervention in politics remains extremely slim. The Greek officer corps appears to have learned from the disastrous seven-year interlude of military rule; there is less arrogance now among officers and less feeling that the army has a "savior mission" on the domestic scene. A widely held conviction among military officers is that Turkey might try to take advantage of any future coup in Greece (as it did in Cyprus in 1974) to create new *faits accomplis* in the Aegean.

On the negative side, the foreign policies of political parties such as PASOK and the KKE (especially with respect to EC and NATO membership) are sharply different from the Western European orientation of the other parties. In foreign policy there remain some signs of the type of polarization that could once more provide the pretext and the opportunity for domestic instability and Great Power intervention.

8

Conclusion

Theodore A. Couloumbis

Greece has been presented in the scholarly and journalistic literature since the early 1920s as a "praetorian state." Clustered with countries such as Portugal, Spain, Italy, and Turkey, Greece has been said to fit very well the profile of praetorian politics.[1]

Praetorian states are rapidly changing societies characteristically faced with an imbalance between popular demands and political institutions. On one side, there are strong pressures for the political, economic, and social mobilization of the masses and on the other, brittle, archaic, and unresponsive institutions which cannot effectively absorb or channel these pressures. The result often is mass-supported political violence, which is then checked by elite-supported (or tolerated) military intervention. The military, once in power, seeks to control or quell public expression and action while attempting, or just promising, to restructure and modernize the institutions.

The record of twentieth-century Greece from 1909 to 1974 seems to fit the praetorian model rather well. A wave of military coups and countercoups plagued Greece in the period between 1909 and 1936. It was followed by the repressive right-wing dictatorship of Ioannis Metaxas (1936–1941) and by Axis occupation, resistance, and civil war in the 1940s. The 1950s and 1960s, despite great progress in economic reconstruction and development, were marred by covert and overt military intervention in politics as well as manipulative and conspiratorial palace politics. Finally, throughout the post–World War II period, influence of the so-called foreign factor was over-

---

[1] For a comprehensive description and development of the praetorian model, see Samuel P. Huntington, *Political Order in Changing Societies* (New Haven: Yale University Press, 1968). Beyond the states of southern Europe, most of the states in Latin America, Africa, and the Middle East, South and Southeast Asia have been described in the postcolonial period as forming a coup d'état zone.

whelming. Since the proclamation of the Truman Doctrine in 1947, the foreign factor has meant the United States.

The military dictatorship that was imposed in April 1967 seems, therefore, to have been a perfect outgrowth of praetorian-style politics. Most commentators portrayed the Greece that fell to the colonels as a politically backward society. Its politicians, they said, were contentious, conspiratorial, and corrupt, while the average Greek citizen possessed deep loyalties to family and friends but virtually no civic consciousness. The political parties they classified as personalistic, clientelistic, nonideological (except for the Greek Communist party), nonprogrammatic, badly organized, centrifugal, and constantly proliferating; the bureaucracy as hydrocephalic (concentrated in Athens), hypertrophic (sheltering hidden unemployment), inefficient, and deeply penetrated by domestic and foreign special-interest groups. The system of education was judged to be stiff, archaic, formalistic, and politically dependent; the church, ritualistic, anachronistic, socially indifferent, and subservient to the state. The press was criticized for being sensational and superficial, as well as penetrated (often funded) by foreign and domestic special interests; the labor unions and other interest groups and associations, for being ineffective, fragmented, and emasculated by either governmental or political party associations. Finally, local government with its limited budget and authority, was seen as relegated to marginal functions such as street cleaning and park beautification.

Up to July 1974 and the collapse of the military dictatorship, Greece's political problem could be summarized as follows: The political establishment had proven unable to manage a continuing crisis of legitimacy or to agree on either the nature or the specifics of the political system.

In the twentieth century the crisis of legitimacy set monarchists against republicans. This division was exacerbated in the 1940s by a bloody clash between the Communists and those favoring a liberal democracy. In foreign policy those who wanted Greece to join with the Central Powers during World War I were pitted against those who thought Greece's interests would have been better served by a pro-Entente orientation. Since World War II, this struggle has been redefined to reflect deep antagonisms between those who favor a Soviet and East European socialist orientation and those who feel that Greece by virtue of its cultural heritage and strategic location belongs to the West.

If one had accepted the premise that people and nations will act in the future as they have generally acted in the past, then the prospects for the new Greek polity back in 1974 would have been dreary indeed. In fact, a number of thoughtful and well-meaning political analysts predicted a bumpy future for Greece after the junta. Specifically, they expected the presidential-parliamentary system of governance to face yet another serious challenge by the supporters of the monarchy (close to 30 percent of the Greek electorate). Economic difficulties and reawakened political passions, it was thought, would unleash a wave of political terrorism sponsored by the extreme left and the extreme right. The political parties that had been formed just prior to the elections of 1974 were supposed to prove fragile and transient—overshadowed by the charismatic personalities of their founders. The military and the security forces—still penetrated by the remnants of the Papadopoulos junta—would continue to interfere in politics and would even (after some regrouping) make a bid to regain power. In short, the specter of praetorianism (what Roy Macridis has called the "niggardly hypothesis" elsewhere in this volume) was still expected to dominate the politics of Greece.

But events seem to have moved in an altogether different direction, one much closer to Roy Macridis's "generous hypothesis." Since July 1974, a new constitution has been adopted, and it appears to be surviving the tests of time, transition, and transfer of power. The elections of 1974 and 1977, the December 1974 referendum on the monarchy, and two sets of municipal elections were conducted quite smoothly by anyone's standards. Few, if any, voices crying "tilt" or "foul" were heard in a country where elections and plebiscites had been frequently manipulated and often denounced as dishonest by the losers.

Wise decisions were made after 1974: to permit the Communist parties to function legally, to try the ringleaders of the military dictatorship but to limit the extent of dejuntification, to settle the thorny language issue by establishing *demotike* (the spoken language) as Greece's official language, and to deal with the monarchy question by a free plebiscite. All these opened wide the way toward national reintegration and a historic reconciliation of the deeply divided population.

Events in the three years since the November 1977 elections seem to lend further support to the generous thesis. It may even be safe to predict that in the future the Greeks will no longer act the way they acted prior to 1974. A major development of the 1977 elections was the concentration of votes in two parties, New Democracy and PASOK, and EDIK's crushing defeat. The center party's bitter experience led to the resignation of its leader, George Mavros. The succession process proved divisive and badly damaging to the party's fortunes. By 1980, EDIK under the aegis of John Zighdis, had been reduced from 20 to 4 deputies in the 300-member Parliament and was but a shadow of its former self. A new Social Democratic party (KODESO) under the leadership of a highly respected Europeanist technocrat, John Pesmazoglu, has sought to fill the vacuum created by EDIK's disintegration, but without overwhelming success.

The center's travails may have opened up a process that will ultimately bridge the political and ideological gaps between PASOK and New Democracy. Sensing that the disorganization and fragmentation of the center parties offered a good opportunity to augment their electoral strength, both New Democracy and PASOK sought to widen their popular bases by coopting as many dissatisfied centrists as they could attract. Both parties have proven moderately successful in attracting prominent political personalities from the center and gradually transforming their popular images for the sake of forming broader based center-right and center-left coalitions. Thus, the migration of centrist elements into the ranks of New Democracy and PASOK has contributed to narrowing the distance that separated these two major parties prior to the 1977 elections.

As the thoughtful chapters by John Loulis and Angelos Elephantis suggest, new forces are emerging in place of the old right and the old left. The "old traditional right," known for its "dynamic" methods such as electoral manipulation, repressive techniques, royal and military intervention in politics, and monopoly control over the army and security services, is being pushed into a far and uncomfortable corner. The "new right," mainly Karamanlis's creation (and by 1980 under the leadership of George Rallis), is a center-right coalition, committed to genuine parliamentary politics, with a Western European orientation and a desire to maintain good contacts with Western conservative and Christian Democratic parties.

On the other side, the "traditional left," known for its commitment to revolutionary confrontation, guerrilla warfare, one-party socialism, and the dictatorship of the proletariat, is being confined to a narrow political corridor (10 to 15 percent of the electorate). PASOK, under the charismatic leadership of Andreas Papandreou, is emerging as a parliamentary-minded, center-left coalition dedicated to a nationalist brand of socialism, but simultaneously able to cooperate with European Socialist and Social Democratic parties. PASOK originally conceived itself in 1974 as a third worldist, socialist, and neutralist protest movement with limited electoral expectations. Six years later it was at the very gates of power, with strong chances of winning the 1981 election. As a party that wants to govern, PASOK is expected to reorder its priorities, policies, and objectives, bringing them within attainable limits.

In May 1980 Constantine Karamanlis was elected president of Greece, replacing the respected octogenarian politician Constantine Tsatsos whose five-year term had nearly expired. Karamanlis stepped down from the premiership of the country and from the chairmanship of the New Democracy party in order to be sworn in as president. Simultaneously, the parliamentary caucus of New Democracy elected George Rallis as the party's new chairman with a razor-thin margin (88–84) over his more conservative rival, Evangelos Averoff, Greece's minister of defense. Rallis formed a reshuffled government, and Averoff agreed to retain the defense portfolio for the sake of party unity.

The events surrounding these transitions lend further credence to the "generous hypothesis" about the Greek polity. Despite the fact that Karamanlis and Rallis were elected to their posts by very narrow margins, the legitimacy of the outcomes was not challenged within New Democracy or by the opposition parties. Nearly all the opposition parties (with the possible exception of EDIK) formally accepted the legitimacy of the elevation of Karamanlis to the presidency even if they had refused to give him their vote in Parliament. In the case of George Rallis's elevation, the two wings of New Democracy (the moderates under Rallis and the conservatives under Averoff) had managed to maintain their unity—proving that a Greek bourgeois party can survive the departure of its charismatic leader.

As we now face the future, the standard projection of Greece watchers is that the next elections will be held sometime between the spring and fall of 1981. By then, Greece will have entered the European Community as its tenth member and will have begun the benefits as well as the costs of membership. The 1981 elections will be held, more than likely, under the existing "reinforced proportional" electoral law. PASOK, which continues to gain in electoral strength, is expected to make a serious bid for power. The outcome of the next election, according to most projections, will be very close. It may, therefore, be necessary for New Democracy or PASOK (whichever secures a plurality of votes) to enter into a coalition with smaller parties such as KODESO (the Socialist Democratic party, led by John Pesmazoglu) or even—as a last resort—with parties of the extreme right and the extreme left.

The chief reasons being offered to support the projection that PASOK's vote will grow are as follows:

1. By 1981 New Democracy will have been in office for seven years. It is, therefore, bound to experience the "natural" erosion that time causes.

2. Greece, like most other European states, has faced difficult

economic problems (25 percent inflation, a worsening balance of payments, low private investment rates, and so on), and the party in power will be held responsible.

3. Karamanlis's absence from the campaign (now that he is president) will cost New Democracy the votes he used to attract solely for his charismatic personality and popular image.

4. Karamanlis as president will be viewed by some voters as a balance and a cushion for a prospective Papandreou government. Karamanlis, that is, will be seen as a counterpoise to Papandreou, with his volatility and populist tendencies. The elder stateman will also be expected to cushion a Papandreou government against any remnants of praetorianism in the armed forces and the security services.

5. In foreign relations, the Greek public is bitterly disappointed in the United States and NATO, which it believes have tilted in favor of Turkey in the Aegean and on Cyprus. This is likely to swing some protest voters to PASOK, which has been arguing since 1974 for greater political and economic independence vis-à-vis the United States and the West.

6. The gradual but steady transformation of PASOK from a third-world-oriented, socialist protest movement to a well-organized and active "Eurosocialist" party with serious chances of acceding to power is likely to attract those who tend to stick with a "winner."

7. Andreas Papandreou will move up a rung to the top of the "charisma ladder" now that Karamanlis will no longer be campaigning.

8. In a country where the voters have bitter memories of political instability caused by party splits and parliamentary defections (especially between 1965 and 1967), a party's ability to maintain its unity is a definite plus. PASOK, unlike most other center and left parties, has managed to hold together its various wings and factions despite considerable ideological diversity in its ranks.

9. PASOK, and Andreas Papandreou specifically, have made a systematic and continuing effort to build bridges to the armed forces and the security services and generally to legitimize their relationships with them. With the armed forces no longer viewed (or viewing themselves) as the exclusive preserve of a narrow, right-wing establishment, a historic reconciliation may be in its final stages. The gulf that was created between the army and the people by the 1967–1974 dictatorship will thus be closed. A feeling of reconciliation, further, will reduce the lingering fear that the armed forces might once more intervene if the political pendulum swings toward the center left.

When it comes to accuracy, prediction in politics rates somewhere between weather forecasting and astrology. It is a very difficult proposition. Still, let us venture this: In case of another New Democracy victory in the next elections, one should expect the continuation of policies (in both domestic and foreign affairs) consistent with the European conservative/Christian democratic pattern. Should PASOK come to power, however, either alone or in coalition with Pesmazoglu's KODESO, the actions and words of Andreas Papandreou since November 1977 suggest that its government would be cautiously revisionist, realist, and pragmatic in its domestic and foreign policies. Without abandoning its long-range goal—to transform Greece into a socialist society—PASOK would try to make clear to the Greek public that fundamental changes cannot take place "overnight."

Andreas Papandreou has repeatedly asserted that PASOK, as a potential government party, will remain democratically accountable both to the people and to Parliament—that it will act not as a revolutionary movement but as a party that expects to move in and out of power. In foreign policy, it has the constitutional obligation to respect the international commitments made by previous elected governments (especially those elected since 1974). At an increasing tempo in the past two years, PASOK has been deepening its contacts with Western European socialist and social democratic parties, while soft-pedaling what used to be its strident opposition to Greece's entry into the European Communities. On the U.S.-operated bases in Greece and on Greek-NATO relations, PASOK's positions remain constant: the total withdrawal of Greece from NATO and an invitation to the United States to vacate its bases. If, on the other hand, PASOK came to power and found a commitment in place (a four-year agreement regarding the status of U.S. bases, for example) it claims that it would have a constitutional duty to respect this agreement for its duration.

The wounds of the Civil War are gradually healing, and no new and unbridgeable cleavages dividing elites and public appear to be in the offing. With well over 70 percent of the population living in urban or semiurban settings, with a high literacy rate, a record in income distribution that is tolerable if not fair, with a "quality of life index" that is competitive by Eastern and Western European standards, and with the armed forces reintegrated into the Greek body politic and properly oriented toward external defense rather than internal policing, the road to consensus politics is now open.

If New Democracy and PASOK maintain their internal cohesiveness, strengthen their party organizations, and continue to effect smooth transitions in party leadership, then Greece will continue to have a variation of a two-party parliamentary system sustained by the reinforced proportional election law. If, on the other hand, New Democracy or PASOK should split and new parties proliferate, the likelihood is that a fragmented Parliament would adopt a centrifugal election law of the "simple proportional" variety. Karamanlis, in such an eventuality, would be more likely to assume a strong presidential profile.

Whether Greece goes in the direction of few parties and a ceremonial president or many parties and a political president, one thing is almost certain: since 1974, praetorian politics has been steadily becoming a thing of the past, a subject for historians, not commentators on the present day.

Appendix A

GREEK BALLOTS, 1977

In Greek elections there is a separate ballot for each party competing in each district. Reproduced here are four of the ballots used in the first and second districts of Athens in the 1977 parliamentary elections. In Athens A the government party, New Democracy (ND), ran a full slate of twenty-two candidates, while the small Communist Revolutionary Movement of Greece (EKKE) ran only seven candidates (none of whom won seats). In Athens B, there were twenty-eight seats, and both the Panhellenic Socialist Movement (PASOK) and the Union of the Democratic Center (EDIK) ran full slates of candidates. The candidates' names are listed in alphabetical order, with one exception: as party leader, Constantine Karamanlis is named at the head of the ND list in Athens A. The original ballots measure 5½ by 9¾ inches.

ΕΝΩΣΗ ΔΗΜΟΚΡΑΤΙΚΟΥ ΚΕΝΤΡΟΥ

ΕΚΛΟΓΙΚΗ ΠΕΡΙΦΕΡΕΙΑ Β' ΑΘΗΝΩΝ

ΑΛΑΒΑΝΟΣ ΚΩΝΣΤΑΝΤΙΝΟΣ τοῦ Νικολάου

ΑΠΟΣΤΟΛΟΠΟΥΛΟΣ ΚΩΝΣΤΑΝΤΙΝΟΣ τοῦ Δημητρίου

ΒΑΣΙΛΑΤΟΣ ΓΕΡΑΣΙΜΟΣ τοῦ Βασιλείου

ΓΕΩΡΓΟΥΤΣΟΣ ΑΧΙΛΛΕΥΣ τοῦ Ἀναστασίου

ΓΚΟΥΒΑΣ ΑΝΔΡΕΑΣ τοῦ Γεωργίου

ΔΑΤΣΕΡΗΣ ΖΑΧΑΡΙΑΣ τοῦ Ἐμμανουήλ

ΔΗΜΗΤΡΕΛΛΟΣ ΧΑΡΑΛΑΜΠΟΣ τοῦ Κωνσταντίνου

ΖΗΚΟΓΙΑΝΝΗΣ ΑΘΑΝΑΣΙΟΣ τοῦ Κωνσταντίνου

ΚΑΜΑΡΑΣ ΑΡΙΣΤΕΙΔΗΣ τοῦ Κωνσταντίνου

ΚΑΝΕΛΛΟΠΟΥΛΟΣ ΠΑΥΣΑΝΙΑΣ ἢ ΒΑΣΙΛΕΙΟΣ τοῦ Ἀντωνίου

ΚΑΡΑΜΠΕΛΑΣ ΘΕΟΔΩΡΟΣ τοῦ Δημητρίου

ΚΛΩΝΙΖΑΚΗΣ ΜΙΛΤΙΑΔΗΣ τοῦ Ἀντωνίου

ΚΟΠΕΛΟΥΖΟΣ ΕΜΜΑΝΟΥΗΛ τοῦ Χρήστου

ΚΟΥΜΑΝΑΚΟΣ ΓΕΩΡΓΙΟΣ τοῦ Εὐστρατίου

ΚΩΣΤΑΚΗΣ ΔΗΜΗΤΡΙΟΣ τοῦ Μιχαήλ

ΛΕΚΑΤΣΑΣ ΠΑΝΑΓΙΩΤΗΣ τοῦ Ἀνδρέου

ΜΑΥΡΟΣ ΦΙΛΙΠΠΟΣ τοῦ Ἰωάννου

ΜΠΑΝΤΟΥΒΑΣ ΕΜΜΑΝΟΥΗΛ τοῦ Ἰωάννου

ΟΙΚΟΝΟΜΟΥ ΠΑΝΑΓΙΩΤΗΣ τοῦ Ἰωάννου

ΠΑΠΑΜΙΧΕΛΑΚΗΣ ΓΕΩΡΓΙΟΣ τοῦ Γρηγορίου

ΠΑΠΑΣΠΥΡΟΥ ΚΩΝΣΤΑΝΤΙΝΟΣ τοῦ Σπυρίδωνος

ΠΑΠΑΤΕΡΠΟΣ ΑΛΕΞΑΝΔΡΟΣ τοῦ Μίλιου

ΣΠΕΝΤΖΟΣ ΙΩΑΝΝΗΣ τοῦ Δημητρίου

ΣΠΥΡΟΠΟΥΛΟΣ ΧΡΗΣΤΟΣ τοῦ Σπυρίδωνος

ΣΤΑΥΡΙΑΝΙΔΗΣ ΙΩΑΝΝΗΣ τοῦ Νικολάου

ΣΤΕΦΑΝΑΚΗΣ ΓΕΩΡΓΙΟΣ τοῦ Ἐμμανουήλ

ΤΣΟΥΔΕΡΟΥ ΒΙΡΓΙΝΙΑ θυγάτηρ τοῦ Ἐμμανουήλ

ΧΑΛΛΟΥΣ ΝΙΚΟΛΑΟΣ τοῦ Ἰσιδώρου

ΝΕΑ ΔΗΜΟΚΡΑΤΙΑ

ΣΥΝΔΥΑΣΜΟΣ
Α΄ ΑΘΗΝΩΝ

ΚΑΡΑΜΑΝΛΗΣ ΚΩΝΣΤΑΝΤΙΝΟΣ τοῦ Γεωργίου

ΑΠΟΣΤΟΛΑΤΟΣ ΓΕΡΑΣΙΜΟΣ τοῦ Κωνσταντίνου

ΒΑΣΙΛΕΙΟΥ ΒΑΣΟΣ τοῦ Ἀνδρέα

ΒΕΡΝΙΚΟΣ ΑΛΕΞΑΝΔΡΟΣ τοῦ Νικολάου

ΒΕΡΡΟΙΟΠΟΥΛΟΣ ΠΑΝΑΓΙΩΤΗΣ τοῦ Κωνσταντίνου

ΔΕΒΛΕΤΟΓΛΟΥ ΕΥΑΓΓΕΛΟΣ τοῦ Ἀθανασίου

ΔΕΜΕΣΤΙΧΑΣ ΙΩΑΝΝΗΣ τοῦ Ἠλία

ΔΡΟΣΟΣ ΓΕΩΡΓΙΟΣ τοῦ Νικολάου

ΕΒΕΡΤ ΜΙΛΤΙΑΔΗΣ τοῦ Ἀγγέλου

ΚΑΡΑΔΟΝΤΗΣ ΠΑΝΑΓΙΩΤΗΣ τοῦ Ἀθανασίου

ΚΑΣΙΜΑΤΗΣ ΓΡΗΓΟΡΙΟΣ τοῦ Παναγιώτου

ΚΟΝΟΦΑΓΟΣ ΚΩΝΣΤΑΝΤΙΝΟΣ τοῦ Ἠλία

ΛΑΜΠΡΙΑΣ ΠΑΝΑΓΙΩΤΗΣ τοῦ Κυριάκου

ΜΑΝΟΣ ΣΤΕΦΑΝΟΣ τοῦ Ἀλεξάνδρου

ΠΑΠΑΔΟΓΓΟΝΑΣ ΑΛΕΞΑΝΔΡΟΣ τοῦ Διονυσίου

ΠΛΥΤΑΣ ΓΕΩΡΓΙΟΣ τοῦ Ἀμβροσίου

ΡΑΛΛΗΣ ΓΕΩΡΓΙΟΣ τοῦ Ἰωάννου

ΣΤΕΦΑΝΑΚΗΣ ΚΩΝΣΤΑΝΤΙΝΟΣ τοῦ Γεωργίου

ΣΥΝΟΔΙΝΟΥ ΑΝΝΑ τοῦ Ἰωάννου

ΤΖΑΝΝΕΤΑΚΗΣ ΤΖΑΝΝΗΣ τοῦ Πέτρου

ΦΙΚΙΩΡΗΣ ΙΩΑΝΝΗΣ τοῦ Βασιλείου

ΧΡΥΣΑΝΘΟΠΟΥΛΟΣ ΚΩΝΣΤΑΝΤΙΝΟΣ τοῦ Μιχαήλ

ΠΑΝΕΛΛΗΝΙΟ ΣΟΣΙΑΛΙΣΤΙΚΟ ΚΙΝΗΜΑ

Β′ ΕΚΛΟΓΙΚΗ ΠΕΡΙΦΕΡΕΙΑ ΑΘΗΝΩΝ

ΑΛΕΞΑΝΔΡΗΣ ΕΥΣΤΑΘΙΟΣ (ΣΤΑΘΗΣ) τοῦ Βασιλείου

ΑΝΑΓΝΩΣΤΟΠΟΥΛΟΣ ΠΑΝΑΓΙΩΤΗΣ τοῦ Ἀθανασίου

ΑΝΤΩΝΟΠΟΥΛΟΣ ΛΥΣΑΝΔΡΟΣ τοῦ Γεωργίου

ΑΣΗΜΑΚΟΠΟΥΛΟΣ ΓΕΩΡΓΙΟΣ τοῦ Σπυρίδωνος

ΒΕΡΥΒΑΚΗΣ ΕΛΕΥΘΕΡΙΟΣ τοῦ Δημητρίου

ΒΛΑΧΟΣ ΑΝΕΣΤΗΣ τοῦ Ἡρακλέους

ΕΥΑΓΓΕΛΑΤΟΣ ΔΗΜΗΤΡΙΟΣ τοῦ Γερασίμου

ΖΑΦΕΙΡΟΠΟΥΛΟΣ ΙΩΑΝΝΗΣ τοῦ Γεωργίου

ΖΕΡΒΑΚΗΣ ΚΩΝΣΤΑΝΤΙΝΟΣ τοῦ Ἰωάννου

ΙΑΣΟΝΙΔΗΣ ΔΗΜΟΣΘΕΝΗΣ τοῦ Ἰωάννου

ΚΑΚΛΑΜΑΝΗΣ ΑΠΟΣΤΟΛΟΣ τοῦ Χρήστου

ΚΑΤΡΙΒΑΝΟΣ ΗΛΙΑΣ τοῦ Χρήστου

ΚΟΝΤΟΓΕΩΡΓΗΣ ΠΑΝΑΓΙΩΤΗΣ τοῦ Ἀθανασίου

ΚΟΥΚΟΥΛΑΚΗΣ ΔΗΜΗΤΡΙΟΣ τοῦ Σταύρου

ΚΡΑΟΥΝΑΚΗΣ ΜΙΧΑΗΛ τοῦ Ἰωάννου

ΚΥΠΡΙΩΤΑΚΗ - ΠΕΡΡΑΚΗ ΜΑΡΙΑ τοῦ Γεωργίου

ΛΑΜΠΡΑΚΗ ΕΙΡΗΝΗ τοῦ Ἀνδρέου

ΜΑΡΓΕΛΗΣ ΓΕΩΡΓΙΟΣ τοῦ Γεωργίου

ΜΑΡΚΟΠΟΥΛΟΣ ΠΑΝΑΓΙΩΤΗΣ τοῦ Ἀναστασίου

ΜΠΑΚΟΓΙΑΝΝΗΣ ΑΓΑΘΟΚΛΗΣ τοῦ Λεωνίδα

ΠΑΝΑΓΟΥΛΗΣ ΕΥΣΤΑΘΙΟΣ (ΣΤΑΘΗΣ) τοῦ Βασιλείου

ΠΑΠΑΔΙΟΝΥΣΙΟΥ ΝΙΚΟΛΑΟΣ τοῦ Κωνσταντίνου

ΠΑΠΑΚΩΝΣΤΑΝΤΙΝΟΥ ΙΩΑΝΝΗΣ τοῦ Κωνσταντίνου

ΠΑΠΑΝΔΡΕΟΥ ΝΙΚΟΛΑΟΣ τοῦ Ἠλία

ΠΕΡΚΙΖΑΣ ΝΙΚΟΛΑΟΣ - ΝΕΑΝΔΡΟΣ τοῦ Ἀνδρέου

ΣΠΗΛΙΟΠΟΥΛΟΣ ΠΑΝΟΣ τοῦ Νικολάου

ΧΑΡΑΛΑΜΠΟΠΟΥΛΟΣ ΙΩΑΝΝΗΣ τοῦ Γεωργίου

ΧΑΡΑΛΑΜΠΟΥΣ ΙΩΑΝΝΗΣ τοῦ Νικολάου

196

ΕΠΑΝΑΣΤΑΤΙΚΟ ΚΟΜΜΟΥΝΙΣΤΙΚΟ ΚΙΝΗΜΑ ΕΛΛΑΔΑΣ
Ε.Κ.Κ.Ε.

ΣΥΝΔΥΑΣΜΟΣ
Α ΕΚΛΟΓΙΚΗΣ ΠΕΡΙΦΕΡΕΙΑΣ ΑΘΗΝΩΝ

ΚΑΪΡΗ - ΔΗΜΑΚΟΠΟΥΛΟΥ ΕΛΕΝΗ τοῦ Λεάνδρου

ΚΑΡΑΚΑΣΟΓΛΟΥ ΑΛΕΞΑΝΔΡΟΣ τοῦ Σταύρου

ΚΟΤΑΝΙΔΗΣ ΓΕΩΡΓΙΟΣ τοῦ Παύλου

ΛΕΖΑΣ ΑΘΑΝΑΣΙΟΣ τοῦ Σπυρίδωνος

ΜΙΧΑΛΙΤΣΙΑΝΟΥ ΣΤΑΓΚΟΥ ΑΝΝΑ συζ. Πέτρου

ΠΑΝΑΓΟΠΟΥΛΟΣ ΙΩΑΝΝΗΣ τοῦ Παναγιώτου

ΠΑΠΑΪΩΑΝΝΟΥ ΑΓΓΕΛΟΣ τοῦ Δημητρίου

Appendix B

GREEK ELECTION RETURNS, 1974 and 1977

Compiled by Richard M. Scammon

GREECE: PARLIAMENTARY ELECTION RETURNS, BY DISTRICT, 1974						
Electoral District	*Valid Vote*	*ND*	*EK-ND*	*PASOK*	*EA*	*Other*[a]
1 Athens-Central	388,882	210,085	78,208	45,432	49,528	5,629
%		54.0	20.1	11.7	12.7	1.4
Seats	22	13	5	2	2	—
2 Athens-Suburban	462,024	215,216	98,309	60,850	82,336	5,313
%		46.6	21.3	13.2	17.8	1.1
Seats	28	15	6	3	4	—
3 Piraeus-Central	146,564	79,582	28,614	18,907	17,981	1,480
%		54.3	19.5	12.9	12.3	1.0
Seats	8	5	2	1	—	—
4 Piraeus-Suburban	135,796	53,831	32,728	16,813	31,433	991
%		39.6	24.1	12.4	23.1	.7
Seats	8	5	2	—	1	—
5 Attica-Remainder	96,648	60,578	16,704	11,544	6,850	972
%		62.7	17.3	11.9	7.1	1.0
Seats	6	5	1	—	—	—
6 Beotia	74,170	44,367	11,436	11,554	4,600	2,213
%		59.8	15.4	15.6	6.2	3.0
Seats	4	4	—	—	—	—
7 Euboia	108,464	63,589	23,766	15,395	4,965	749
%		58.6	21.9	14.2	4.6	.7
Seats	6	4	2	—	—	—

Electoral District	Valid Vote	ND	EK-ND	PASOK	EA	Other[a]
8 Phthiotis	103,256	67,678	21,302	8,022	4,683	1,571
%		65.5	20.6	7.8	4.5	1.5
Seats	6	5	1	—	—	—
9 Phokis	32,690	21,718	6,086	2,777	1,239	870
%		66.4	18.6	8.5	3.8	2.7
Seats	2	2	—	—	—	—
10 Argolis	50,448	34,324	6,514	7,887	977	746
%		68.0	12.9	15.6	1.9	1.5
Seats	3	3	—	—	—	—
11 Arcadia	80,086	52,179	17,569	7,546	2,156	636
%		65.2	21.9	9.4	2.7	.8
Seats	5	4	1	—	—	—
12 Corinth	73,729	47,031	10,632	13,243	2,119	704
%		63.8	14.4	18.0	2.9	1.0
Seats	4	4	—	—	—	—
13 Laconia	59,345	45,127	7,670	4,191	1,809	548
%		76.0	12.9	7.1	3.0	.9
Seats	4	3	1	—	—	—
14 Messinia	113,962	71,296	19,717	15,431	5,068	2,450
%		62.6	17.3	13.5	4.4	2.1
Seats	7	6	1	—	—	—
15 Aetolia-Acarnania	134,076	80,290	20,817	21,231	9,424	2,314
%		59.9	15.5	15.8	7.0	1.7
Seats	9	6	2	1	—	—
16 Achaia	138,392	71,979	19,782	34,345	11,261	1,025
%		52.0	14.3	24.8	8.1	.7
Seats	8	6	1	1	—	—
17 Evritania	24,992	16,065	5,181	3,285	461	—
%		64.3	20.7	13.1	1.8	—
Seats	2	2	—	—	—	—
18 Zanthe	19,171	10,188	6,337	931	1,509	206
%		53.1	33.1	4.9	7.9	1.1
Seats	1	1	—	—	—	—
19 Elia	109,483	58,286	30,457	16,184	2,857	1,699
%		53.2	27.8	14.8	2.6	1.6
Seats	7	4	2	1	—	—
20 Cephalonia	23,611	13,586	5,237	1,832	2,863	93
%		57.5	22.2	7.8	12.1	.4
Seats	2	2	—	—	—	—

(Table continues on next page)

Electoral District	Valid Vote	ND	EK-ND	PASOK	EA	Other[a]
21 Arta	48,349	31,285	5,738	7,438	2,346	1,542
%		64.7	11.9	15.4	4.9	3.2
Seats	3	2	1	—	—	—
22 Thesprotia	22,413	13,822	4,858	3,183	484	66
%		61.7	21.7	14.2	2.2	.3
Seats	2	2	—	—	—	—
23 Ioannina	91,115	56,517	18,176	8,780	7,058	584
%		62.0	19.9	9.6	7.7	.6
Seats	5	5	—	—	—	—
24 Corfu	57,349	27,683	10,702	12,900	5,791	273
%		48.3	18.7	22.5	10.1	.5
Seats	3	3	—	—	—	—
25 Lefkas	16,553	7,774	3,017	1,107	4,493	162
%		47.0	18.2	6.7	27.1	1.0
Seats	1	1	—	—	—	—
26 Preveza	33,299	19,638	5,456	5,702	1,670	833
%		59.0	16.4	17.1	5.0	2.5
Seats	2	2	—	—	—	—
27 Grevena	26,064	15,459	5,578	3,511	1,407	109
%		59.3	21.4	13.5	5.4	.4
Seats	2	2	—	—	—	—
28 Karditsa	91,750	48,216	17,428	12,175	7,888	6,043
%		52.6	19.0	13.3	8.6	6.6
Seats	6	5	1	—	—	—
29 Kozani	88,040	54,875	16,734	10,704	4,866	861
%		62.3	19.0	12.2	5.5	1.0
Seats	5	5	—	—	—	—
30 Larissa	137,814	73,961	28,057	18,429	16,385	982
%		53.7	20.4	13.4	11.9	.7
Seats	8	5	2	1	—	—
31 Magnesia	104,363	53,699	26,325	8,869	15,469	1
%		51.5	25.2	8.5	14.8	—
Seats	6	4	2	—	—	—
32 Thikkala	86,488	46,552	18,338	9,677	8,328	3,593
%		53.8	21.2	11.2	9.6	4.2
Seats	5	3	2	—	—	—
33 Imathia	70,787	38,878	14,615	11,065	5,917	312
%		54.9	20.6	15.6	8.4	.4
Seats	4	3	1	—	—	—

Electoral District	Valid Vote	ND	EK-ND	PASOK	EA	Other[a]
34 Thessaloniki City	206,027	112,301	35,702	22,505	32,698	2,821
%		54.5	17.3	10.9	15.9	1.4
Seats	12	8	2	1	1	—
35 Thessaloniki-Remainder	118,421	67,434	18,205	17,692	14,014	1,076
%		56.9	15.4	14.9	11.8	.9
Seats	6	5	1	—	—	—
36 Castoria	25,424	16,117	5,612	1,186	419	2,090
%		63.4	22.1	4.7	1.6	8.2
Seats	1	1	—	—	—	—
37 Kilkis	59,119	33,864	9,235	7,150	6,186	2,684
%		57.3	15.6	12.1	10.5	4.5
Seats	3	3	—	—	—	—
38 Pella	81,559	49,406	13,263	13,867	3,899	1,124
%		60.6	16.3	17.0	4.8	1.4
Seats	5	4	1	—	—	—
39 Pieria	55,543	35,006	9,634	6,519	3,879	505
%		63.0	17.3	11.7	7.0	.9
Seats	3	3	—	—	—	—
40 Serres	143,500	95,825	19,098	17,503	10,584	490
%		66.8	13.3	12.2	7.4	.3
Seats	8	7	1	—	—	—
41 Florina	31,458	22,220	5,825	1,879	1,274	260
%		70.6	18.5	6.0	4.0	.8
Seats	2	2	—	—	—	—
42 Chalkidiki	54,369	36,151	8,953	6,582	2,414	269
%		66.5	16.5	12.1	4.4	.5
Seats	3	3	—	—	—	—
43 Drama	62,781	36,773	9,841	11,229	2,836	2,102
%		58.6	15.7	17.9	4.5	3.3
Seats	3	3	—	—	—	—
44 Evros	86,674	55,449	16,522	9,984	3,601	1,118
%		64.0	19.1	11.5	4.2	1.3
Seats	5	4	1	—	—	—
45 Kavalla	83,017	47,317	14,923	9,584	9,658	1,535
%		57.0	18.0	11.5	11.6	1.8
Seats	4	4	—	—	—	—
46 Xanthi	48,029	25,249	11,355	3,957	941	6,527
%		52.6	23.6	8.2	2.0	13.6
Seats	3	2	1	—	—	—

(Table continues on next page)

Electoral District	Valid Vote	ND	EK-ND	PASOK	EA	Other[a]
47 Rodope	62,020	27,723	24,400	4,722	1,010	4,165
%		44.7	39.3	7.6	1.6	6.7
Seats	4	2	2	—	—	—
48 Dodekanese	61,574	27,928	10,457	12,937	1,472	8,780
%		45.4	17.0	21.0	2.4	14.3
Seats	4	3	1	—	—	—
49 Cyclades	64,449	40,548	15,351	6,729	1,296	525
%		62.9	23.8	10.4	2.0	.8
Seats	4	3	1	—	—	—
50 Lesbos	74,413	31,911	12,480	11,267	18,268	487
%		42.9	16.8	15.1	24.5	.7
Seats	4	3	1	—	—	—
51 Samos	28,020	14,352	6,870	2,022	4,589	187
%		51.2	24.5	7.2	16.4	.7
Seats	2	2	—	—	—	—
52 Chios	32,371	17,219	9,481	3,527	1,938	206
%		53.2	29.3	10.9	6.0	.6
Seats	2	2	—	—	—	—
53 Heraklion	122,771	32,231	47,566	34,142	8,561	271
%		26.3	38.7	27.8	7.0	.2
Seats	7	2	4	1	—	—
54 Lassithion	45,787	13,851	21,062	9,345	976	553
%		30.3	46.0	20.4	2.1	1.2
Seats	3	1	2	—	—	—
55 Rethymnon	39,585	13,933	7,381	8,125	1,223	8,923
%		35.2	18.6	20.5	3.1	22.5
Seats	2	2	—	—	—	—
56 Canea	71,890	10,971	27,255	13,020	6,830	13,814
%		15.3	37.9	18.1	9.5	19.2
Seats	4	1	3	—	—	—
Total Vote	4,908,974	2,669,133	1,002,559	666,413	464,787	106,082
Percent		54.4	20.4	13.6	9.5	2.2
District Seats	288	211	57	12	8	—
National Seats	12	9	3	—	—	—
Total Seats	300	220	60	12	8	—

[a] The other vote was as follows: EDE (National Democratic Union) 52,768; DEK (Union of the Democratic Center) 8,509; EKKE (Communist Revolutionary Movement of Greece) 1,539; Coalition of Liberal Democratic Union and Socialist party of Greece 975; independent candidates 42,291.

SOURCE: Election Directorate, Ministry of the Interior, *Apotelesmata ton Voulef-tikon Eklogon tis 17is Noemvriou 1974* [Results of the parliamentary elections of November 17, 1974], vol. 1 (Athens: National Printing Office, 1976).

GREECE: PARLIAMENTARY ELECTION RETURNS, BY DISTRICT, 1977

Electoral District	Valid Vote	ND	PASOK	EDIK (EK-ND)	KKE	National Alignment	SPAD	New Liberal	Other[a]
1 Athens-Central	408,469	174,945	92,235	37,502	47,028	27,183	24,507	2,166	2,903
%		42.8	22.6	9.2	11.5	6.7	6.0	.5	.7
Seats	22	10	6	2	2	1	1	—	—
2 Athens-Suburban	511,464	184,830	141,120	42,447	82,262	26,297	26,558	3,169	4,781
%		36.1	27.6	8.3	16.1	5.1	5.2	.6	.9
Seats	28	11	9	2	4	1	1	—	—
3 Piraeus-Central	150,475	66,098	35,918	16,512	16,616	7,358	6,322	559	1,092
%		43.9	23.9	11.0	11.0	4.9	4.2	.4	.7
Seats	8	4	3	1	—	—	—	—	—
4 Piraeus-Suburban	143,847	46,622	38,084	17,241	27,818	4,295	7,464	668	1,655
%		32.4	26.5	12.0	19.3	3.0	5.2	.5	1.2
Seats	8	3	3	1	1	—	—	—	—
5 Attica-Remainder	106,652	48,100	29,942	11,825	8,130	5,842	1,923	—	890
%		45.1	28.1	11.1	7.6	5.5	1.8	—	.8
Seats	6	4	2	—	—	—	—	—	—
6 Beotia	71,528	28,182	22,163	8,555	5,275	5,710	1,223	—	420
%		39.4	31.0	12.0	7.4	8.0	1.7	—	.6
Seats	4	3	1	—	—	—	—	—	—
7 Euboia	116,736	49,874	32,313	15,273	6,169	6,585	1,230	—	5,292
%		42.7	27.7	13.1	5.3	5.6	1.1	—	4.5
Seats	6	4	2	—	—	—	—	—	—

(Table continues on next page)

Electoral District	Valid Vote	ND	PASOK	EDIK (EK-ND)	KKE	National Alignment	SPAD	New Liberal	Other[a]
8 Phthiotis	106,226	46,710	24,093	15,042	6,099	11,697	1,181	759	645
%		44.0	22.7	14.2	5.7	11.0	1.1	.7	.6
Seats	6	4	2	—					
9 Phokis	32,506	17,838	7,789	1,261	1,594	3,441	330	248	—
%		54.9	24.0	3.9	4.9	10.6	1.0	.8	—
Seats	2	2	—	—					
10 Argolis	53,417	24,579	13,620	5,556	1,843	6,623	527	651	18
%		46.0	25.5	10.4	3.5	12.4	1.0	1.2	—
Seats	3	2	1	—					
11 Arcadia	80,761	39,364	17,321	9,862	4,064	9,044	897	—	209
%		48.7	21.4	12.2	5.0	11.2	1.1	—	.3
Seats	5	3	2	—					
12 Corinth	77,250	36,380	23,070	7,513	2,995	4,755	1,148	1,128	261
%		47.1	29.9	9.7	3.9	6.2	1.5	1.5	.3
Seats	4	3	1	—					
13 Laconia	59,410	32,675	9,643	4,179	2,475	9,651	521	78	188
%		55.0	16.2	7.0	4.2	16.2	.9	.1	.3
Seats	4	4	—	—					
14 Messinia	116,459	51,740	27,215	12,746	7,076	16,362	1,006	—	314
%		44.4	23.4	10.9	6.1	14.0	.9	—	.3
Seats	7	4	2	—		1			
15 Aetolia-Acarnania	140,656	69,265	36,575	14,543	10,660	6,771	1,762	494	586
%		49.2	26.0	10.3	7.6	4.8	1.3	.4	.4
Seats	9	5	3	1					

Region	Total								
16 Achaia	146,527	58,609	54,589	8,312	11,932	9,464	2,964	—	657
%		40.0	37.3	5.7	8.1	6.5	2.0	—	.4
Seats	8	4	4	—	—	—	—	—	—
17 Evritania	21,868	10,153	6,219	2,990	667	1,477	122	240	—
%		46.4	28.4	13.7	3.1	6.8	.6	1.1	—
Seats	1	1	—	—	—	—	—	—	—
18 Zanthe	20,002	7,266	4,078	1,476	3,159	3,050	400	573	—
%		36.3	20.4	7.4	15.8	15.3	2.0	2.9	—
Seats	1	1	—	—	—	—	—	—	—
19 Elia	111,696	39,366	34,624	20,228	4,130	11,856	1,063	—	429
%		35.2	31.0	18.1	3.7	10.6	1.0	—	.4
Seats	7	4	2	1	—	—	—	—	—
20 Cephalonia	23,199	9,202	5,580	2,264	3,034	2,627	492	—	—
%		39.7	24.1	9.8	13.1	11.3	2.1	—	—
Seats	2	2	—	—	—	—	—	—	—
21 Arta	51,408	20,214	14,350	6,475	3,270	6,198	612	149	140
%		39.3	27.9	12.6	6.4	12.1	1.2	.3	.3
Seats	3	1	2	—	—	—	—	—	—
22 Thesprotia	24,806	8,458	7,578	6,136	1,128	1,319	187	—	—
%		34.1	30.5	24.7	4.5	5.3	.8	—	—
Seats	2	1	1	—	—	—	—	—	—
23 Ioannina	95,367	44,118	23,636	8,173	7,731	7,221	2,390	1,644	454
%		46.3	24.8	8.6	8.1	7.6	2.5	1.7	.5
Seats	5	3	2	—	—	—	—	—	—

(Table continues on next page)

Electoral District	Valid Vote	ND	PASOK	EDIK (EK-ND)	KKE	National Alignment	SPAD	New Liberal	Other[a]
24 Corfu	57,600	20,413	18,471	4,404	5,779	5,737	1,653	148	995
%		35.4	32.1	7.6	10.0	10.0	2.9	.3	1.7
Seats	3	2	1	—	—	—	—	—	—
25 Lefkas	17,273	5,509	2,863	3,232	3,120	1,412	780	47	310
%		31.9	16.6	18.7	18.1	8.2	4.5	.3	1.8
Seats	1	1	—	—	—	—	—	—	—
26 Preveza	34,319	15,174	11,796	1,334	2,556	3,045	414	—	—
%		44.2	34.4	3.9	7.4	8.9	1.2	—	—
Seats	2	1	1	—	—	—	—	—	—
27 Grevena	27,487	8,917	4,973	7,417	2,213	2,836	279	623	229
%		32.4	18.1	27.0	8.1	10.3	1.0	2.3	.8
Seats	1	1	—	—	—	—	—	—	—
28 Karditsa	95,064	34,721	25,253	9,674	10,422	13,587	960	—	447
%		36.5	26.6	10.2	11.0	14.3	1.0	—	.5
Seats	6	3	2	—	—	1	—	—	—
29 Kozani	89,698	44,684	21,257	12,184	5,023	4,797	1,616	—	137
%		49.8	23.7	13.6	5.6	5.4	1.8	—	.2
Seats	5	3	2	—	—	—	—	—	—
30 Larissa	143,455	52,937	32,003	16,628	21,608	14,785	3,321	—	2,173
%		36.9	22.3	11.6	15.1	10.3	2.3	—	1.5
Seats	8	4	2	1	1	—	—	—	—
31 Magnesia	105,633	44,813	20,640	14,961	15,337	5,692	3,509	—	681
%		42.4	19.5	14.2	14.5	5.4	3.3	—	.6
Seats	6	4	1	—	1	—	—	—	—

32 Thikkala	91,754	34,115	20,500	17,486	11,106	7,221	1,038	—	288
%		37.2	22.3	19.1	12.1	7.9	1.1	—	.3
Seats	5	3	1	1					
33 Imathia	75,196	32,590	23,024	8,226	6,352	3,129	1,530	78	267
%		43.3	30.6	10.9	8.4	4.2	2.0	.1	.4
Seats	4	3	1						
34 Thessaloniki City	217,708	99,702	48,167	19,639	26,073	9,110	11,994	926	2,097
%		45.8	22.1	9.0	12.0	4.2	5.5	.4	1.0
Seats	12	7	3	1	1				
35 Thessaloniki-Remainder	126,203	58,299	34,766	9,396	12,636	6,718	2,568	1,220	600
%		46.2	27.5	7.4	10.0	5.3	2.0	1.0	.5
Seats	7	4	3						
36 Castoria	27,174	12,014	5,295	2,708	766	3,665	277	—	2,449
%		44.2	19.5	10.0	2.8	13.5	1.0	—	9.0
Seats	1	1							
37 Kilkis	62,031	26,660	14,644	5,671	6,329	7,038	1,033	319	337
%		43.0	23.6	9.1	10.2	11.3	1.7	.5	.5
Seats	3	2	1						
38 Pella	87,546	38,700	27,301	9,612	3,996	6,433	1,191	85	228
%		44.2	31.2	11.0	4.6	7.3	1.4	.1	.3
Seats	5	3	2						
39 Pieria	61,501	27,086	14,643	9,254	4,032	5,096	1,167	—	223
%		44.0	23.8	15.0	6.6	8.3	1.9	—	.4
Seats	3	3							

(Table continues on next page)

Electoral District	Valid Vote	ND	PASOK	EDIK (EK-ND)	KKE	National Alignment	SPAD	New Liberal	Other[a]
40 Serres	150,558	79,122	34,776	14,565	10,387	8,422	2,738	—	548
%		52.6	23.1	9.7	6.9	5.6	1.8	—	.4
Seats	8	5	3	—	—	—	—	—	—
41 Florina	34,594	16,271	5,404	6,631	1,661	2,793	320	—	1,514
%		47.0	15.6	19.2	4.8	8.1	.9	—	4.4
Seats	2	2	—	—	—	—	—	—	—
42 Chalkidiki	56,128	29,647	14,488	6,007	2,334	2,419	937	94	202
%		52.8	25.8	10.7	4.2	4.3	1.7	.2	.4
Seats	3	2	1	—	—	—	—	—	—
43 Drama	66,897	26,533	18,251	4,852	2,408	6,844	1,013	90	6,906
%		39.7	27.3	7.3	3.6	10.2	1.5	.1	10.3
Seats	3	2	1	—	—	—	—	—	—
44 Evros	87,540	47,906	19,052	11,388	3,236	3,796	1,485	—	677
%		54.7	21.8	13.0	3.7	4.3	1.7	—	.8
Seats	5	3	2	—	—	—	—	—	—
45 Kavalla	86,820	43,843	20,230	8,138	6,460	3,426	3,323	233	1,167
%		50.5	23.3	9.4	7.4	3.9	3.8	.3	1.3
Seats	4	3	1	—	—	—	—	—	—
46 Xanthi	49,433	21,680	11,099	11,861	1,021	2,669	510	—	593
%		43.9	22.5	24.0	2.1	5.4	1.0	—	1.2
Seats	3	2	1	—	—	—	—	—	—
' Rodope	62,103	22,192	10,357	10,558	1,548	16,963	485	—	—
%		35.7	16.7	17.0	2.5	27.3	.8	—	—
Seats	4	2	1	—	—	1	—	—	—

48 Dodekanese	65,022	26,866	18,016	16,295	1,768	1,330	747	—	—
%		41.3	27.7	25.1	2.7	2.0	1.1	—	—
Seats	4	2	1	1	—	—	—	—	—
49 Cyclades	62,994	34,618	14,441	7,946	2,175	1,918	1,500	252	144
%		55.0	22.9	12.6	3.5	3.0	2.4	.4	.2
Seats	4	3	1	1	—	—	—	—	—
50 Lesbos	72,708	31,099	15,117	5,787	17,543	829	1,778	485	70
%		42.8	20.8	8.0	24.1	1.1	2.4	.7	.1
Seats	4	2	1	—	1	—	—	—	—
51 Samos	27,659	12,001	3,008	5,959	4,862	813	849	—	167
%		43.4	10.9	21.5	17.6	2.9	3.1	—	.6
Seats	2	2	—	—	—	—	—	—	—
52 Chios	31,339	14,967	4,910	8,470	1,692	630	670	—	—
%		47.8	15.7	27.0	5.4	2.0	2.1	—	—
Seats	2	2	—	—	—	—	—	—	—
53 Heraklion	125,705	31,296	44,445	31,537	9,094	901	2,741	5,221	470
%		24.9	35.4	25.1	7.2	.7	2.2	4.2	.4
Seats	7	2	3	2	—	—	—	—	—
54 Lassithion	45,540	13,485	11,924	14,104	1,910	207	303	3,607	—
%		29.6	26.2	31.0	4.2	.5	.7	7.9	—
Seats	3	1	1	1	—	—	—	—	—
55 Rethymnon	41,562	12,258	10,091	5,790	1,899	213	358	10,818	135
%		29.5	24.3	13.9	4.6	.5	.9	26.0	.3
Seats	3	1	1	—	—	—	—	1	—

(Table continues on next page)

Electoral District	Valid Vote	ND	PASOK	EDIK (EK-ND)	KKE	National Alignment	SPAD	New Liberal	Other[a]
56 Canea	72,798	11,654	17,065	14,961	7,771	688	1,440	18,722	497
%		16.0	23.4	20.6	10.7	.9	2.0	25.7	.7
Seats		—	2	1	—	—	—	1	—
Total Vote	5,129,771	2,146,365	1,300,025	612,786	480,272	349,988	139,356	55,494	45,485
Percent		41.8	25.3	11.9	9.4	6.8	2.7	1.1	.9
District Seats	288	164	88	16	11	5	2	2	—
National Seats	12	7	5	—	—	—	—	—	—
Total Seats	300	171	93	16	11	5	2	2	—

[a] The other vote was as follows: EKKE (Communist Revolutionary Movement of Greece) 11,895; LDE (People's Democratic Unity) 8,839; EDE (Workers Internationalist Union) 1,032; EHE (Greek Christian Social Union) 777; Communist Organization, Fighter 321; EKE (Social party of Stock Farmers) 170; Workers and Peasants party 84; ODI (Olympic Democracy) 19; independent lists and candidates 22,348.

Source: Election Directorate, Ministry of the Interior, *Apotelesmata ton Vouleftikon Eklogon tis 20is Noemvriou 1977* [Results of the parliamentary elections of November 20, 1977], vol. 1 (Athens: National Printing Office, 1979).

Contributors

THEODORE A. COULOUMBIS is professor of international relations at the School of International Service of the American University. He is the author of *Greek Political Reaction to American and NATO Influences* and coeditor of and contributor to *Greek-American Relations: A Critical Review*.

ANGELOS ELEPHANTIS is founder and managing editor of the monthly review *O Politis*. His publications include a history of the Greek Communist party from its origins in 1918 up to World War II.

J. C. LOULIS is director of studies at the Center for Political Research and Information (KPEE) in Athens and editor of its journal, *Epikentra*. He has written extensively on Greek party politics and on the place of the new liberalism in political thought. His book, *The Greek Communist Party: 1940–44*, will be published shortly by Croom-Helm.

ROY C. MACRIDIS is Wein Professor of International Cooperation in the department of politics at Brandeis University. He is the author of *Contemporary Ideologies: Movements and Regimes, French Politics in Transition*, as well as many other works.

MICHALIS PAPAYANNAKIS lectures on development economics at the Mediterranean Agronomic Institute at Montpellier and is pursuing research at the Hellenic Mediterranean Center for Arab and Islamic Studies in Athens. He has written widely on Greek economics and politics.

RICHARD M. SCAMMON, coauthor of *This U.S.A.* and *The Real Majority*, is director of the Elections Research Center in Washington, D.C. He has edited the biennial series *America Votes* since 1956.

PHAEDO VEGLERIS is professor emeritus at the University of Athens. He has written widely in Greek and French on problems of Greek and comparative constitutional law, jurisprudence, human rights, and administration including the judicial control of administration.

THANOS VEREMIS lectures on modern Greek history at the Pantios School of Political Science. His works include studies of Greek security considerations and military intervention in Greek politics.

Index

Administrative Committee of ND, 69, 70, 71, 79, 81; composition of, 80
Aegean islands, fortification of, 169–70
Aegean seabed dispute, 68, 98, 169–70; EDIK policy and, 181; ND policy and, 177
Age: of ND cabinet members, 63–64; ND voting and, 77; of PASOK M.P.s, 128; voting, 26, 27
Age distribution of electorate, 12
Agriculture, 4, 116; EC and, 100; low production rate and, 3; the ND party and, 66; reform in, landowners and, 5
Air-space question, 168–69
Alavanos, Constantine, 100, 104
Angellousis, Angelos, 92
Apostolou, Lefteris, 136
Assembly. *See* National Assembly
Athens Polytechnic Institute, 64, 148–49
Averoff, Evangelos, 63, 64, 189

Balance of payments, 65, 66, 67
Ballot: of 1977, 192; secrecy of, 23; simultaneous, 28; valid, 46
Berlinguer, Enrico, 113
Black, C. E., 4
Britain, 162, 163, 164, 169
Broad district electoral system, 30
Brzezinski, Z. K., 52
Bureaucracy, 186; inflated, ND party and, 66; party organization and, 50; patron-client patterns and, 3

Cabinets, 18; instability of, 3; ND party, 63–64; number of (1946–1951), 8

Campaign funding, EDIK, 99
Campaigning: EDIK organization and, 99; EK-ND (1974), 91; KKE, 152, 154–56; National Democracy (1977), 74–79; PASOK and, 115–16; on personal basis, 50–51
Campaign issues, 152; Center Union, 87, 90, 91–92, 98–99, 100, 101; KKE, 150, 154, 155–56; Movement of New Political Forces, 90; National Democracy, 60, 61, 75; in 1974, 10–12; in 1977, 16–17; party coalitions and, 7–8; PASOK, 98, 100, 115–16, 150, 156
Candidates: EDIK, 102–103; electoral system characteristics and, 39–40; eligibility and, 28–29; former prime ministers as, 36; objections and, 41, 42–43; PASOK, 124; selection of (regional), 71; state deputy, 36
Capital: export of, 3; PASOK theory and, 112; "state monopoly," KKE and, 182
Caretaker governments, 37
Carter, Jimmy, 115
Center for Educational Training and Research (KEME), 67
Center for Political Research and Information (KPEE), 66–67, 75
Center Union, 7, 102, 103, 104, 105, 107; anticommunism and, 55; EDIK formation and, 86–89, 92; the king's interference with, 56; monarchy referendum and, 15; results of 1974 election and, 13–14, 60; results of 1977 election and, 16
Center Union–New Forces (EK–ND),

36, 90, 131, 150, 151; campaign of, 91

Central Committee of KKE, 142; KKE split and, 147

Central Committee of PASOK, 107, 122, 123, 125; members expelled from, 108

Centralists, 60; Liberals as, 88; results of 1974 election and, 13–14; results of 1977 election and, 16

Christian Democracy, 90, 130, 154, 155; composition of, 131

Church, the, 6

Citizenship, 26–27

Clientelism. *See* Patron-client pattern

Coalitions, 10, 46 n.35, 74, 188; Center Union, 90, 98; Communist, 7, 131, 181, 183; forming and reforming of, 2–3; future elections and, 20; People's party, 51; political parties and, 7–8; right-wing, 102

Commission for Parliamentary Control and Documentation (PASOK), 124

Committee for Analysis and Programming (PASOK), 124

Committee of Financial Control (PASOK), 122

Communist International, KKE and, 135–36

Communist party of Greece (KKE): coalitions and, 7, 10, 131; Communist International and, 135–36; congress of, 148, 158; coup d'état of 1967 and, 144–47; during the 1930s, 51; elections of 1974 and, 132, 149–52; elections of 1977 and, 127, 131, 132, 152–59; electoral base of, 135; foreign policy and, 162, 171, 181–82; history of, 134–44; leadership of, 135–36, 140, 141–42; after liberation, 52–53; occupation years and, 52, 137–38; organization of, 135; PASOK and, 129; proportional representation and, 35; Soviets and, 136–37, 140, 143; split in, 130–31, 143, 147–49

Communist party of Greece–Interior (KKE-Interior): coalitions and, 131, 181, 183; congress of, 148, 158; coup d'état of 1967 and, 145–47; elections of 1977 and, 127, 131, 152, 154–59; foreign policy and, 171, 181, 183; PASOK and, 129; Soviets and, 147–48; split from KKE, 130–31, 138, 143, 147–49

Communists, 12, 117, 121, 163; defeat of (1949), 85–86; EDA and, 140; Eurocommunist parties and, 113, 134, 136, 158, 183; fear of, 52–53, 55; Liberals and, 92; ND party and, 65; organization and, 50; outlawing of (1947), 25; PASOK and, 113; reinstatement of (1974), 62, 166, 187; results of 1974 election and, 13–14; results of 1977 election and, 16–17, 79; socialist ideology and, 117

Conservatives: coalition of, 74; disagreement with the king and, 56; government stability and, 54–55; Greek Rally and, 54; ideology and, 58; Karamanlis and, 61–62; language reform and, 67; movement of, rejuvenated, 59; People's party and, 53; weakness/strength of, 81

Constantine I, 38 n.22, 85, 135, 163

Constantine II, 55–56, 88

Constituencies: electoral system and, 29–30; proportional representation and, 33–34; constitution and, 46

Constitution, 1, 187; electoral law disputes and, 45, 46, 47; electoral system and, 21–26; the French constitution and, 17, 18; Karamanlis's views on, 63; referendums and, 38; validation of elections and, 40, 41, 43 n.30

Coordinating Council of PASOK, 123

Council of Ministers, 25

Council of State, 40; electoral law review and, 45–47

Coups d'état, 49, 56, 64, 185. *See also* Military junta, 1967–1974

Crete, 6, 13

Cultural division, 162

Cyprus, 11, 26, 57, 67, 68, 97, 101, 115, 118, 145, 149, 164, 165, 190; EDIK policy and, 180, 181; as foreign policy problem, 166–68; ND policy and, 176–77; PASOK policy and, 179

DeGaulle, Charles, 10, 17–18

Deliyannis, Theodore, 85, 161

Democracy: history of Greek, 22–24; Karamanlis's views on, 64; reinstatement of Greek, 1–2

Democratic Defense (DA), 105, 131, 146, 149

Dependence, 6–7, 111, 161

Devletoglou, Nikos, 74

Dictatorship, ideology and, 117–18

Disciplinary Board of PASOK, 122

Dodecanese islands, fortification of, 169–70

Dovas, General Constantine, 87

EA. *See* United Left (EA)

EADE. *See* National Democratic Antidictatorial Unity (EADE)

EAM. *See* National Liberation Front (EAM)

EAS. *See* National Resistance Council (EAS)

EC. *See* European Economic Community (EC)

Economic Committee of ND, 70, 71

Economic issues, 187; ideological crisis and, 118; Mediterranean profile and, 3–4, 5; ND party and, 61, 65–67; Papandreou's theory and, 112, 178

EDA. *See* United Democratic Left (EDA)

EDIK. *See* Union of the Democratic Center (EDIK)

EDIN. *See* Youth Movements, Center Union (EDIN)

Education, 64, 67

EK. *See* Union of the Center (EK)

EK-ND. *See* Center Union–New Forces (EK-ND)

ELAS. *See* National Popular Liberation Army (ELAS)

Elective office, eligibility for, 28–29

Elections: announcing, 45 n.32; Center Union and 1974, 13–14, 60; Center Union and 1977, 16; foreign policy trends and, 170–71, 172–75; general results of 1974, 13–14, 194–206; general results of 1977, 14, 16–17, 194–206; indirect, 46; KKE and 1974, 132, 149–52; KKE and 1977, 127, 131, 132, 152–59; local, 39–40; New Democracy and 1974, 62, 67, 150, 151; New Democracy and 1977, 14, 16–17, 73–79; in 1958, 132; in 1951/1952, 53; in 1956, 141; in 1946, 131; in 1963, 87; parliamentary, 30, 39–40; parliamentary, validations of, 40–48; PASOK and 1974, 13–14, 16, 72, 126–29, 132, 156, 157; PASOK and 1977, 16, 78–79, 98, 101, 102, 106, 126–29, 156, 157; patron-client pattern and, 3, 50, 73; presidential (1980), 17–19; Union of Democratic Center (EDIK) and 1974, 89–92; Union of Democratic Center (EDIK) and 1977, 78–79, 97–104, 127

Electoral law: constitution and, 21–26; electoral system and, 29–30; judicial review of, 45–47; right to vote and run for office and, 22–29

Electoral system: caretaker governments and, 37; characteristics of, 39–40; defining, 21–22; local elections and, 29–40; proportional, 33–36; referendums and, 37–39; state deputies and, 36–37

Electorate, changes in (1964–1974), 12–13

Employment, 4

EP. *See* National Camp (EP)

EPEK. *See* National Progressive Union of the Center (EPEK)

ERE. *See* National Radical Union (ERE)

Eurocommunist movement, 113, 134, 136, 158, 183. *See also* Communist party of Greece; Communist party of Greece–Interior; Communists

European Economic Community (EC), 2, 26, 64, 68, 73, 91, 98, 100, 114, 155–56, 167, 189; EDIK policy and, 180; KKE policy and, 182; ND policy and, 176; PASOK policy and, 178, 179

Executive branch, 23; dissolution of parliament and, 26

Executive Bureau of PASOK, 122–23

Executive Committee of ND, 69, 71, 80

Factions, Liberal party, 7

Foreign intervention, 6–7, 111, 161–62, 163, 185–86

Foreign investment, 4, 7. *See also* Investment policies

Foreign policy, 6, 19, 190; air-space question and, 168–69; early twentieth century, 162–63; Eurocommunist movement and, 183; hawks and doves and, 161; KKE and, 162, 171, 181–82; National Camp and, 182–83; the ND party and, 64, 67–68, 171–77; since 1974, 165–70; nineteenth-century legacy and, 160–62; PASOK and, 112–13, 162, 177–80; political parties and, 161, 170–83; problems with (1974–1978), 166–70; Union of Democratic Center (EDIK) and, 104, 180–81; United States and, 163–65

Fortification of islands, 169–70

Free Greeks (movement), 146

Friedrich, C. J., 52

Generous hypothesis, 2, 20, 187
George II, 51, 85, 92
German occupation (1941–1944), 85;
  KKE and, 52, 137–38
Giscard d'Estaing, Valéry, 11, 17–18
Gizikis, General Pahedon, 64 n.55
Grass-Roots Development Committees
  of PASOK, 124–25
Greece: democracy in, 1–2, 22–24, 64;
  foreign policy/Karamanlis and,
  67–68; foreign policy profile of,
  160–63, 165–70; language reform in,
  67, 187; Mediterranean profile and,
  2–9; nineteenth-century political
  parties in, 84–85; Papandreou's
  theory and, 111–12; political parties/
  foreign policy and, 170–83;
  praetorian politics and, 185; United
  States and, 163–65
Greek Rally (party), 53, 54, 59, 60
Greek Resistance (movement), 146
Greek War of Independence, 161–62

Hagenback-Bischoff PR system, 33
Houtas, Stylianos, 92

Ideology: conservative, 58; coup of
  1967 and, 56; Metaxas's, 52; National
  Radical Union (ERE), 55; New
  Democracy (ND), 59–68, 81–82;
  People's party's lack of coherent, 50,
  51; of populism, social roots and,
  116–22; Union of Democratic Center
  (EDIK), 91–92
Iliou, Ilias, 157
Income inequalities, 3
Income redistribution, 66, 115
Industrialization, 5
Inflation, 65, 66, 67
Interest groups, 186
Interior Bureau of KKE, 147
International Civil Aviation
  Organization (ICAO), 168
Intervention. See State intervention
Investment policies, 7; public, 66.
  See also Foreign investment
Ioannidis, Brigadier Dimitrios, 59;
  prison sentence of, 65
Ionian islands, 62

Judicial validation, 40–41, 45–48.
  See also Validation of parliamentary
  elections
Junta. See Military junta (1967–1974)

Kanellopoulos, Athanasios, 103
Kanellopoulos, Panayotis, 89
Kapodistrias, John, 85
Karamanlis, Constantine, 1, 10, 11, 86,
  87, 88, 93, 97, 149, 166, 176, 188, 190;
  junta of 1967 and, 57; National
  Radical Union and, 54–57; New
  Democracy and, 57–58, 59, 61, 62–63,
  64, 67–68, 81; 1974 election results
  and, 13; 1977 election results and,
  73, 74, 76, 77, 101; presidential
  election of 1980 and, 17–19, 189;
  resignation (1963) of, 87
King, 6, 20; disagreement of, with
  conservative leaders, 55–56; history
  of Greek democracy and, 23–24;
  Liberals and, 92. See also
  Constantine I; Constantine II;
  George II; Monarchists (royalists);
  Monarchy
KKE. See Communist party of Greece
  (KKE)
KKE-Interior. See Communist party of
  Greece–Interior (KKE-Interior)
KODESCO. See Social Democratic
  party (KODESCO)
Kokevis, Andreas, 92
Koumoundouros, Alexander, 85, 161
Kyprianou, Spyros, 181

Laiko Komma. See People's party
Land ownership, agrarian reform
  and, 5
Language reforms, 67, 187
LaPalombara, Joseph, 3
Leaders, 54; campaigning and, 50–51;
  candidate selection and, 71; EDA,
  141; EDIK, problem with, 93–97,
  104; ERE, power of, 55; KKE, 135–36,
  140, 141–42; ND party, 72, 81, 82;
  PASOK, 106–110, 117; proportional
  representation system and, 36;
  revival of parties and, 10; state
  deputies and, 46
Left, the, 7, 107; history of, 134–49;
  non-Communist, 88, 143; overview
  of, 130–34; proportional representation and, 35; results of 1974 election
  and, 13–14; results of 1977 election
  and, 157; traditional, 188
Legg, Keith, 8
Legislative branch: electoral rules and,
  21–22, 23; state deputies and, 36
Legitimacy, 3; Karamanlis and, 54;
  leader-follower relationship and,

109–110; military dictatorship and, 117; twentieth-century crisis of, 186
Liberal governments, 86
Liberal party, 49, 51, 84, 85; factions of, 7. *See also* Union of the Democratic Center (EDIK)

Macridis, Roy, 187
Majority electoral system, 30
Makarios, President, 149, 167
Mangakis, George Alexander, 90, 93, 100
Maniadakis, Constantine, 55
Manufacturing, 5, 67
Maris, Giannis, 64 n.55
Markezinis, Spyzos, 149
Mavrocordatos, Alexander, 85, 161
Mavromichalis, Kyriakoulis, 85
Mavros, George, 88, 89, 91, 99, 103, 150, 171; EDIK's leadership and, 93–97; election of 1977 and, 98, 187; television appearances of, 101
Media. *See* Newspapers; Television
Mediterranean community, PASOK and, 114, 179
Mediterranean profile (economic and social), 2–9
Megali Idea, 161
Men, voting and, 13, 26
Metaxas, General Ioannis, 55, 56–57; dictatorship of, 51–52, 85, 137, 185
Meynaud, Jean, 8
Middle class: disagreements within, 6; radicalization of masses and, 120, 121. *See also* Social classes
Military junta (1967–1974), 1, 9, 56–57, 89, 184; analysis of, 186; Communists and, 144–47; fall of, populism and, 119
Minis, Anastasios, 93, 100
Minorities question (Greek/Turkish), 170
Mitsotakis, Constantine, 88
Mobility: geographical, 4; of workers, 3
Monarchists (royalists), 19, 163; People's party and, 49, 52–53
Monarchy, the, 6, 74, 187; referendum and, 14–16, 24, 37–38, 139, 151, 187; revival of, 53; reviving sentiment for, 52; unpopularity of, 51. *See also* King
Movement of the New Political Forces, 90, 104
Mylonas, George, 104, 149

Narrow district electoral system, 30
National Alignment, 16, 17
National Assembly, 18, 20
National Camp (EP), 58, 74, 77, 79; foreign policy and, 171, 182–83
National Democratic Antidictatorial Unity (EADE), 151–52, 154, 158
National Democratic Union (NDU), 58, 62, 73, 77
National identity, 6; ND party and, 61
Nationalizations, 61
National Liberation Front (EAM), 137
National Popular Liberation Army (ELAS), 137
National Progressive Union of the Center (EPEK), 86
National Radical Union (ERE), 13, 59, 60, 87, 145; establishment of, 54–57
National Resistance Council (EAS), 146
NATO, 10, 11, 16, 17, 68, 91, 100, 111, 115, 150, 190, 191; EDIK policy and, 180; Eurocommunists and, 183; foreign policy and, 163–65, 166–67, 168; Greece's withdrawal from military wing of, 67, 176; KKE policy and, 182; ND policy and, 176; PASOK policy and, 178, 179
ND. *See* New Democracy party (ND)
NDU. *See* National Democratic Union (NDU)
New Democracy party (ND), 36, 106, 187, 189, 190, 191; Administrative Committee and, 80; charter of, 69, 70–71, 80–81; coalitions and, 7; congress of, 71, 79–80, 81, 82; division in, 19–20; foreign policy and, 64, 67–68, 171–77; ideology and performance of, 59–68, 81–82; membership figures for, 71; monarchy referendum and, 14–16, 63; organization and structure of, 68–73, 77, 82–83; as outgrowth of People's party, 49–59; party leadership and, 72, 81, 82; posters of, 99; presidential election (1980) and, 17; proportional representation and, 35; results of 1974 election and, 13–14, 62, 72, 150, 151; results of 1977 election and, 14, 16–17, 73–79; revival of 10, 11
Newspapers, 74, 186; conservative nature of, 55; foundation of PASOK and, 109; Karamanlis's foreign policy

and, 68; ND's, 74; ND's liberalism and, 65; voluntary closing of (protesting junta), 57
Niggardly hypothesis, 2, 20

Objections to parliamentary elections, 41, 42–43. *See also* Validation of parliamentary elections
Office. *See* Elective office
Opinion polls: first in Greece (1974), 63; in 1977 election, 77
Ottoman Empire, 160, 161, 162

PAK. *See* Panhellenic Liberation Movement (PAK)
PAM. *See* Patriotic Antidictatorial Front (PAM)
Panagoulis, Alexander, 100, 146
Panhellenic Liberation Movement (PAK), 105, 146, 149, 150
Panhellenic Socialist Movement (PASOK), 1, 7, 36, 68, 75, 91, 102, 103, 104, 150, 151, 152, 153, 156, 159, 187, 188, 189, 190, 191; alliances of, 113–14; congress of, 122; elections of 1974 and, 13–14, 16, 72, 126–29, 132, 156, 157; elections of 1977 and, 16, 78–79, 98, 101, 102, 106, 126–29, 156, 157; electoral tactics of, 115–16; European Community and, 114–15; foreign policy and, 112–13, 162, 177–80; formation of, 90 n.11, 105–106; ideology of, 116–22; leadership of, 106–10; as main opposition party, 126–28; members of Parliament and, 127–28; membership figures for, 72; membership increase and, 125–26; monarchy referendum and, 15; organization of, 71–72, 107, 110, 122–26; political orientation of, 110–16; populism and, 19; posters of, 99; principles of, 105, 108, 122; proportional representation and, 35; revival of, 10–11; social base of, 120–22; younger voters and, 77
Papadopoulos, George (dictator), 100 n.25, 145, 146, 149; prison sentence of, 65
Papagos, General Alexandros, 53, 54, 86, 141
Papakonstandinou, Theofylaktis, 63
Papaligouras, Panayiotis, 59, 63, 65 n.58; income distribution and, 66
Papandreou, Andreas, 10, 17, 20, 88,

89, 97, 104, 131, 149, 150, 165, **190, 191**; EC and, 114; election of 1977 and, 98, 101, 122; foreign policy and, 113, 177, 178 n.14; formation of PASOK and, 90 n.11; grass-root organization and, 124–25; ideology of populism and, 117; leadership of, 106–10; organizational control of, 124; party principles and, 105; PASOK campaign and, 91, 93; political theory of, 111–12; populism and, 19; social programs and, 116; the superpowers and, 114–15
Papandreou, George, 121, 132, 144, 145; arrest of, 59; Center Union and, 55, 86, 87, 88, 89, 91, 92; death of (1968), 91; resignation of, 56, 88
Papaspirou, Demetrios, 89
Parliament (Vouli): allocation of seats in, 33–34, 36, 42; constitution and, 21, 22, 23–24; dissolution of, 25–26, 45 n.32; electoral law and, 30, 39–40; number of members in, 30; PASOK M.P.s in, 124, 127–28; regional differences and, 8; term of, 25; validation of elections and, 40–48
Parliamentary Work Sections (PASOK), 123
Participation (electoral), 3; percentages, 12–13; threshold of, 34–35
Parties. *See* Political parties; *names of specific political parties*
PASOK. *See* Panhellenic Socialist Movement (PASOK)
Passalidis, Yannis, 140, 141
Patriotic Antidictatorial Front (PAM), 146
Patron-client pattern: elections and, 3; ND and, 73; political parties and, 50
Peasants, 6, 120
Penalties, registration/voting, 28
People's party (Laiko Komma), 7; development of New Democracy party and, 49–59
Pesmazoglu, John, 90, 100, 104
Plastiras, Nicolas, 86, 127
Platforms. *See* Campaign issues
Political Bureau of KKE, 142, 147
Political development, 5; in late 1970s, 9–19
Political parties: citizen classification of, 186; divisions in, 20; Euro-communist, 113, 134, 136, 158, 183; "foreign" (factions/1830s and 1840s),

162; foreign policy and, 161, 162, 170–83; freedom to found, 25; large, PR and, 35; Mediterranean profile and, 2–3; of nineteenth century (Greek), 84–85; organizational structure and, 50; proportional representation and, 33–34; revival of, after junta, 9–12; small, PR and, 35; Socialist, as PASOK allies, 113–14; state deputies and, 36; structure of, fragility and, 7–9. See also names of specific political parties

Political theory, PASOK and, 111–12
Polling stations, 27
Population (legal), 46
Populism, 19, 85; ideology of, social roots and, 116–22; Papandreou's leadership and, 109–10, 119–20
Posters, 99
PR. See Proportional representation (PR)
Praetorian state, Greece as, 185
Prefecture Assembly of PASOK, 123
President, 15, 20; dissolution of Parliament and, 25–26; duties of, 18; electoral system and, 39; the 1980 election for, 17–19; referendums and, 38
Press. See Newspapers
Prime minister, 20; Karamanlis as, 18
Proportional representation (PR), 33–36
Protopapas, Haralambos, 90
Protopapas, Evangelos, 104
Public Law of the Greeks, 23
Public sector, 66, 67

Rallies: KKE, 155; ND, 77; PASOK, 77
Rallis, George, 63, 64, 67, 188, 189
Referendums, 49; disputed, 44; the electoral system and, 37–39; the monarchy and, 14–16, 24, 53, 63, 139, 151, 187
Regional Assemblies of ND, 71
Regional Development Committees of PASOK, 125
Regional differences, 6; political parties and, 8
Registration: electoral law and, 27–28; objections and, 41; percentages by sex, 13; registered citizen and, 26–27
Representative system, principles of, 24–26
Republicans ("democrats"), 19, 49

Right, the, 7, 86, 102; conservative split and, 53; language reform and, 67; "new," 188; PASOK theory and, 111; People's party and, 51, 53; women voters and, 13
Rural sector: election of 1974 and, 62; election of 1977 and, 79

SDE. See Social Democratic party of Greece (SDE)
Seabed dispute. See Aegean seabed dispute
Sesmik I (survey ship), 68
Simitis, Constantine, 100
Slogans, 162; of EDIK, 99; ideology underlying, 120; of KKE, 135, 155; of ND party, 75, 77; of PASOK, 112 ,150
Social classes: divisions in, PASOK and, 111, 112; ideology and, 117, 118; income redistribution and, 66; international revolution and, 113; PASOK's social base and, 120–22; political instability and, 6. See also Middle class
Social Democratic party (KODESO), 188, 189, 191
Social Democratic party of Greece (SDE), 90
Socialism, ideological crisis and, 117, 118–19
Social issues: Mediterranean profile and, 3, 4–5; ND party and, 60, 66; PASOK and, 115–16; radicalization and, 120–22
Socialist Initiative, 130, 154, 155
Socialist March, 130, 154, 155; formation of, 108, 131
Socialists, 188, 190, 191; PASOK alliances and, 113–14. See also Panhellenic Socialist Movement (PASOK)
Social radicalism, 117–19, 120
Special interest groups, 186
Stalin, Joseph, 140
State deputies, 36–37, 46
State intervention, ND and, 60, 61, 66, 82
Stefanopoulos, Konstantine, 82
Stefanopoulos, Stefanos, 74, 88
Suffrage: universal, 23, 27; valid ballots and, 46
Supreme Special Court (SSC), electoral validation and, 40, 42, 43, 44–45, 46 n.35, 47

Television: EDIK campaign and, 101; ND campaign and, 75–76
Territorial waters question, 169. *See also* Aegean seabed dispute
Terrorism, 187
Theodorakis, Mikis, 132
Theotokis, Georgios, 85
Theotokis, Spyros, 63, 73, 74
Tourism, 5, 120
Trade deficit, 3
Tricoupis, Charilaos, 85, 161
Tsatsos, Constantine, 17, 63, 73, 189
Tsatsos, Demetrios, 90, 93
Tsirimokos, Elias, 88
Tsouderou, Virginia, 100, 104
Turkey, 11, 17, 26, 67, 73, 97, 98, 100, 115, 118, 149, 164, 190; Aegean seabed dispute and, 68, 98, 169–70; air-space question and, 168–69; EDIK policy and, 180–81; friendship with, Karamanlis and, 68; as Greece's greatest threat, 166; invasion of Cyprus/foreign policy and, 166–68; KKE policy and, 182; minorities and, 170; ND policy and, 176–77; PASOK policy and, 179

Unemployment, 120
Union of the Center (EK), 143, 144, 145, 150, 153, 159
Union of the Democratic Center (EDIK), 106, 121, 128, 129, 132, 153, 171, 187–88; activities of, between 1974–1977, 92–97; charter and organization of, 92; congress of, 90; elections of 1974 and, 89–92; elections of 1977 and, 78–79, 97–104, 127; foreign policy and, 104, 180–81; ideology and, 91–92; leadership problems of, 93–97; organization of, 192, 194–96; party history, 85–89, 102–103; postelection (1977) developments and, 103–104; proportional representation and, 35
United Democratic Left (EDA), 7, 87–88, 130, 132, 140, 141, 150, 154, 155, 156, 157, 158, 181; split in, 131, 148; structure of, 142–43

United Left (EA), 10, 12; monarchy referendum and, 15; results of 1974 election and, 13, 131, 150
United Nationalist Front, 53
United States, 111, 114–15, 150, 177–78, 180, 183; Greek foreign policy and, 163–65
Urbanization, social change and, 4–5, 118
Urban sector: EDIK and, 103; election of 1974 and, 62; election of 1977 and, 78; voting percentages and, 12
USSR, 114–15, 178; Cyprus issue and, 167; Czechoslovakian invasion and, 147; KKE and, 136–37, 140, 143

Validation of parliamentary elections: consequences of, 44–45; disputed referendums and, 44; grounds for objection and, 42–43; judicial review of electoral laws and, 45–47; principle of judicial, 40–41, 47–48
Vance, Cyrus, 115
Venizelos, Eleftherios, 38 n.22, 50, 51, 53, 84, 85, 99, 163
Venizelos, Sophocles, 88
Villages, 6; decline of, 4, 12
Vlachos, Helen, 57
Voter registration. *See* Registration
Voting: compulsory, 26, 28; local elections and, 39; the right of, 26–27. *See also* Men; Women
Voting participation. *See* Participation
Voting percentages, 12–13
Vouli (Parliament). *See* Parliament (Vouli)

Women, voting and, 13, 26
Workers: exodus of young, 3; nonresident, voting and, 28; remittances of emigrated, 120

Youth movements, 110; Center Union (EDIN), 128; Communist, 137; of EDIK, 97, 99; of ND party, 80

Zighdis, John, 89, 90, 103, 187

AEI's *At the Polls* Studies

Australia at the Polls: The National Elections of 1975, Howard R. Penniman, ed.

The Australian National Elections of 1977, Howard R. Penniman, ed.

Britain at the Polls: The Parliamentary Elections of 1974, Howard R. Penniman, ed.

Britain Says Yes: The 1975 Referendum on the Common Market, Anthony King

Britain at the Polls, 1979: A Study of the General Election, Howard R. Penniman, ed.

Canada at the Polls: The General Elections of 1974, Howard R. Penniman, ed.

France at the Polls: The Presidential Elections of 1974, Howard R. Penniman, ed.

The French National Assembly Elections of 1978, Howard R. Penniman, ed.

Germany at the Polls: The Bundestag Election of 1976, Karl Cerny, ed.

India at the Polls: The Parliamentary Elections of 1977, Myron Weiner

Ireland at the Polls: The Dáil Elections of 1977, Howard R. Penniman, ed.

Israel at the Polls: The Knesset Elections of 1977, Howard R. Penniman, ed.

Italy at the Polls: The Parliamentary Elections of 1976, Howard R. Penniman, ed.

Japan at the Polls: The House of Councillors Election of 1974, Michael K. Blaker, ed.

A Season of Voting: The Japanese Elections of 1976 and 1977, Herbert Passin, ed.

New Zealand at the Polls: The General Elections of 1978, Howard R. Penniman, ed.

Scandinavia at the Polls: Recent Political Trends in Denmark, Norway, and Sweden, Karl H. Cerny, ed.

Venezuela at the Polls: The National Elections of 1978, Howard R. Penniman, ed.

Democracy at the Polls: A Comparative Study of Competitive National Elections, David Butler, Howard R. Penniman, and Austin Ranney, eds.

Referendums: A Comparative Study of Practice and Theory, David Butler and Austin Ranney, eds.

Studies are forthcoming on the latest national elections in Belgium, Canada, Denmark, France, Germany, Italy, India, Israel, Jamaica, Japan, the Netherlands, Norway, Portugal, Spain, Sweden, and Switzerland and on the first elections of the European Parliament. Also *The American Elections of 1980*, edited by Austin Ranney.

SELECTED AEI PUBLICATIONS

AEI ASSOCIATES PROGRAM